A Year of
Assemblies Book 1

Redvers Brandling

First published in 1993 in Great Britain by
Simon & Schuster Education

This edition published in 2000 by
Stanley Thornes (Publishers) Ltd
Delta Place
27 Bath Road
CHELTENHAM GL53 7TH
England

00 01 02 03 04 / 10 9 8 7 6 5 4 3 2 1

A catalogue record for this book is available from the British Library.

ISBN 0-7487-5836-4

Typeset by Florence Production Ltd, Stoodleigh, Devon
Printed and Bound in Great Britain
by T. J. International Ltd., Padstow, Cornwall

Contents

Acknowledgements

For many years the staff and children of Dewhurst St. Mary School, Cheshunt, were a receptive audience for material such as is contained in this book. They were also a source of both information and inspiration with their own presentations. I will always be grateful to them.

The material contained in *A Year of Assemblies Book 1* originally made up part of the *Autumn*, *Spring* and *Summer* assembly books.

It should also be mentioned that some of the stories in these books have been used, heard and re-adapted several times in assemblies. In consequence their original sources are not remembered and if this has unwittingly caused the infringement of copyright, the author apologises and will correct this omission in future editions, if notified.

Introduction

The preparation of regular, effective assemblies is no easy task, but the rewards for good presentations are considerable. In examining this statement it is useful to look at some of the comments made in the Secretary of State's proposals in the review of the National Curriculum in England (QCA 1999). These comments highlight some consistent aims:

to establish more explicit and coherent provision in the areas of personal, social . . . education and responsibility'

'develop pupils' knowledge and understanding of their role and responsibilities as active citizens in a modern democracy'

'equip them with the values, skills and knowledge to deal with the difficult moral and social questions they face'

'to be aware that people and other living things have needs, and that pupils have some responsibility in meeting them'

'to identify and show respect for differences and similarities between people'

'to recognise that family and friends care for each other'

Where better to achieve these aims than in a school assembly? In seeking to do so, and suggesting how they might be achieved, there still seems no better description of what is required than the list proposed in *Collective Worship for Schools in Hertfordshire*:

'In achieving this meaningful act . . . valid are . . . stories and readings, dance and drama, prayers/meditations, creative silence, songs/hymns/music, sacred/secular readings, artefacts and natural materials, children's contributions, visual aids.'

A Year of Assemblies Book 1 and *Book 2* seek to provide constructive and practical help for assemblies throughout the school year. Each book contains eighty ready-made assemblies.

These are divided up into presentations for each month and they are 'instant' inasmuch as they provide an introduction, story and a suggested hymn and prayer as well as additional information for the teacher. It is also recommended that any pre-assembly reflection and preparation can add considerably to the material's potential.

Complete assemblies

September

1 She's new

Introduction

Starting a new school in a new place where you don't know anybody can be quite frightening. How would you help somebody in this situation?

Story

Padma was . . . well . . . just miserable.

During August she had, unexpectedly, come from India to live in England. Now, having moved into her new home just one week ago, here she was in a new school. She knew nobody, could hardly understand the way all the other children talked, and felt cold all the time. She was miserable.

Mrs Gillespie, the teacher, tried to help. She put Padma in one of the friendliest groups and asked everybody to help her settle in. But, there were thirty-four other children in the class and everybody seemed so *busy* with their own affairs and their own friends. In fact, in every spare moment the other children on Padma's table seemed to be working away at something between them, but when Padma tried to get a look at it someone always seemed to get in her way. She felt terribly left out.

The days passed with agonising slowness. Eventually it was Friday. Soon she could escape this awful place for two whole days.

When Padma went into the classroom that Friday morning she could sense a different atmosphere. Everybody seemed to be waiting for something. Mrs Gillespie spoke.

'Is it ready now, Julie?'

'Yes, miss,' replied one of the girls on Padma's table. 'Come on Wayne, let's carry it out.'

Julie and Wayne carried a roll of thick card out to the front. Padma realised it was what the group had been working on since Tuesday – if only they'd let her help, after all she was quite a good painter.

'Right,' said Mrs Gillespie. 'Open it out.'

Slowly Wayne and Julie unrolled the card and, as they did so, the other children clapped. As more of the card came into view Padma began to feel her eyes tingle and her tummy grow strangely tight. Soon the whole card was stretched out across the front of the room.

'WELCOME, PADMA' it said in big letters, and underneath were the names of everybody in the class.

Now Padma knew why ... but what could she ... it was ... suddenly Padma didn't feel miserable at all.

Information for the teacher

This is a familiar theme in many schools in September. One 9-year-old child captured its essence in the following words:

> A loving arm
> Shelters me
> From any harm.
>
> The shelteredness
> Of kindness
> Flows around me.

Hymn suggestion

Come and Praise Vol 2 'It's a new day' No 106

Prayer

Let us think this morning about being a good friend. Let us try always to treat others as we would like them to treat us. Let us try to really understand what we mean by the word 'welcome'.

2 Keeping a diary

Introduction

One of the most famous events ever to happen in this country took place in September, 1666. This was the Great Fire of London – but how do we know so much about it?

Story

The Great Fire of London destroyed two-thirds of the city: 13,200 houses, 430 streets and 89 churches. The fire could be seen from forty miles round the capital.

The reason we know so many details about the fire is that two men who were alive at the time kept diaries in which they described the dramatic events. The names of these two people were John Evelyn and Samuel Pepys.

Other famous people who have kept diaries were Queen Victoria and Captain Scott. Queen Victoria started completing diaries when she was 13 years old and continued throughout her life. But for Captain Scott's diary we would know very little about his brave but unsuccessful attempt to lead the first party of men ever to reach the South Pole. His diary was found after his death.

Another diary which was found after its owner's death was that of Anne Frank. In it, a young girl describes what it was like to have to hide for months and months in the upstairs room of a house during the Second World War.

Here are some notes from a girl's diary of today:

4th September: Back to school. I sit next to Aliya. Our new teacher's name is Miss Hawksmith.

5th September: My turn to have a go on the computer, it was great. Brownies tonight.

6th September: Mum's birthday. Dylan and I bought her a cake and it's not yuk. She says she's twenty-one, but we know she's not.

Perhaps one of the most interesting things about diaries is that they focus our attention on time – what we did yesterday, and the day before, last week and last month. When we think more carefully about time we realise how precious it is. Once it has gone we can never get it back again. How important it is therefore never to waste time.

Information for the teacher

1   Some actual quotes from Pepys' diary might be useful:

2nd September: '. . . walked to the Tower and there I did see the houses at that end of the bridge all on fire . . .'

4th September: '. . . the sky looks all on fire in the night . . .'

7th September: '. . . saw all the towne burned and a miserable sight of St Paul's church burned, and Fleet Street.'

2   'Don't waste time' is a philosophy which has been pursued in various poems and sayings. It might be useful to have some Biblical comment here:

'Be most careful how you conduct yourselves, like sensible men, not simpletons. Use the present opportunity to the full . . . do not be fools.' (Ephesians 5, 15–17)

Prayer

Dear God, Help us to use time wisely. Help us to learn from the past and make the most of the present. Teach us to value our time at school so that we can prepare for the future. Amen.

3 Laurence

Introduction

Is your name Laurence? Do you know anybody called Laurence? The following story would be of very great interest to anybody with this name, but apart from that, it is a tale of great courage about a man we can all admire.

Story

The Roman Emperor Valerian stroked his chin and looked at the officers surrounding him.

'These Christians have got to be stamped out,' he said. 'They are a danger to the empire.'

'I agree, your majesty,' said a tall, sly-looking minister. 'But whilst we are getting rid of them why don't we make it profitable at the same time?'

'What do you mean by that?' snapped the Emperor.

'Well, why don't we command that deacon fellow – Laurence – to collect and bring to you all the wealth of all the Christian churches in Rome?'

Valerian sat silently. In his mind's eye he could already see the caskets of jewels and money this order would bring in. 'Not a bad idea at all,' he thought to himself. His face gave none of his thoughts away. Leaning forward he spoke brusquely.

'See to it.'

So in the year 258 AD the order went out. Laurence, a young deacon of the Christian church, was ordered to collect and bring the churches' treasure to the Emperor's palace.

A few days later he stood in the courtyard of the palace. The imperial officer whose idea it had all been came out to meet him.

'What are all these people doing with you?' asked the officer. 'Are they all carrying treasure?'

'None of them is carrying anything,' replied Laurence. 'You asked to receive the treasure of the Christian church – here it is.'

The officer looked puzzled, and then Laurence waved his hand at the huge crowd gathered behind him. 'It is the people of the Christian church who are its greatest treasure!'

For a minute there was a stunned silence, and then the officer screamed to the guards to arrest Laurence. For his 'insulting behaviour' in response to the Emperor's orders, Laurence was sentenced to death.

Like many other martyrs, however, Laurence became an inspiration to others who followed him. He was declared a Saint of the Church and finally, in 312 AD, the Roman Emperor became a Christian and the persecution of Christians throughout the Roman Empire stopped.

Information for the teacher

1   St Laurence's feast day is 10th August and there are about two hundred and fifty churches in England dedicated to him.

2   The Escorial Palace in Madrid, built in 1563, stands on the site of a monastery dedicated to St Laurence who was thought to have been born in Spain.

3   September link – getting to know new children's names.

Hymn suggestion

Come and Praise Vol 1 'The Building Song' No 61

Prayer

Dear God, Let us give thanks for those people whose courage acts as an inspiration to us all. Amen.

4 Marooned

Introduction

If you had to go, alone, to a desert island, what things would you take with you? What would you miss most? What would worry you most? The following story might make you think about these things.

Story

A few clothes, a knife, a hatchet, a kettle, a Bible – Alexander Selkirk looked at these things as the hot sun shone down on him. They were now all he had in the world.

An hour or two earlier he had been a member of the crew of the sailing ship 'Cinque Ports'. Then, after the captain had accused him of preparing to lead a mutiny, he had been rowed ashore to the tiny, lonely Pacific island of Juan Fernandez, and left on his own.

The date was September, 1704. Questions burned through Alexander's head. How would he live? Was he here for ever? Would he never see another human being again? Feeling himself beginning to panic the lonely sailor decided to explore the island.

Some time later he knew that there were no other humans on the island, but that there was plenty of material to build a hut. Working hard, he spent the next few days building one hut to live in and another for storage and cooking. He became an expert fisherman and hunter very quickly and lived on fish and goat meat. He used the goat skins for clothes.

As time went on Alexander's shoes wore out so he ran along the stones on the beach until his feet were as hard and tough as leather. Every day he read the Bible. The thing it took him longest to get used to was the loneliness. Then he had an idea.

The island was full of wild cats – what if he tamed them? Starting by giving them food he soon made friends of these savage creatures. When he had done so, dozens of them came to lie on his bed at night and keep him company.

For four years and four months Alexander Selkirk lived like this, and then, on 1st February 1709, a British ship anchored offshore and a landing party found the abandoned sailor. Alexander was fantastically excited to have been found but it had been so long since he had spoken to anybody that it took him days to be able to speak properly again.

Eventually the ship, 'Duke', which had found Alexander, got back to London. Within a very short time his story made him famous. A writer called Daniel Defoe heard of Alexander's adventures and decided to write a book based on them. You may have read this book, and you will certainly have heard of it. It is called *Robinson Crusoe*.

Information for the teacher

1 Juan Fernandez is a remote island in the South Pacific.

2 Defoe was a prolific writer who published his own newspaper. *Robinson Crusoe* was written when he was 58 and its profits helped him to face debt and ill health.

3 Selkirk was 27 when he was marooned.

4 He returned to sea and in 1720 set sail on a voyage to Africa. He never returned, dying of yellow fever on the voyage.

Hymn suggestion

Come and Praise Vol 2 'Give us hope Lord' No 87

Prayer

Dear God, Give us the courage, strength and skill to deal with the unexpected in our lives. Help us to make the most of the abilities you have given us and teach us to value everything we learn. Amen.

5 What do we see?

Introduction

Elizabeth once said to her mother: 'I like bananas because it's only when you peel off the skin that you find out how good they are inside.'

In some ways this is a bit like people. What they look like on the outside doesn't tell us about the qualities they have 'inside' – and sometimes they are just waiting to show these qualities. This morning's story is about just such a person.

Story

The sun beat down fiercely on the old town of Capernaum. Clouds of dust rose round the feet of travellers as they made their way through the great gate of the town. The man who sat at the gate mopped his sweating brow as he arranged the piles of money on a table in front of him.

Two men stood outside the gate and watched him.

'No wonder he looks miserable.'

'Nobody will have anything to do with him, will they?'

'Well – do you blame them? There he is, a Jew, collecting taxes from his own people to give to the Romans!'

'Yes, and I bet some of the money goes into his pocket too.'

As the two men talked, others handed over their taxes to Matthew, for that was the tax collector's name. As they did so they muttered harsh and unkind things to him. He said nothing in return, just keeping his eyes down and fingering the piles of money on the dust-covered table. It was then that Matthew heard another voice.

'Matthew, come and follow me and we will teach men about a better life.'

Looking up, Matthew saw Jesus standing in front of him. He had already heard something of this man. Could Jesus really be asking him, Matthew the hated tax collector, to join him in his wonderful work? In a second the mean, closed-in look disappeared from Matthew's face. With a smile he stepped round his table of money.

'I'm ready, Master,' he said, 'and thank you.'

Information for the teacher

1   September 21st is St Matthew's Day.

2   There is more about the recruitment of the first disciples in Matthew 4. A list of all twelve disciples can be found in Mark 3, 16–19.

3   A useful class follow-up to this story might be to ask individual children to name what they think others in the class do well. Teacher tact is necessary here and the scope should be as wide-ranging as possible.

Hymn suggestion

Come and Praise Vol 2 'Sad, puzzled eyes' No 74

Prayer

Dear God, Help us to see the good in people. Let us not pay too much attention to appearances, but to try and get to know what qualities people around us have.

Let us pray that we may be given the strength and wisdom to show, and use, our good qualities. Amen.

6 For good and evil . . .

Introduction

Close your mouths tightly. Now run your tongue round your teeth inside your mouth. Press it against the front teeth. Lick your lips with it. Now listen to this morning's story which is about . . .

Story

Long ago people in the West Indies believed that there was a god called Orula, who ruled the earth. How he got this job was one of their favourite stories.

The chief of all the gods decided that he would test the young god Orula to see if he was suitable for this difficult task.

He summoned Orula to him and said, 'Prepare me the best meal you can possibly think of.'

Orula bowed low and then went to do this. Some time later he came back with a large plate and set it down before the chief of the gods.

Round the outside of the plate were small pieces of salad, nuts and vegetables. In the centre of it was a large slice of cooked tongue. The chief eyed it hungrily and then ate it all.

When he had finished he looked at Orula and nodded. 'That was splendid. I enjoyed it very much indeed. Tell me, why did you choose tongue?'

'Well,' replied Orula, 'it was really to show you how much good the tongue does on earth. It comforts people when they are worried, encourages them when they need help, explains their difficulties, speaks words of love and kindness – and can even tell jokes!'

'Hmm,' muttered the chief, stroking his chin, 'a good answer . . . yes, a good answer.'

There was a pause and then he spoke again.

'Now – bring me the worst meal you can think of.'

Once again Orula disappeared, to return shortly with another large plate. Lying on it was a thick slice of . . . cooked tongue. With raised eyebrows the chief bit into a slice. Immediately his face creased and he spat it out.

'Ugh! That is disgusting, absolutely disgusting. Whatever made you choose tongue again?'

'Ah,' said Orula. 'We have heard how the tongue is an instrument for good – but it can also lie, spread false rumours, say hurtful things, cause trouble.'

The chief held up his hand. 'You're right of course – and such wisdom makes you the ideal person to rule the earth and deal with all its problems.'

And so Orula became god of the earth.

Information for the teacher

1   A possible follow-up could be to discuss some useful sayings, proverbs, etc. To make a September link, one the most famous men of words was Dr Johnson. He was born on 18th September, 1709. Examples of his sayings:

'When two Englishmen meet their first talk is of the weather.'

'When a man is tired of London he is tired of life.'

2   Some useful quotations from religious and other sources could include:

If a man speaks or acts
With an evil thought,
Pain follows him.
A tamed mind
Brings happiness
                                        (Buddha)

Whoever loves life and would see good days
Must restrain his tongue from evil
And his lips from deceit;
Must turn from wrong and do good,
Seek peace and preserve it.
                    (The Bible, Peter 3, 8–11)

O God
Let us be united
Let us speak in harmony
                                        (Hindu prayer)

A word is like water,
Once spilled it cannot be gathered again.
                                        (African proverb)

Hymn suggestion

Come and Praise Vol 1 'Go tell it on the mountain' No 24

Prayer

One of the passages from Teacher Information could be used here.

7 Jane

Introduction

People who are handicapped sometimes need help. Blind people, for instance, are tremendously grateful for the wonderful work which is done by their guide dogs.

This morning's story is about Jane, a golden retriever guide dog. Jane not only looked after her mistress well, but also found time to help a person who could see!

Story

'Right Jane, I know we're coming to the road.'

Miss Lorann spoke to Jane, her guide dog, as if she were a human being, she relied on her so much.

Miss Lorann could hear but not see the busy traffic moving along the street of the town. Jane could both hear and see it, and she knew how dangerous it was.

When they reached the point where Miss Lorann usually crossed the road, Jane sat obediently on the kerb waiting for her mistress's signal saying that she was ready to cross.

Suddenly Miss Lorann heard a shout and then, with a terrible shock, she felt Jane's harness torn from her hand. There followed a whole series of noises which were quite terrifying for the blind woman. A car's tyres screeched in protest to an emergency stop, a child screamed and then began to cry, footsteps pounded around her and voices shouted nearby.

Miss Lorann was near to panic when she suddenly felt Jane's warm body press reassuringly against her legs.

'Oh Jane, thank goodness you're safe. What has happened?'

A man's voice spoke over the child's sobbing. 'That's a wonderful dog you've got there. She just saved a little girl's life.'

'But how . . .' began Miss Lorann, when a young woman's voice interrupted her and she felt herself being hugged.

'How can I ever thank you and your dog enough?' she gasped. 'Becky – that's my little girl – ran away from me and was just about to dash into the road when your dog saw her. The dog jumped in front of her and knocked her out of the way of the car you heard skidding.'

Miss Lorann smiled and held onto the young woman tightly for a few seconds. 'I'm so pleased Jane was able to help,' she said, 'but I'm not surprised. Jane is really a wonderful friend.'

Jane's story appeared in the newspapers and she was awarded a medal for her quick thinking and swift action.

Information for the teacher

1   The address for Guide Dogs for the Blind Association is:

Hillfields, Burghfield Common, Reading RG7 3YG, www.gdba.org.uk/

2   70 per cent of guide dogs are labradors and 70 per cent are bitches. The training period lasts from six to eight months.

3   The September link is that the first training of dogs for use with blind people began in Germany in 1916.

4   The 'animal VC' is the Dickin Medal, instituted by Mrs Maria Dickin in 1943.

Hymn suggestion

Come and Praise Vol 1 'Cross over the road' No 70

Prayer

Let us think this morning of those who are handicapped in some way. Let us pray that they may be given hope and help. Amen.

October

8 A tale of two sisters

Introduction

Lots of stories follow a similar pattern. There are good and bad people in them and at first it seems as if everything is going best for the bad person. Then there is a surprise twist which results in a happy ending.

Story

The sun shone down brightly on grass glistening after the shower. Jemila pushed her way along the path towards the pool. It was very hot, as usual.

As she walked, Jemila thought about her sister Ama.

'Go and get some water from the pool, Jemila,' Ama had said, 'and hurry up about it.'

She never seemed to say anything gently or politely, thought Jemila. And yet she was so beautiful, easily the loveliest girl in the village.

'Well nobody would ever say I was beautiful,' thought Jemila as she glimpsed her reflection in a large puddle of water on the ground. A large, round, rather heavy face looked back at her.

Parting the last clump of bushes, Jemila arrived at the pool and got a surprise. There, sitting by the water, was an incredibly old woman. Feebly she was trying to wash her back.

Seeing the old woman's difficulties Jemila called out to her. 'It's all right – let me help you. I can wash your back for you quite easily.'

The old woman's back was hard and scaly and Jemila had to wash very hard to soften and clean it. At last she finished.

'You're so kind,' said the old woman in a surprisingly gentle voice. 'How nice of you to give so much of your time to a miserable old woman.'

'Oh, don't say that,' replied Jemila, 'it wasn't anything; I'm just glad I was able to help.'

'Well,' went on the old woman, 'I'd like to reward you for your kindness, my dear. You can have any wish you like.'

'Oh, I couldn't possibly take anything,' replied Jemila. 'I'm just glad that we've met and had a chance to talk.'

The old woman smiled.

'Look in the water my dear.'

Jemila did so – and gasped. The face that looked back at her was still her own, but different. The round, heavy look had gone and, there was no doubt about it, she was beautiful.

'Oh ... but ... thank ...'

She looked up, but the old woman had vanished.

When Jemila got home Ama didn't recognise her at first, but after listening to only part of the story she snapped in her usual unkind way. 'Trust you to have all the luck. I suppose you think you are more beautiful than me now. Well you're not and nobody else will think so either.'

But even while she was talking Ama was thinking how she could get something for herself. As soon as Jemila was out of the way she hurried to the pool.

'What did that sister of mine say?' she muttered to herself as she hurried along the path. 'There was somebody who told her she could have anything she liked. Wait till I find this person, I'm going to ask to be the richest girl in the world.'

Impatiently she burst through the bushes surrounding the pool – and saw an old, feeble woman by the water.

'Could you . . . could you help me wash my back please?' asked the old woman in a thin, wavering voice.

'This creature can't be granting wishes,' thought Ama contemptuously, and snapped angrily at the old woman.

'Get out of my way. I'm looking for somebody important. Come on – move!'

A tired smile flickered across the old woman's face. 'As you are so rude and impatient perhaps you'd better look like me,' she said.

At once Ama changed from a beautiful girl into a gnarled and tired looking old woman.

Information for the teacher

1   This story is an adaptation of a West Indian folk tale and is similar to many such stories which can be found in children's anthologies. Teachers might find the Biblical tale of the unforgiving servant a useful link. It can be found in Matthew 18, 23–34.

2   An October link for this story is that various towns in England hold Festivals of literature at this time of the year, and these provide an excellent opportunity to look at the messages of stories.

Hymn suggestion

Come and Praise Vol 1 'God knows me' No 15

Prayer

Dear God, Let us think this morning about some words, and what they mean – kindness, helpfulness, selfishness, greed, forgiveness.

Give us the strength to be kind and thoughtful to everyone with whom we come in contact. Help us always to be considerate people. Amen.

9 Mums

Introduction

This morning's assembly is about mums. Listen to what some children have written.

Story

1) One of my best times in the week is on a Wednesday night when I go swimming with my mum. We have a cup of tea really early and then later we drive down to Waltham Abbey and go to the pool.

My mum is a real good swimmer and she always dives in. I'm a bit scared and sometimes I jump in. Then we swim together up and down the pool doing breaststroke and backstroke. We have a lot of fun in the changing room and we have a hot shower.

Then we run to the car and on our way home we stop and buy fish and chips. When we get home dad is back from work and he is pleased to see us – and the fish and chips!

2) One of the worst times I have ever had was when mum was in hospital for a week. Every night we went to see her and she was in her dressing gown and I wanted her to come home with us. I thought she looked sad when we left even though she was smiling.

My dad is quite a good cook but sometimes he burns stuff. And he forgot to make the bed properly this morning, because I looked in their room. I didn't like seeing all mum's stuff, her lipstick and things, when she wasn't there.

When mum came home it was good, and I hope she doesn't go to hospital again.

3) I want to tell you about my mum. She's quite big really and has blonde hair. She wears jeans in the house but dresses when she goes out. Her favourite food is lasagne and she likes mints. She sometimes wears high heeled shoes but she says they kill her feet. She's got quite a soft voice but when she laughs it's loud. She laughs a lot because she likes jokes.

4) My mum has got lovely hands and I love to feel them on my face.

Information for the teacher

1   This material could obviously be supplemented or replaced by passages written by children known to the teacher.

2   An October link for this material is with the Hindu festival of Durga (which takes place in the month of *Asvin*). The goddess Durga, 'the divine mother' in one of her forms, is particularly remembered on Durga Puja (1st Asvin), when daughters return to their mother's homes for feasting, celebrations and the giving of presents.

Hymn suggestion

Come and Praise Vol 2 'Love will never come to an end' No 99

Prayer

Dear God, Help us to think for a moment about mothers all over the world. Let us give thanks for their love by saying the following prayer together. (*The children could repeat the words one line at a time after the teacher*):

> Where love is
> There riches be.
> Keep us all
> From poverty
>   (Old Medieval Prayer)

10 Learning a lesson

Introduction

Long ago, in the days before banks, people who saved money had plenty of worries about keeping it safe. Should they hide it? If so where? Or could they give it to someone powerful to look after it for them? Listen to what happened to one unfortunate man.

Story

'You see, sir,' said the poor man, 'I have saved one hundred crowns but need another fifty before I can go back to my wife and children and buy a small piece of land.'

'Go on,' said the rich merchant.

'Well I know you have many servants to look after your property and I have heard you are an honest man. Will you look after my hundred crowns until I can save the rest and return to my family? I will pay for your help.'

'Pay?' smiled the merchant. 'Don't worry about that – I'm a man who likes to help when he can. Your money will be safe with me.'

'Thank you,' replied Abraham, for that was the poor man's name.

Back to the fields he went to work long and tiring days. He hadn't seen his family for three years . . . but soon, he could return and care for them. The months passed and finally Abraham had the rest of his money. He then went to see the merchant.

'A hundred crowns! What are you talking about? I've never seen you before in my life. Servants – throw this scoundrel out!'

Abraham couldn't believe his ears when he heard the merchant's angry roaring. Within minutes he was lying bruised and bleeding in the street, where he had been thrown by the servants. His precious hundred crowns! Gone! Nobody would ever believe his side of the story . . . three years' work for nothing. Abraham clasped his hands over his face in despair.

What's the matter old chap? It can't be as bad as all that.' A kind voice interrupted Abraham's thoughts and a friendly arm held his shoulder. Looking up, Abraham saw a man with sharp, intelligent eyes who was well spoken and well dressed. Desperate with disappointment and frustration Abraham told the stranger the whole story.

Hmm, seems like our friend needs a lesson,' said the stranger. 'This is what we'll do.'

The next day the well-spoken stranger stood in front of the merchant.

'I've heard you are a man to be trusted,' he said. 'I too am a merchant making a journey to lands of the east. However, I am worried about carrying my fortune with me. Would you look after half of it for me until I get back?'

The merchant's eyes glinted greedily. Quickly he smiled and replied in a fawning voice.

'Oh you can certainly trust me, sir. Shall we get on with making the arrangements about . . .'

Before he could go on there was an interruption and a servant showed Abraham into the room.

'Oh no,' thought the treacherous merchant. 'What a time for him to appear again.' But before he could speak he got a surprise.

'Sir,' said Abraham politely, as if nothing had happened on his previous visit. 'I've come to collect my hundred crowns.'

The merchant did some quick thinking. He needed to impress the stranger who was obviously going to leave a far greater sum of money so . . .

'Of course, my friend,' he said, pretending too that nothing had happened between them. 'At once, at once.'

Within minutes Abraham had his hundred coins and hurried out.

'There you are – you see how reliable I am,' said the merchant, turning to his rich visitor, but in the commotion with Abraham the mysterious stranger had slipped away.

Later that night, as Abraham and the stranger journeyed far from the town the two men smiled at each other.

'Thanks,' said Abraham, 'somebody learned a lesson in honesty today.'

Information for the teacher

1   A possible October reference here is to Al Capone. The American gangster who thought he could live beyond the law was sent to prison for income tax evasion on 17th October, 1931.

Hymn suggestion

Come and Praise Vol 2 'A still, small voice' No 96

Prayer

Let us think this morning of the 'still, small voice' of our conscience. Let us ask that we might learn the lessons of honesty. Let us behave towards others as we would like them to behave to us.

Let us pray that our thoughts, words and deeds are guided towards these aims.

11 Honesty

Introduction

Unfortunately all of us are tempted to do something we shouldn't at some time or other. This morning's story is about a man who learned his lesson in a very unusual way.

Story

Johann and Karl made violins. Johann was getting old and relied more and more on his younger partner, Karl.

One day the old man put his arm round his young partner's shoulders. 'Karl,' he said, 'for years we've made the finest violins in the world. Great musicians have played them and thanked us for their quality.'

'That's true,' replied Karl, 'and we have played them ourselves in many concerts too.'

'Right,' went on Johann, 'but I'm getting old and tired my friend – and I want you to do me one last favour.'

'Anything,' said Karl.

'Well, the doctor says I must take a long holiday in the mountains. When I come back I would like a really great violin to play. Will you make me this great violin whilst I am away?'

'Of course I will,' answered Karl. 'It will be ready for you to come back to.'

'Remember,' continued Johann, 'use only the very finest materials; make it as only you know how.'

Soon the older man was away in the mountains. Karl sat alone in their workshop surrounded by the wood, strings and varnish. As he looked into the dancing flames of the open fire he thought deeply.

'I've got lots of work to do,' he thought. 'I haven't really got time to make this special violin for Johann ... but ... now he is so old, he'll never know if I use poorer materials and fake it up to look good. It will never last, of course, but he won't be around long enough to find out.'

So Karl got on with making other violins and when he had a spare moment he worked on Johann's, using just enough time and skill to make it look good, even though it wasn't.

'In five years' time this will just be scrap,' he thought, as he picked up another piece of poor wood and began to smooth it. He quickly put the thought out of his head.

Then came the day when Johann returned. Looking ill but rested, he came into the workshop.

'Johann, my old friend,' Karl greeted him warmly.

'Well,' said the old man, 'have you got it?'

Karl went to the cupboard and came back with the gleaming new violin. He held it out to Johann.

'Try it.'

'No, no,' said the old man. 'I know you will have used the best possible materials, and spared no time or expense on it. I will give you the money for all that.'

'Yes, but ...'

'The violin is my present to you, Karl – in thanks for all our work together and all your help. I know you still play at many concerts and I want you to have a fine instrument which will sound beautiful and look good for years. Knowing you as I do I thought that this was the best way for you to get such an instrument.'

Information for the teacher

1   An October link for this honesty and dishonesty theme could be made on the 12th of the month – the date on which Elizabeth Fry, reformer of English prisons, died in 1845.

2   The theme of this particular story could be adapted to other products and situations quite easily. In any of its guises it is particularly well suited to drama.

3   There is a nice simple Biblical reference here: 'God loves people who tell the truth' (Proverbs 12, 22).

Hymn suggestion

Come and Praise Vol 2 'Make us worthy Lord' No 94

Prayer

Do all the good you can,
By all the means you can,
In all the places you can,
At all the times you can,
To all the people you can,
As long as ever you can.

(John Wesley)

12 A father's choice

Introduction

Have you ever wanted something really desperately? It might have been a computer, or a new bike, or a TV in your bedroom. Did you get it? If not, why not?

Story

Darren had just got his driving licence and he wanted a car. He had no money to buy one but he had an idea.

'Dad,' he said one morning to his father after breakfast. 'I want to talk to you for a few minutes.'

'Certainly, son, what is it?'

'Well, both Chris and I work for you in the family business. That means that when you ... er ... when you ...'

'Yes, yes, when I die. Come on, get to the point.'

'Well the business will be shared between us then, Dad, but I want to leave the firm and have my share of the money now.'

There was a long pause whilst Darren's father looked at him very seriously.

'Very well,' he said finally. 'I'll let you have your share tomorrow.'

So Darren got half of the money due to him from the family business. The next day he was at a new car showroom in the nearest town.

'I was thinking of getting something second hand,' he thought, 'but now I've got plenty of money I might as well get just what I want.'

Two days later Darren was behind the wheel of a shiny new red sports car. With two cases in the back he was leaving home for ever to find adventure. When he reached the big city he rented a flat in an expensive district. His car attracted a lot of interest and in no time he had a group of good friends.

'How fast can it go, Darren?'

'Why don't we take a trip to the coast?'

'Let's take your car, Darren, it's better than any of ours.'

Life was exciting. There always seemed to be something happening and Darren couldn't believe his popularity as he took his friends here, there and everywhere.

Then one day he realised that his money was beginning to run out.

'It'll be all right though,' he thought. 'I'll soon get a job and until I do my friends will see me OK.'

It was then that Darren got the first of a few unpleasant surprises. When he wasn't providing the transport his so-called friends lost interest in him. Desperate to keep their friendship, he set about finding a job to increase his rapidly falling money supply.

Times were hard though and he couldn't get the sort of job for which his father had trained him. He had to take a poorer job, with poorer wages. This meant moving to a rented room in a less attractive part of town. Now his lovely car had to stand out on a dark and dirty street.

Then came another dreadful day.

'Want to see you,' said the boss when Darren got to work. 'Afraid we're losing business so you'll have to go. Finish tonight.'

Depressed, Darren walked back through the rain to his room and there, outside on the street, stood his car – tyres slashed and paintwork scratched all over. As he now had no money he couldn't get it repaired and had to sell it as it was, for just a fraction of what he had paid for it.

A week later Darren sat in his cold, gloomy room. He hadn't been able to get another job, his last few pounds had gone to pay the rent and all he could afford for a meal was a cheap tin of beans.

His mind turned to home. He thought of his old room, the lovely meals his mother made, the kindness of his father.

'I'll go back,' he said to himself, 'but I'll ask my father if I can be just an ordinary worker – I'm not fit to be called his son.'

A few days later Darren climbed down from the cab of the lorry which had given him a lift. He was tired, dirty and hungry because he had been travelling for two days. He hadn't been able to afford the fare for either bus or train but now, standing outside the garden gate of his old house, he felt a great surge of relief sweep over him. It was then that his father, who happened to be looking out of the window, saw Darren. Dropping everything he rushed outside and hugged his son.

'You're back, you're back!' he cried. 'How wonderful. We'll have the best meal we've ever had in this house tonight!'

'But Dad,' mumbled Darren. 'I'm so ashamed. I've let you down, I've lost . . .'

'Come in, come in – let's get this party organised.'

And so the family was together again. At first, Darren's brother Chris was not very happy about all the fuss being made over someone who had wasted his father's money. The boys' father took Chris to one side.

'I know how you feel,' he said. 'But remember, everything I have is yours and it was certainly right for me to welcome Darren back. After all he was lost and now he's found again.'

Information for the teacher

1 A comparison between this modern version and the original story of the prodigal son can be made by referring to Luke 15. Some questions might be put to the children after reading the original – the son's thoughts when he was at his lowest ebb (verses 17–19); the father's joy at his son's return (verse 20); the father's comments (verse 24). St Luke's Day is 18th October.

2 This story could lead to some work on an enlarged theme of forgiveness. A useful quotation here might be:

'Lord, how often am I to forgive my brother if he goes on worrying me? As many as seven times?'
Jesus replied, 'I do not say seven times, I say seventy times seven.' (Matthew 18, 21–22)

Hymn suggestion

Come and Praise Vol 2 'Let the world rejoice together' No 148

Prayer

Dear God, Help us to know when we are wrong about something. Help us to say sorry and ask for forgiveness. Please help us also to forgive other people who may at times be thoughtless and unkind.

Let us learn from your example. Amen.

13 A life's work

Introduction

Can you name some of the famous buildings in London? (*In answer to this question it should not be long before somebody says* St Paul's Cathedral.)

Story

A small, frail man stepped carefully amongst the charred timbers and shattered walls of ruined London. It was 1666 and the city had just been devastated by the Great Fire.

'What an opportunity!' muttered the man to himself. 'Now everything can be rebuilt in a beautiful, spacious way. There will be wide roads and leafy parks – no more of those crowded, unhealthy slums.'

So said Christopher Wren, a young architect, whose dreams of rebuilding London caused him to work day and night on the plans. Finally he finished and took his work to King Charles II.

'Marvellous,' exclaimed the king. 'Now we will have a city to be proud of; but first of all we'll have to get the rich merchants of the city to put up the money for the rebuilding.'

It was then that Christopher got his first shock.

'Far, far too expensive!' the merchants claimed. 'Out of the question.'

So what might have been a wonderful city disappeared before it got beyond the planning stage – but there was some consolation for Christopher Wren.

'You can plan and rebuild St Paul's Cathedral.'

On 21st June 1675, the first stone of the new cathedral was laid. For the next thirty-five years the building of the great cathedral was the life's work of Christopher Wren.

Finally, when he was seventy-eight years old, in 1710, the building was finished. Once a year after that the ailing architect was carried up to the top of the great dome to look out over the ever-growing London.

Was he disappointed that this was not being developed in the way he thought it should be? We will never know, but his own great work still stands proudly in his memory.

Information for the teacher

1   The October link for this story could be the date of birth of Sir Christopher Wren – 20th October, 1632. He was the son of the

Dean of Windsor, chaplain to King Charles I. From childhood he showed great ability. He died on 25th February, 1723, and was buried ceremonially in St Paul's Cathedral. He was responsible for many other London buildings as well.

2   A possible Biblical link with this story is that of the Tower of Babel and why it failed (Genesis 11).

Hymn suggestion

Come and Praise Vol 2 'You can build a wall' No 91

Prayer

Let us give thanks this morning for the skill of men who have made the world a more beautiful place by their work. Let us think particularly of architects and builders whose work has to be so carefully planned and with so much attention to detail.

Let us also think of the designers and builders of religious buildings throughout the world. Amen.

November

14 The friend

Introduction

There is an old saying: 'A friend in need is a friend indeed'. This morning's story shows us exactly what that saying means.

Story

Damon and Pythias were very good friends. They did as much as they could together and always enjoyed each other's company. They lived in a city called Syracuse and the man who ruled it was cruel and ruthless. His name was Dionysus.

Damon said to Pythias, 'That Dionysus is not fit to rule this great city. Somebody else should have the job.'

'It's dangerous to go round saying things like that,' replied Pythias. 'You want to be careful.'

But Damon wasn't careful. Finally he was arrested and taken before Dionysus.

'You'd like to get rid of me, I hear,' said the ruler, 'so you must be a dangerous man to have around.' With a wave of his hand Dionysus summoned two of his soldiers. 'Throw this wretch in prison. He dies in three days.'

Damon was shocked but not surprised at these dreadful words. Bowing his head, he asked Dionysus if he could say farewell to his family before the execution. They lived a day's journey away.

Dionysus stared at his prisoner for a while, and then a sly grin came over his face. 'Yes,' he said finally. 'You can do that – but Pythias must take your place whilst you are away. If you're not back in three days he dies in your place.'

Secretly Dionysus thought that this was a wonderful idea. He was sure Damon would not return. Then he would kill Pythias, another trouble maker, and after that send his soldiers to find and kill Damon. In this way he would get rid of both men.

So Damon left the city and Pythias took his place in prison.

After saying a tearful farewell to his family, Damon called for his horse to return to Syracuse.

'It's gone, sir,' said his servant.

'Gone? Gone? What do you mean?'

'I sold it . . . now you can't return to die . . . you can stay here and . . .'

Damon looked at his kind old servant, then without a word, he turned and began to run back to Syracuse. After hours of desperate effort he was tired, dirty and knew that he could never reach the city in time. Then he saw a man with a horse. Giving the stranger every penny he possessed he leapt on the horse and galloped on his way.

Meanwhile, back in Syracuse the deadline had been reached. Dionysus stood smiling in front of a group of soldiers. Amongst them knelt Pythias, who was about to be beheaded.

'So much for friends,' smirked Dionysus, when suddenly a horse pounded into the courtyard and Damon threw himself down from it.

'My friend,' he cried, rushing up to Pythias, 'thank goodness I'm in time!'

Dionysus was dumbfounded.

'You've come back,' he gasped.

'Wait,' he went on as the soldiers closed in on the two friends. 'This is really true friendship. Neither of you will be hurt – and I hope I can learn from your example. Perhaps then I might be called a friend of yours too.'

Information for the teacher

1   A useful Biblical link is the story of David and Jonathan (Samuel 1, 18–20).

2   Damon's actions were certainly 'saintly' and some further follow-ups could be linked with All Saints Day on 1st November.

3   The story of Damon, Pythias and Dionysus is a traditional Greek legend.

Hymn suggestion

Come and Praise Vol 1 'Man for all the people' No 27

Prayer

Let us think this morning about keeping our word, no matter how difficult this may be. Let us remember that promises are made to be kept and we should never say we will do something unless we really mean to. Let us also give thanks for loyal friends everywhere.

15 Happiness

Introduction

Let us spend half a minute in absolute silence thinking about things which make us really happy ... now listen to this morning's story.

Story

Ghandar had one great aim in life.

'If only I had one of those magnificent silk-lined cloaks,' he thought to himself. 'Then everybody would see how rich and important I have become.'

Now Ghandar made his money by buying things cheaply and selling them expensively. He also worked hard and spent all his time earning money. He had no wife or children, nor any real friends – he hadn't time for such things.

Well, of course, he got rich and the great moment came when he chose his cloak. It really was magnificent. It was purple and, as everyone knew, that was the most expensive colour anybody could have. It was huge and almost wrapped round Ghandar twice. Its lining was of the finest silk and it fastened with a precious stone.

'Fantastic,' thought Ghandar, 'what happiness, what a wonderful cloak. How other people must admire and envy me.'

At home that night Ghandar didn't take his cloak off once. He stroked it and fingered it and smoothed it over his arms.

'Wonderful,' he kept muttering.

Finally, after hanging his cloak up very carefully, he went to bed. That night whilst he was asleep a thief broke into his house and stole the cloak.

When he awoke and found his precious cloak had gone Ghandar was heartbroken. All that money he had spent so much time earning so that he could buy the cloak – all that and the cloak – gone. Now he had nothing.

In the same town lived a young man called Bhattabhatika. At about the time Ghandar was discovering his loss, Bhattabhatika was preparing to leave home to go and seek his fortune in the world.

'Mother,' he said, 'what shall I do to find happiness in the world?'

His mother smiled. 'What you do doesn't matter as much as how you do it,' she said. 'Always do your best and treat everybody you meet with kindness and consideration. That's the way to find happiness.'

Information for the teacher

1   A very useful Bible reference here is Matthew 6, 19–21.

2   The Buddha's teaching was that the ideal state of Nirvana could only be reached through kindliness, compassion and the joy of inner peace.

3   A useful calendar link with this story is that 2nd November is the anniversary of the founding of the Samaritans in 1953. 'Giving to those in need' can be explored in various themes.

Hymn suggestion

Come and Praise Vol 2 'I come like a beggar' No 90

Prayer

> Let us try to be:
> Loving instead of angry
> Kind instead of greedy,
> Truthful instead of deceitful.

Let us try and remember
That we gain the most
By giving the most.
  (Adapted from Buddhist scriptures)

16 John and Errol

Introduction

If you have ever been in hospital you will know what a difference it makes to meet somebody there who is always cheerful.

Story

One day John woke up and he couldn't open his eyes. He was very frightened. He rubbed them and they felt swollen and sore. He couldn't get them to open and he couldn't see.

'Mum,' he cried out, '*MUM*!'

Hearing his frightened cry, John's mother rushed into his bedroom. 'What is it ... oh dear.'

Soon the doctor arrived to see if he could help. 'I think I know what the problem is,' he said, 'but it will take time to get things put right. Meanwhile John will have to go to hospital.'

Later that day John was lying in bed in the local hospital. He was very miserable and frightened. He couldn't control his muffled sobs.

'What's the matter?' asked a voice.

John knew that the voice belonged to the boy who was in the next bed. The nurse had told him there were only two of them in the room.

'I can't see,' said John ... 'and I'm scared.'

'Don't worry,' replied the other boy in a cheerful tone. 'My name is Errol and I'll soon cheer you up. I'm only in here 'cos I broke my leg.'

Soon the two boys were talking together.

'What's it like in here?' asked John.

'What do you mean?' asked Errol.

'Well ... what it looks like ... and everything.'

There was a very long pause.

'Errol? Did you hear what I said?' asked John.

'Oh ... yeah ... yeah. Well it's ... sort of very bright. The door is bright yellow, the curtains have got big flowers on them and the nurse is very pretty. There's lots of things you can see through the window too.'

'Tell me some more,' whispered John.

For the next few days Errol kept cheering John up with his tales of what he could see going on all around – how the nurse looked, what the weather was like, kinds of cars he could see outside and so on. His constant cheery chatter made John forget about his eyes until . . . one morning he woke . . . and he could see again!

'Errol!' he cried. 'Errol . . . I can see . . . I can *see*!'

'Oh . . . that's great John, really great.'

'Now you won't have to keep telling me about things I can see for mys . . .'

Suddenly John stopped talking as he looked round. There were no low windows in this room . . . the door was a dark brown colour . . . there were no flowery curtains . . .

John looked across at Errol, who had a plaster cast on his leg but was sitting up in bed and staring straight ahead . . . with sightless eyes.

'OK, OK,' said Errol, 'now you know. Well I had to cheer you up, didn't I? And I *have* got a broken leg. Now – you can tell me what it's like in here!'

Information for the teacher

1   A strong November link in the 'those who care for us' theme relates to 5th November 1855, the date when Florence Nightingale arrived in Scutari. For those who want to pursue the sight aspect, then Louis Braille was born on 4th January 1809.

2   Two addresses which might be useful are:

Guide Dogs for the Blind, Hillfields, Burghfield Common, Reading, RG7 3YG, www.gdba.org.uk/

Royal National Institute for the Blind, 224 Great Portland Street, London W1N 6AA, www.rnib.org.uk

Hymn suggestion

Come and Praise Vol 1 'From the darkness came light' No 29

Prayer

Dear God, Teach us to be thankful for our senses. Help us to use them as fully as we can to enjoy so much that is beautiful in the world.

Please help those unfortunate people who are handicapped in some way and cannot enjoy all their senses as we do. Amen.

17 Know your strengths

Introduction

It is very easy to be flattered. For instance somebody might say to you 'You are a really lovely singer', when you know you are not. But perhaps when this is said, you start to believe it. Now in this morning's story . . .

Story

The pale moon shone down over the field. The shadows of the trees and hedges sharpened and blurred as scattered clouds scudded across the sky. One shadow moved. Slowly and carefully it crept and stopped and edged forwards. The wolf was closing in on his prey.

The shepherd and his dogs slept, the sheep and lambs huddled close to each other. The wolf got nearer. He had spotted a lamb on the outside of the flock. Stealthily he moved towards it, and then with a fierce swoop he had it in his jaws and was dragging it off to a nearby hill where he could enjoy his supper.

Awake and terrified, the lamb realised she was in terrible danger.

'Mr Wolf, Mr Wolf,' she cried, as the wolf surged strongly up the slope of the hill. Keeping the lamb firmly in his jaws the wolf simply growled.

'Mr Wolf,' went on the lamb, 'I know you've caught me fair and square . . . but . . . please . . . one last request before I die.'

'This is a very strange lamb,' thought the wolf, but his curiosity was aroused. Stopping on his upward path, he relaxed his savage jaws and snarled.

'What is it then?'

'Well . . .' went on the lamb, 'one of my great regrets – if I am to die – is that I have never heard your voice.'

'What do you mean?'

'My parents told me so much about you – not only are you fierce and strong and independent – but you also have such a wonderful singing voice.'

'A what?' muttered the surprised wolf.

'All the flock knows about it. They might be terrified of you, but they also know what a marvellous singer you are. They've heard you. Please, before you eat me – will you sing just one short song?'

'I . . .' the wolf was flattered.

Putting one paw firmly on the lamb he threw back his head and began to howl, long and loud.

Instantly the shepherd and the guard dogs were awakened. Recognising the wolf's howl and fearing for the flock, they raced towards the sound.

Far from being his usual cautious, crafty self the wolf, with his eyes closed, continued to lift his head in 'song'. With a rush the dogs were on him. Bruised and cut he managed to fight them off and dash away safely up the hill.

Finally, when the shepherd, dogs and rescued lamb returned to the flock he sat, panting and sore, looking down on them. He had learnt a lesson tonight.

Information for the teacher

1 A possible November link for this story could be the fact that Peter Tchaikovsky, the Russian composer, died on 6th November, 1893. 'Peter and the Wolf' would be very evocative music to introduce and conclude the assembly.

2 A Biblical story which conveys the theme of flattery undoing strength is Samson and Delilah. It can be found in Judges 16.

3 For older children this theme could be developed one stage further – what motivation do people often have when they say flattering things about a person, or an object (a car they want to sell for instance)? This could obviously lead on to areas like honesty and would provide good discussion material for Year 6 children.

Hymn suggestion

Come and Praise Vol 2 ' 'Tis the gift to be simple' No 97

Prayer

Dear God, Give us the wisdom to know ourselves. Let us not be deceived by false words. Help us to be honest with ourselves and others. Amen.

18 The beggar

Introduction

It is easy to give presents to people we know well and like. It is more difficult to give to strangers, particularly if what we give is something we very much want to keep for ourselves.

Story

The wind whistled round the line of soldiers as they made their way across the bleak countryside to the city in the distance.

'I'll be glad to be inside in front of a warm fire,' said one.

'Me too,' agreed his companion.

The soldiers were Romans and they were on duty in Gaul. Each was well equipped and had a thick cloak to keep out the biting wind.

As they reached the city gate they heard a moaning sound above the noise of the wind.

'Help me ... please ... food ... anything.'

The moans and pleas came from a beggar. Dressed in filthy rags, he lay on the ground beside the city gate. As the soldiers drew nearer he increased his begging cries.

'What a welcome!' muttered one Roman.

'You're going to catch cold lying there,' shouted another.

'Maybe he's too warm inside,' snorted a third.

There was a roar of laughter from the group, and one of the soldiers moved over to give the beggar a kick as he walked past.

But one of the Romans didn't feel the same as the others. 'That poor, miserable man,' he thought. 'How desperately cold and poor he must be. If only I had something to give him.'

But as the soldier, whose name was Martin, fingered his empty purse he knew that he had nothing ... or had he?

'Yes,' he thought suddenly. Stopping beside the beggar, he unfastened his thick cloak at the neck and swept it off his shoulders. With a stroke from his sword he cut it in two.

Then, carefully, he wrapped one half round the shivering man. When he had done this he shrugged into what was left of his cloak and hurried to catch up with his colleagues.

The other soldiers looked at him in amazement, said nothing and avoided his eye.

Soon they were inside the city and warmed by food and shelter. With the others Martin lay down to sleep. It seemed that his head had hardly touched the pillow when he began to dream.

In his dream Martin saw the half of his cloak which he had torn and given away. It was no longer being worn by a beggar, it was wrapped round the shoulders of a man Martin recognised as Jesus. As the dream continued Martin thought he could hear Jesus telling a group of people round him how he had been given the cloak.

With a start the soldier awoke. He lay in the darkness trying to collect his thoughts. Then he sat up. 'I've got work to do,' he said to himself.

Shortly after this he left the army and became a monk. For many years he travelled round Gaul, preaching about Jesus and helping people in any way he could. Finally he settled in the city of Tours and became a bishop there.

When he died in 397, Martin had become famous for his concern for, and kindness to, others. He is especially remembered every year on 11th November and many churches are named after him.

Information for the teacher

1   Martin was born in Hungary where his father was a Roman soldier. Following in his father's footsteps he too became a soldier at the age of fifteen. It is thought that the famous incident described here took place when he was about eighteen.

2   There may well be a St Martin's Church known to the children locally. Probably the most famous one in England in St Martin's-in-the-Fields in London.

Hymn suggestion

Come and Praise Vol 2 'I come like a beggar' No 90

Prayer

Let us think this morning about the following words:

> We love our friends
> That is easy.
> Let us learn to love others
> Near and far,
> Known and unknown to us.
> Let us learn that
> What hurts them also hurts us.
> Teach us to share
> All that we have
> With those who have nothing
>   (Adapted from an original African prayer)

19 *War and peace*

Introduction

Dreadful things happen in wartime, but sometimes strange events and acts of kindness take place too.

Story

Bullets whistled overhead as Lieutenant Paul George, a vet, ran crouching along the muddy trench during a day's action in the First World War. English and German soldiers faced each other in hundreds of miles of trenches. From time to time huge shells dropped on either side and threw up great mounds of earth. There was never any peace from the rifle and machine gun fire.

Then, above the hideous noise, Lieutenant George heard a pitiful whining. Turning a corner in the trench he saw a German Shepherd dog lying on its side, bleeding from a wound.

'Now old chap, we'll soon fix this up,' he said as he bent over the dog. For the next few minutes the vet cleaned and bandaged the wound as the dog gratefully licked his hand.

Lieutenant George knew that both sides used dogs to carry messages but he got a surprise when he looked at the wounded dog's collar and saw '1826 Karl' – it was obviously a dog used by the Germans.

Looking down at his patient, Lieutenant George knew that the dog needed further careful treatment and that he would be better getting it where he felt at home. The vet came to a decision.

Putting his hands to his mouth the lieutenant shouted at the top of his voice: '1826 Karl'. There was a slight pause in the gunfire and he took advantage of this to shout again: '1826 Karl – to come home'.

This time the firing ceased all together.

Lieutenant George stood up and climbed out of the trench with the wounded dog following him painfully. The two of them stood there in No Man's Land with hundreds of eyes watching them and dozens of guns stilled.

Speaking gently, Lieutenant George patted the dog and sent him limping and bandaged on his way to the German lines.

A week later, under cloudy skies, the noise of gunfire rolled again over the long trenches. Then, suddenly, there came a cry from the German lines '1826 Karl'. There was a lessening of the fire, and the shout came again: '1826 Karl'.

This time every gun stopped. There was sudden complete silence. It was as if hundreds of men were holding their breath. Then, slowly, from out of the German trenches there climbed a dog handler. After him climbed a fit and healthy Karl. The German soldier bent down and put a leash on Karl, then carefully he walked the fully recovered dog for a hundred yards between the lines of trenches.

The silence lasted for perhaps a minute longer, and then it was broken by the first cheer. Suddenly the air was full of the sound of cheers, clapping hands and whistles. Those tired, battle-weary men were giving thanks that one dog had been restored to fitness and health.

Information for the teacher

1   This assembly could be used on, or near, Remembrance Day, 11th November. Just one of the many dreadful statistics of the First World War: eight million five hundred thousand soldiers were killed during the fighting.

2   A very evocative piece of prose written by a twelve-year-old boy could be used in connection with thoughts on the distress caused by war:

> 'When they dropped the atom bomb there was a terrible explosion and a terrifically strong blast. People were blown against trees and buildings. When it was over only shadows were left in the slight breeze.'
>
> (Originally published in *Assembly* by Redvers Brandling (Macmillan))

3   Some thoughtful work could be done on the 'bitter sweet' popular songs associated with the First World War – 'Goodbyee', 'It's a long way to Tipperary', etc.

Hymn suggestion

Come and Praise Vol 1 'Peace, perfect peace' No 53

Prayer

Dear God, Please give men wisdom that they might forever be without war. Teach us to avoid the faults which cause argument and distress. Help us to be free from greed, selfishness and prejudice. Amen.

20 A long tongue makes for a short life

Introduction

The Armenian proverb which is the title of this morning's story is one to make us think. It could be linked to another wise saying: 'Actions speak louder than words'.

Story

Long ago a fox, a wolf and a camel were making a long journey together. They had become friends, but the journey was long and tiring and they were often hungry. One day as they trudged along, the camel, who was much taller than the other two, saw something lying on the trail ahead.

'Something lying on the ground up there,' he said in his usual terse way.

'I wonder what it can be?' said the fox excitedly.

'Let's hurry up and find out,' added the wolf.

Soon the animals reached the spot where the object was lying on the ground. To their delight they found that it was a loaf of bread which had obviously been dropped by some other travellers.

'Food,' cried the fox. 'Just what we can do with.'

'Great,' went on the wolf, 'but of course there's only enough for one of us.'

'What do you mean?' replied the fox irritably. 'If there's only enough for one of us – which one?'

'That's easy,' growled the wolf. 'The oldest of the three of us should have the bread and I'd like to point out that that's me.'

'Rubbish,' snapped the fox, 'I'm old enough to be your Dad.'

'Bah, I'd like you to prove that.'

'All right, that shouldn't be too difficult . . .'

For the next five minutes the fox and the wolf argued and insulted each other. Suddenly in the middle of this war of words, they both stopped and looked at the ground nearby. The bread was gone.

'What . . .'

'Who could have . . .?'

Slowly they both turned to look at the camel – just in time to see his jaws finish chewing.

'Ah,' he said. 'I thought you two had lost interest in the bread as you were talking so much. It was good.'

Looking at their tall companion, the fox and the wolf could only growl hungrily at each other before continuing the journey.

(Adapted from an Armenian folk tale)

Information for the teacher

1   A useful calendar link for this story is 18th November. In 1307 this was the date on which William Tell supposedly shot the apple from his son's head – truly an action which spoke louder than words.

This story of William Tell is in its own right very good assembly material. Gessler was an Austrian bailiff who ruled harshly over the people of Schwytz, Uri and Unterwald. William Tell, a hunter, refused to bow to Gessler's hat in the market place. He was arrested and ordered by Gessler to shoot an apple from his son's head, or die. The feat was accomplished in the market place.

2   There is a very evocative African proverb which is well suited to the theme of this story:

> A word is like water,
> Once spilled it cannot be gathered again.

Hymn suggestion

Come and Praise Vol 2 'A still, small voice' No 96

Prayer

Let us think this morning about how we speak.
Let us always try to speak kind, thoughtful, helpful, sensible words.
Let us try to avoid speaking words which are thoughtless, cruel, meaningless or untrue.
Let us never make promises we don't keep.
Let us never waste words.
Let us learn the value of listening.
Let us learn to know when actions and not words are needed.

December

21 Giving

Introduction

As we move into December our thoughts turn to Christmas. Christmas is a time for giving and this morning's story is about a man who found doing this very difficult.

Story

Isaac and Jacob sat at a table drinking coffee.
   'Fools they were – all of them,' said Isaac once again.
   'You mean your ancestors?' replied Jacob.

'That's who I mean – my father, his father before him, and the one before that too. All of them made lots of money and then died before they could spend it! Madness. I'm going to make sure that doesn't happen to me.'

'Really?' smiled Jacob. 'Well here's the waiter with our bill, you can make a start on spending now.'

'Ah,' frowned Isaac, patting his pockets. 'Ah, well I haven't any money with me at the moment. Do you mind?'

Later that night there was a knock at Isaac's door. When he answered it he found a shabby, exhausted-looking man there.

'Excuse me, sir,' said the man. 'I'm afraid things have been going badly for me. I had to leave my job to look after my sick wife. Now she has died and as I couldn't pay the rent I've lost my home as well. Have you any work I can do for you in return for a meal?'

Isaac scowled. His first thought was to send this nuisance away with a good ticking-off ... but then ... perhaps he could make something out of this situation.

'I've got plenty of work here. You can work for a year – no wages but one meal a day and you can sleep in the shed at the bottom of the garden.'

'Thank you, sir,' said the stranger, whose name was Saul, 'you won't regret your decision.'

After six months Isaac couldn't believe his luck. Saul was a fantastic worker. Already he'd created a beautiful garden, re-painted the magnificent house, repaired machinery from clocks to carriages.

'I'm richer than ever,' thought Isaac, 'and all this is costing me nothing except one miserable meal a day.'

A short while later Isaac was walking in his garden when he heard voices. On the other side of the hedge Saul was talking to someone. Peeping through the hedge Isaac saw that the other person was a poor thin-looking man.

'Anything would help,' he was saying.

'Well, I'll tell you what,' said Saul. 'My master is very fair, he gives me one meal a day and lets me sleep in a little bed in the shed. Why don't you sleep in my bed for a couple of nights until you are feeling better? I'll sleep on the floor, and you can share my meal with me.'

As Isaac listened to these words he felt an icy chill go through his body.

'I've never given anything away in my life,' he thought. 'I'm getting richer and richer and yet this Saul – who has nothing – is prepared to give his bed and half his measly food to a stranger.'

Isaac suddenly stood up straight and marched round the hedge. 'Let me help,' he said humbly.

After helping Saul and the stranger as much as he could, Isaac spent the rest of his life looking for ways to use his money to help as many people as possible.

Information for the teacher

1   Some useful December anniversaries associated with giving could include: 3rd December 1838, birthdate of Octavia Hill who 'gave' the country the National Trust; 4th December 1865, birthdate of Edith Cavell who gave her life in helping British soldiers to escape in the First World War; 5th December 1901, birthdate of Walt Disney whose work gave children so much pleasure; 6th December, feast day of St Nicholas, model for Santa Claus.

2   This theme could lead on to a consideration of what the school or class might give to the local community at Christmas.

Hymn suggestion

Come and Praise Vol 2 'Give us hope Lord' No 87

Prayer

Dear God, Help us to give as generously as we can, and to remember that we can give of our time and talents as well as material things. Teach us what is really important in this world of ours. Amen.

22 STOP!

Introduction

When you think about it – *STOP* – is a very important word. If somebody shouts it to a group of people, they pay attention and immediately wonder what has happened. It is a word which is important in this morning's story.

Story

The Buddha was a great religious teacher. He lived in India about two thousand five hundred years ago and taught that it is very important to care for each other.

Once the Buddha was visiting a city called Savatthi. He found the people there very worried.

'It's awful,' one of them said. 'There's the most terrible bandit lurking outside the city.'

'Nobody dares go out alone,' said another resident. 'He lies in wait and robs people regularly.'

'We can't catch him and he's got everybody terrified.'

'Hmm,' said the Buddha. 'I'll have to see what I can do to help.'

'You must be careful, Lord, he's very dangerous.'

So the Buddha left the city and walked slowly out into the countryside. It was hot and dusty and the sun shone down fiercely on the rough country track.

Unknown to the Buddha the bandit had watched him leave the city and then hurried to the spot where he regularly ambushed his victims. He gripped the huge sword he used to terrorise them firmly in his right hand. He waited until the Buddha reached the clump of trees behind which he was hiding, and then leapt out into the road.

'Hand over your money or . . .'

The bandit shouted out his threat, but the Buddha must have been walking faster than he thought because he was already past the clump and walking on down the road.

The bandit turned angrily and, with a shout, began chasing his victim. But strange things started happening.

No matter how loud the bandit shouted, the Buddha paid no attention. Even stranger was the fact that the Buddha just seemed to be strolling along whilst the bandit was running flat out – but just couldn't catch up.

Finally, gasping with exhaustion and frustration, the bandit let out one more yell.

'*Stop*! Hey you, just *stop* will you!'

At once the Buddha turned and said, 'I have stopped, will you?'

'What? What do you mean?' gasped the bandit.

'I've heard of your thieving and cruelty and the way you are making other people's lives miserable. Don't you think you should stop doing that?'

For a moment the bandit looked dazed and worried. Then, unnerved by the strange events which had taken place, and suddenly sorry for all the dreadful things he had done, he dropped to his knees in front of the Buddha.

'You're right,' he cried. 'I've behaved dreadfully. How can I show how sorry I am?'

'Well,' said the Buddha, laying his hand on the bandit's head, 'you can become a follower of mine, and you can go back to Savatthi and return all the things you have stolen. Then people will realise you are a changed man and want to live an honest and caring life.'

Information for the teacher

1   A simple and effective way to introduce this story might be to have three pieces of card with the words: *STOP, LOOK* and *LISTEN* printed on them.

2   The link between this assembly and December stems from the fact that Bodhi Day is celebrated by Buddhists in this month each year. It commemorates the occasion when Prince Gautama discovered enlightenment sitting under a Bodhi tree and became the Buddha.
One form the celebrations assume is the placing of flowers in Buddhist temples as offerings to, and thanksgiving for, the Buddha.

Hymn suggestion

Come and Praise Vol 2 'Lead us from death to life' No 140

Prayer

Let us listen to some words from the Buddha, and then spend some time thinking about them. The words are:

'All that we are is the result of our thoughts'.

23 Tough?

Introduction

The 10th December is a day which was specially set aside to think about caring for each other, and trying to make sure everyone has a fair life.

In times past this was often very difficult. This morning's assembly is about events which took place about five hundred years before Jesus was born.

Story

Aristotle was unhappy and worried. Life in Athens had been wonderful. It was a beautiful city, he had lived with his mother and father . . . and then had come the terrible day of the accident. Now he was in Sparta, an orphan, living with his uncle.

Sparta was so different. Here, to be tough meant everything, and today he had heard about this great festival of toughness from the boys who lived nearby.

'It's great, you'll see.'

'How do you mean?'

'Well, it's a battle.'

'Will . . . will . . . I be in it?'

' 'Course not. You're too young and too small. It's for the bigger boys.'

'But what happens?'

'Well you know that field which is surrounded by the river – two armies of boys meet there to see who wins the fight.'

'Do they have spears and swords?'

'No, nothing like that. All the fighting is done with bare hands.'

Aristotle shuddered and yet at the same time felt a strange excitement. The other boys could talk of nothing else and were obviously looking forward to the great fight.

The day of the battle finally arrived. The whole city had a carnival atmosphere. Men, women and children made their way to the field by the river in order to get good viewing positions. Food sellers shouted cheerfully to advertise what they were selling and everyone seemed in a good mood.

Suddenly a cry went up.

'Here's the first lot.'

A team of some of Sparta's biggest and strongest boys came marching through the crowd. They crossed the bridge into the field and, lifting their arms, gave a great shout that was half battle-cry and half challenge.

The shout was answered by the second team of boys who were now marching through the crowds towards the bridge. Soon they were across it too, and facing their opponents.

A hush fell over the watchers and Aristotle could feel the excitement and anticipation all around him. Suddenly, with a gigantic roar, the two sets of boys charged at each other.

Aristotle saw blows and punches rained on heads and bodies. Boys took terrible blows and fell to the ground beneath charging feet. Screams of pain mixed with the frantic cheering of the crowd.

Information for the teacher

1   This story could end on a questioning note of concern and could then be used to promote reflections about Human Rights Day, which is on the 10th December. This day was established by the United Nations General Assembly, and it is also the day when prizes are announced for those whose achievements have enhanced human rights and benefited mankind. These are the

Nobel prizes. They originate from the fortune of Alfred Nobel who died on 10th December, 1896. He was an industrialist and invented dynamite.

Hymn suggestion

Come and Praise Vol 2 'Sad, puzzled eyes' No 74

Prayer

Lord, help us to work for peace.
Where there is hatred, let us show love;
Where there is injury, pardon;
Where there is discord, union;
Where there is doubt, faith;
Where there is darkness, light;
Where there is sadness, joy;
Where there is despair, hope;
For you and for everyone. Amen.

(Prayer of St Francis)

24 The organist

Introduction

Sometimes in life we experience something so good that we never ever forget it. Let's imagine this morning that we are not in a school but in a village church. It is getting near Christmas and the organist is in the church by himself – practising hard for all the playing he will shortly have to do.

Story

John sat at the organ. The church was empty and still. For the twentieth time his fingers attempted to play the difficult piece in front of him – and for the twentieth time he made half a dozen mistakes as he played.

'Ohh,' he groaned to himself. 'I know I'm not really a very good organist, but this is such a lovely piece, I wish I could play it better.'

He sighed and looked again at the music. The composer's name stood out clearly on the sheet in front of him – Felix Mendelssohn.

'Well . . . must try again . . .'

Then John was suddenly aware that somebody was standing at the back of the church. He felt annoyed.

'Just what I don't want,' he muttered. He started to play again, but became more annoyed when he saw the visitor walking slowly up the aisle towards him.

John took his hands off the keyboard just as the stranger spoke.

'Excuse me,' said the man, 'I was passing by and I heard you playing that piece on the organ. Would you mind if I had a try at playing it?'

John could hardly believe his ears. Of all the cheek!

'Not a chance, I'm afraid. I'm the organist here and I'm afraid we can't let just anybody who fancies it play on this valuable instrument. Besides, it's a very difficult piece.'

'Oh,' replied the stranger and to John's annoyance he sat down in one of the front seats.

John started playing again. He tried to ignore the quiet man sitting there and concentrate on the music. Gradually he laboured through the piece.

'Excuse me.'

It was the stranger again.

'Yes?'

'I really wouldn't hurt the organ if I played it. I have got some experience.'

John sighed with exasperation.

'Perhaps if I let him have a go he'll clear off and I'll be able to get on with it,' he thought to himself. 'All right,' he said aloud. 'Try for a couple of minutes then.'

John climbed down from the organ seat and busied himself with some piles of music.

'Thank you,' said the stranger, and put his hands on the keyboard. At once music swelled through the church. Its beauty caused John to stop what he was doing just to listen.

As the magnificent playing continued, John gasped with astonishment. The stranger was playing the difficult piece which he had struggled so desperately with – and what's more, he was playing it with his eyes tightly closed!

As suddenly as it had started the wonderful music stopped and the stranger climbed down.

'Thank you,' he said in his quiet voice.

John finally recovered from his shock.

'That was . . . that was . . . it was just wonderful,' he said, 'but . . . but . . . who are you?

'Oh, my name is Felix Mendelssohn,' said the stranger as he walked away up the aisle.

Information for the teacher

1 Felix Mendelssohn Bartholdy was born in Hamburg in 1809 and died in Leipzig in 1847. Son of a wealthy father, he composed prolifically ('A Midsummer Night's Dream', 'Fingal's Cave', 'Italian Symphony', etc.) and during his travels he visited England. He composed the overture to 'A Midsummer Night's Dream' when he was only seventeen.

2 The idea of travelling musicians is a very old one. The 'minstrels' of Hebrew times (II Kings 3, 15) were also metal workers who travelled round from community to community both playing and repairing things.
Throughout Biblical history musicians were highly honoured – they were found in prestigious places near kings and priests and were often spared execution when savage changes of power took place.

Hymn suggestion

Come and Praise Vol 2 'Sing, people sing' No 110

Prayer

Let us think this morning about the pleasure which music gives to so many people. Let us give thanks for talented musicians whose skills and compositions we can enjoy. Let us also give thanks for those technicians whose skills make it possible for us to listen to music on discs and tapes.

25 What's in a carol?

Introduction

One of the most famous carols sung at Christmas is 'Good King Wenceslas'. Let me remind you of some of the words:

'Good King Wenceslas looked out
On the feast of Stephen,
Where the snow lay round about
Deep and crisp and even.
Brightly shone the moon that night,

47

>   Though the frost was cruel,
>   When a poor man came in sight
>   Gathering winter fuel.'

Who was Wenceslas? How did the carol come about?

Story

The story of Wenceslas is really one which centres round three main characters. These were: Wenceslas, a young prince who became King of Bohemia in 921; Boleslav, his brother, who wanted to rule the country instead of Wenceslas; Henry I, ruler of the Germans who wanted to invade Bohemia and make it part of his empire.

Wenceslas, before becoming king, had spent most of his life in a monastery. He was gentle and kind and firmly believed that all people should be treated with goodwill. As soon as he became king he began to put his ideas into practice. Calling his ministers together he gave them some orders.

'Those gallows which stand in so many public places – take them down. We don't want to remind people of bad things. Let's be encouraging. The same goes for the dungeons – there will be no more torture down there, no matter what the crime.'

Such moves made Wenceslas very popular with his subjects. Gradually they became less fearful.

'Wenceslas is young but he's got the right ideas.'

'He means what he says.'

'Yes . . . if only we could all live in peace . . .'

'. . . And stop worrying about armies and wars.'

But Boleslav thought his brother was wrong. 'It's no good being soft like this. The Germans are just waiting to invade us. We've got to be tough on our people, make them ready to fight and die if necessary.'

In 928 Henry I and the Germans invaded Bohemia. In a very short time they were at the gates of Prague. Wenceslas stayed calm and once again called his ministers to him.

'If we fight, thousands of people will be killed or injured and we will probably still lose. Let's try the peaceful approach. I will go to the city gates and welcome Henry myself.'

Was Wenceslas right? Boleslav and his followers didn't think so, because just a year later they murdered Wenceslas. The Czech people had different ideas though. They remembered Wenceslas for his concern for others, his kindness and his many Christian acts. That is why St Wenceslas is one of the most famous saints in Czechoslovakia.

But what about the carol? Well, the tune is a very old one which dates back to about 1250. The words which we sing were put to this tune by a man called John Neale in the nineteenth century. He probably didn't know any more about Wenceslas than we do, but his work helps us all to remember a Christian who lived in very difficult times.

Information for the teacher

1   In Wenceslas Square in Prague the statue of the King-Saint carries an epitaph beneath it: 'St Wenceslas suffer not us nor our children to perish'.

2   If the carol aspect of this story is enlarged then the story of another carol always interests children. This is of course 'Silent Night'.

In 1818, in the village of Obendorf in Austria, the priest Joseph Mohr discovered just before Christmas that mice had damaged the bellows of the church organ. Anxious to divert the congregation's attention away from this lack of musical accompaniment, Mohr and the organist Franz Gruber composed a new carol for the Christmas service. With Gruber accompanying the singing on a guitar, 'Silent Night' had its first public performance at the village Christmas service.

This story has marvellous dramatic possibilities.

Hymn suggestion

The obvious choice here is the carol which is central to this morning's theme.

Prayer

Dear God, Let us think this morning about decisions. As we get older we have more and more difficult decisions to make. Give us the strength and wisdom to choose wisely when we are in these situations. Amen.

26 An unusual Christmas dinner

Introduction

Let's think about Christmas dinner – what sort of food do we eat at this time of the year? (*Pause for answers!*)

This morning's story tells of one of the strangest Christmas dinners you could imagine. Here's how it came about.

Story

On 21st December 1908 a man wrote the following words in his diary: 'We are very hungry . . . our beards are masses of ice all day long.'

The man was called Ernest Shackleton and he was the leader of a group of men who were trying to be the first explorers to reach the South Pole. Already they had been travelling for two months on their mission and things had been very difficult for them.

'It was hard going up those icy mountains,' called Eric Marshall to his colleagues.

'It wouldn't have been so bad if all the ponies hadn't died. Then we wouldn't have had to pull these sledges ourselves, would we?' answered Frank Wild.

'You're right there,' said Eric. 'They're a terrible weight. Still, we've a treat to look forward to soon.'

'What's that?'

'Christmas dinner – what else?'

In the bitter wind, fingering his cut and frostbitten nose, Ernest Shackleton couldn't resist a smile. Despite the savagery of the weather his men had remained cheerful.

They had had to abandon all but the very bare essentials because they were too exhausted to pull much on the sledges. They had only the clothes they stood up in – and they were still many, many miles from the Pole.

By six o'clock on Christmas Day they had covered only a few more miles. The wind howled relentlessly over the snow and they bent their tired and aching bodies to the task of putting up their little tent.

Once this was done the four men crouched inside in their thick fur clothes. The thoughts of all of them were far away – back home with their families and friends.

'Right,' said Ernest. 'This is what we've been waiting for – anybody hungry?'

There was a great cheer from the three men as Shackleton set the little stove going and prepared to make the feast.

'I've never been so hungry in my whole life,' muttered Lieutenant Adams. 'Never.'

'Never mind, Christmas dinner coming up soon – I can hardly wait, replied Eric Marshall.

'First course on its way,' called out Ernest, who had been doing the cooking.

Each man grasped his tin plate and looked at the steaming pile which lay upon it.

'Oh, it's hoosh,' said Frank.

'Hoosh' was a ration for the dead ponies which had been boiled up with a strange kind of dried meat called pemmican.

'What's next?'

There was a clinking noise as the next course came round. This was one dried biscuit each. The third course was half a cup of Oxo each, and then came the highlight of the meal.

Through all the difficulties and abandoning of equipment Ernest had held onto a tiny Christmas pudding. Now, he boiled up a little cocoa water and then dropped the Christmas pudding into it. When the water boiled again and steam rose into the tiny tent the leader divided the small pudding with his spoon and carefully laid a piece on each man's plate.

'Merry Christmas,' he said.

'Merry Christmas,' they all replied, thinking they had never tasted anything so wonderful in their whole lives.

Information for the teacher

1 Shackleton's 1908–09 mission to reach the South Pole failed. With food supplies almost completely finished, and suffering from acute stomach pains after having eaten some undercooked rice, the men were totally exhausted by early January. On 7th January they encountered the worst snow storm yet – 'a blinding, shrieking blizzard' wrote Shackleton. They could go no further and began the return journey.
   Despite the expedition's failure, Shackleton was knighted for his bravery when he returned to England.

2 The theme of 'what we enjoy when we are really desperately hungry' is a far-reaching one with lots of thought-provoking possibilities at this time of the year.

3 There is a quotation from the Bible which could be used to provoke a great deal of thought in the context of this story. It is: 'A man's spirit may sustain him'. (Proverbs 18, 4)

Hymn suggestion

Come and Praise Vol 1 'When a knight won his spurs' No 50

Prayer

Let us think this morning of the courage of explorers, whose discoveries have so increased our knowledge of the world. Let us learn from their self-sacrifice and determination. Let us also appreciate the good food and good fortune which so many of us enjoy.

27 Christmas around the world

Introduction

Many people celebrate Christmas all over the world. In different places some things are done very differently, as you will hear.

Story

At Christmas the Post Office receives many letters from children addressed to Father Christmas at the North Pole. In Germany, when the children have written their letters, they put them in envelopes and then spread glue lightly over each envelope. Next they scatter sugar on the glue so that the letters glitter. Then, on Christmas Eve, the glittering letters are put outside on window sills to await collection.

In Poland it is very important to watch for the first star on Christmas Eve. When it appears the whole family sits down to a Christmas feast. This begins with the passing round of a thin piece of bread which is called an *oplatek*. There is a picture of Mary, Joseph and Jesus on the *oplatek* and each member of the family breaks a piece of it when it reaches them. Usually two empty places are left at the feast table so that if Mary and Joseph were to arrive there would be places for them.

In Finland, where it is very cold in December, children make a point of putting out special feasts for birds and animals at Christmas. Long poles are sometimes stuck in the ground and pieces of suet hung from them. Nuts are strung from trees in long chains.

If you lived in Finland you would look forward to very different food from that which we enjoy in Britain at Christmas. You might sit down to a feast of cold ham and pickled herrings!

In Norway too, animals are thought of at Christmas. Norwegian children remember the story of a little gnome who was supposed to guard animals, and they put out bowls of porridge for him at this time of the year.

Swedish children remember that Jesus lay in a manger of straw, so they make many of their Christmas decorations from straw. In France, when everybody had open fires and not central heating, it was important to keep the fire going all night on Christmas Eve in case Mary should pass by and need warmth and shelter.

Italy is the country with which we associate Christmas cribs. St Francis made one in his home town of Greccio to remind people of where and how Jesus was born. From this beginning Italian families began to make model cribs in their homes and eventually the idea spread around the world.

In far away Australia, Christmas comes in the middle of the summer, when the weather is very hot. People go to famous beaches like Bondi in Sydney to eat their turkey and pudding at picnics. When they go home, though, they still have decorations of Christmas trees and evergreens in their houses.

Information for the teacher

1   This assembly could be presented in tableau form, whereby pictures, models and dramatic re-enactments reflect each of the aspects shown, and the whole thing is linked by the words of the passage.

2   Whilst on the international aspect of Christmas, the idea of wishing people 'Merry Christmas' in different languages is always one that appeals to Junior School children. Thus the following might be useful:

Czechoslovakian	*Vesele Vanoch*
Dutch	*Gelukkig Kerstfeest*
Finnish	*Hauskaa Joulua*
French	*Joyeux Noël*
German	*Fröhliche Weinachten*
Italian	*Buone Feste Natalizie*
Norwegian	*Gledig Jul*
Polish	*Bozego Narodzenia*
Spanish	*Feliz Navidad*
Swedish	*Glad Jul*

Hymn suggestion

Come and Praise Vol 2 'As I went riding by' No 120

Prayer

When we think of our own Christmas we so often think of warmth, family gatherings, kindness – all those things which make this time so special. Let us listen now to some words about that first Christmas:

> Winds through the olive trees
> Softly did blow,
> Round little Bethlehem
> Long, long ago.
>
> Sheep on the hillside lay
> Whiter than snow;
> Shepherds were watching them,
> Long, long ago.
>
> Then from the happy sky,
> Angels bent low,
> Singing their songs of joy,
> Long, long ago.
>
> For in a manger bed,
> Cradled we know,
> Christ came to Bethlehem
> Long, long ago.
>
> (Author unknown)

January

28 This month

Introduction

January is the month we say 'Happy New Year' to each other. We think about new beginnings – and learning from our mistakes of the last year. January is also the month when it seems as if winter is going on for ever ... but it isn't.

Story

January is often the coldest month of the year, but there are strange contrasts during this month.

When there is frost and snow there are problems both in town and country. Roads become dangerous, pipes freeze and stored potatoes have to be protected with straw or even heaters. Small birds are in danger when it is cold. This is because the surface area of a small bird is large compared with the rest of its body. Surfaces lose warmth quickly so the bird's body gets cold quickly. We can help by putting out plenty of food on the bird table. When it eats, the bird gets both heat and energy from the food.

At the same time, however, January does promise the end of winter. If you look carefully at the tips of branches you can see that leaf buds are already beginning to swell, and yellow hazel catkins start to come out during this month. Masses of starlings start to swirl about the sky just before it gets dark, and if there is a really sunny day during the month squirrels start to appear more often. The first baby lambs are born in January. Flowers are very few but yellow gorse can be seen on commons and hillsides and the first snowdrops are starting to peep through.

The first Monday after the Twelve Days of Christmas used to be a day when ploughmen all over the country had parties and went from door to door collecting money. The reason for this was that they were marking the end of their holidays with a special occasion and preparing to start work again. You might think of this when you see tractors and ploughs cutting their furrows through the bare fields.

Information for the teacher

1   Quite a few schools have tailor's dummies on which school uniforms or other costumes are displayed. In this assembly it would be useful to dress up the dummy for the assembly in what seems the most appropriate clothing for the month. As the month progresses, the children can reflect on the appropriateness of this clothing to the prevailing weather.

2   Primary school children are fascinated by the line of thought that January is named after the Roman god Janus, and that the Latin word '*jauna*' means 'door'. Thus we move through the door into the new year, leaving disappointments behind and striving for better things to come.

3   The 6th of the month is the celebration of the Feast of the Epiphany in the Christian Church. This is the time when the three kings supposedly arrived in Bethlehem.

4   Bearing in mind the idea that January offers the opportunity to 'turn over a new leaf', reference to the Bible might be useful in locating passages which suggest admirable virtues. Possible references might be: Matthew 15, 29–31 for determination; Luke 16, 19–31 for concern and kindness; Romans 12, 1–5 for unselfishness.

Hymn suggestion

Come and Praise Vol 2 'It's a new day' No 106

Prayer

Let us bow our heads and think this morning of January in Britain. It is a time when, beneath the cold and darkness, preparations are being made for new life.

Let us think about our own lives and ways in which we can try to be more helpful and considerate people.

29 The hero

Introduction

Have you got a hero? Do you admire someone for their talent, or a skill, or any actions? Is there anybody about whom you would like to say, 'I wish I was like that'? This morning's story is about an unusual hero.

Story

'Those monkeys are too noisy,' said the king to one of his ministers. 'I'm going to get rid of them for ever.'

'Yes, your majesty,' replied the minister, bowing low.

Then he listened carefully to the king's plans.

A few days later the king and the minister, together with a squad of soldiers armed with spears and bows and arrows, set out for the huge trees where all the monkeys lived. Several eyes watched their progress.

Within minutes the movement of the soldiers was being reported to the leader of the monkeys.

'They're coming – lots of men with weapons! They're going to surround the tree and kill us all – I know it!'

'Keep calm, keep calm,' said the monkey leader. 'I know a way in which we can escape.'

Meanwhile the king and his soldiers had reached the tree. The soldiers began to push their way through the bushes and soon the tree was surrounded.

'When you're all in position I'll give the order to fire,' said the king. 'Then we'll be rid of these nuisances for ever.'

The leader of the monkeys heard the movement and voices as he worked desperately to save his friends. Running alongside the great tree was a river, and on the other side of the river was another tree with great creepers hanging down from it.

'Now, I can jump the river,' thought the monkey leader, 'and then swing back on one of those creepers. If I tie it to this tree all the monkeys can use it as a bridge and escape to the other side.'

So, as the soldiers moved into position, the monkey leader crossed the river, chose the longest creeper, and swung back to the home tree with it ... but there was a snag. The creeper was just not quite long enough to reach between the two trees.

'No problem,' thought the leader. 'I'll make up the distance with my own body.' So, with one arm hanging onto the tree and the other arm outstretched to grip the creeper, the monkey leader was suspended in space – the last link of his bridge.

Now things started to happen quickly, Seeing their escape route ready and hearing their leader's instructions, the monkeys began to pour over the bridge to safety. Furious at the thought of them escaping, the king called out to his soldiers, 'Fire – before they all escape!'

Struggling to get their bows ready, the soldiers managed to get a few arrows off but none of the monkeys was hit. Then a terrible thing happened.

The last monkey in the home tree was one who for years had been jealous of the leader. He was filled with envy and hatred and suddenly he saw the chance to get rid of his rival and become leader himself.

Leaping from the tree, he crashed feet first into the tired and aching back of the monkey leader, smashing him away from the tree. With a terrible cry of pain the monkey leader fell to the ground while his evil rival grabbed the creeper and swung away to safety.

From the ground the king had seen all this happen. As the monkey leader crashed to the ground, he called out to his men, 'Stop firing! Stop firing at once.'

Pushing desperately through the bushes, the king reached the monkey leader. He saw at once that the leader was in great pain and dying.

'A doctor!' cried the king. 'To the palace at once and get a doctor.'

It was no use. The monkey leader died as the group of men stood round him. The king spoke with bowed head to them all.

'Never in my life have I seen a braver action than this. This monkey will be buried as if he were a king and the story of his courage will be told to all children and never forgotten.'

Information for the teacher

1 This is an adaptation from an old Buddhist story from the *Jataka* tales. The king was the King of Benares and the evil monkey was called Devadatta. This story is an excellent one for reflecting the Four Noble Truths of the Buddhist religion. These are:

- suffering is a part of life;
- selfishness is the cause of suffering;
- if selfishness is overcome then suffering will stop;
- following the 'eightfold path' towards perfection will bring suffering to an end.

The Buddha also told his followers that three of the greatest selfish evils were greed, hatred and laziness.

2 A possible calendar link is with Education Sunday which is held in some Christian churches during this month. Buddhism is very much concerned with teaching. *'Dharma'* is the name given to the Buddha's teaching.

Hymn suggestion

Come and Praise Vol 2 'All the animals' No 80

Prayer

Let us bow our heads and think this morning about some of the advice given in the words of the Buddhist religion: 'Mules and horses and elephants are excellent when trained, but more excellent is the man who has trained himself.'

30 A helping paw

Introduction

Some wild animals are very frightening. For instance, how would you like to come face to face with a lion . . . ?

Story

The afternoon light was fading as the group of monks sat in the chapel. One was reading aloud while the others were still and quiet, listening. Suddenly they were aware of movement at the back of the chapel. Turning, they saw that limping slowly down the aisle was an enormous lion!

There were gasps and cries and, in an undignified scuffle, the monks bundled past each other – all trying to get out of the chapel before the lion reached them. All, that is, except a monk called Jerome. He saw the lion too, but he took the trouble to look at it a little more closely.

'He's hurt,' Jerome muttered to himself as the lion limped nearer. Getting up from his seat, he turned and walked slowly towards the lion.

'You're hurt, old friend,' he said in a quiet voice. 'You're hurt. How can I help?'

As if he understood, and without pausing in his limping stride, the lion came right up to the monk and lifted up his front paw.

'Ah, this is the problem, is it?' said Jerome. 'Well, let's have a close look at it.

Bending down, the monk examined the paw carefully. It was swollen and badly cut. 'Looks as if you've torn that on some thorns,' murmured Jerome. 'It needs bathing and some ointment on it and in a few days it will be as good as new.'

The lion followed Jerome as the monk set about treating its paw. Within a few days it had healed properly. By this time the other monks had got over their fear of the creature because he went about the monastery almost as a pet.

'Now,' said Jerome one day when the lion was completely cured, 'we must think about our friend the lion. We must find him work to do which is useful and suited to him. Have you any suggestions?'

'I've got one,' said one monk straight away. 'You know we've got that donkey to carry wood for our fires? Well, when we're out with him we're always scared some fierce creature is going to attack. Now if he had a guard . . .'

'Excellent,' replied Jerome, 'excellent.'

And so it came about that the lion worked every day protecting the donkey from harm and making sure that the monks got plenty of wood for their fires.

Information for the teacher

1 The themes of hasty reactions to animals could be developed by reflecting on a very different story. This is that of the prince who came home and found his baby's cot covered in blood, with his dog covered in blood too. Suspecting the worst, he slew his dog immediately, only to find that it had dragged the baby to safety and then fought off the attacking animal which had sought to kill them both.

2 A possibly useful calendar link here is that Gerald Durrell was born on 7th January 1925. He founded the Wildlife Preservation Trust.

Hymn suggestion

Come and Praise Vol 2 'All the animals' No 80

Prayer

Make us worthy, Lord,
To care for each other
And for all living creatures

Give us courage, Lord,
To give help when it is needed
In difficult or frightening circumstances

Give us faith, Lord,
That you will guide us
And make our efforts worthwhile

Amen.

31 The weekend

Introduction

Sometimes in our lives we meet people for a very short period of time. How they remember us often depends upon how we behaved that time . . .

Story

This is a true story. It is about a family, and a young woman who had recently become a widow.

'We'll go away for the weekend – it's not every day I get a new job,' said Mum.

'All right,' replied Dad. 'The kids will love that. But where will we go?'

'As a matter of fact I've already booked somewhere,' Mum went on. 'I saw an advert in the evening paper. It sounds like a nice house down by the sea near Brighton.'

'Yippee!' cried Emily, Jacob and Lynn when they heard the news.

Meanwhile, in 'the nice house by the sea', Barbara Jackson was worried. Her husband had died six months ago and she had decided to rent out part of her house to holidaymakers so that she could earn a living. Now her first guests were coming for a weekend – a mum, dad, and three children. How would she cope? Could she give them enough food? Would they mess up the bedrooms?

On Friday night Barbara met Geoffrey and Thelma Johnson and Emily, Jacob and Lynn. From the start it was a great weekend for everybody. Geoffrey and Thelma loved the house, the kids loved the games room in the cellar and they all found Barbara and her Great Dane, Alphonse, good company.

'From my point of view, it's just a great relief,' thought Barbara. 'They're such nice people and they're obviously enjoying themselves.'

Sunday afternoon came round all too quickly.

'Go and get the car sorted out – I'll pay the bill,' said Geoffrey Johnson, and Thelma went outside to pack the car.

Soon, after the farewells, the family were on their way back to London. But an hour after Barbara had waved them off, after tidying up, she made an unpleasant discovery.

'How could I?' she said to herself. 'I've charged them for only one room instead of two. Now, instead of making a small profit, I've lost money I could ill afford. Oh dear . . . well, they must be laughing about it. I suppose I've learnt an expensive lesson.'

She had just finished giving Alphonse his tea when there was a knock on the front door. Opening it, Barbara found Thelma Johnson standing there. 'We got talking about the bill on our journey home and we realised you must have made a mistake – so we've come back to pay you what we owe you.'

'But . . . you must have been nearly halfway home,' gasped Barbara.

'Perhaps – but after such a lovely weekend we couldn't let you think we'd cheat you in any way. We just had to come back straight away.'

Minutes later the Johnsons were on their way again. As she waved once more, Barbara's head was full of thoughts. 'If I have ten thousand guests – I'll never forget the Johnsons,' she smiled to herself.

Information for the teacher

1   A nice little anecdote to use in conjunction with this story is the derivation of the word 'sincere'. Marble craftsmen of long ago tricked customers by putting melted wax in flaws in the marble. The more reputable of them gave customers a guarantee saying their work was not fraudulent in this way. The guarantee said SINE CERA (in Latin this meant 'without [*sine*] wax [*cera*]'). From this we get the word 'sincere'.

2   One possible calendar link for this story is the 8th of the month. This was the date in 1941 that Lord Baden Powell died. His insistence on 'honourable' behaviour was one of the keystones of the Boy Scout movement and, later, of the Girl Guides.

Hymn suggestion

Come and Praise Vol 1 'Make us worthy, Lord' No 94

Prayer

Dear God,

Help us to be honest enough to admit our own mistakes. Give us the strength to be honest when it is easier to tell a lie or say nothing. Help us to be honest at all times in both word and deed.

Amen.

32 Here he comes

Introduction

Have you ever noticed how people are superstitious? They won't walk under ladders, they 'touch wood' or 'keep their fingers crossed'. This morning's story is about a woman who thought bad luck would come her way because of the actions of one man . . .

Story

It was terribly hot in the city of Mecca. The air seemed to press down heavily and the dusty street was still and silent. A first man appeared, to be followed by another, and another. Women and children arrived too, and all crowded in small patches of shade. They made sure they could all see the street.

Soon a whisper went up. 'Here he comes.'

'Get ready!'

'She hasn't appeared yet.'

'Don't worry, she has never missed.'

Walking steadily along the street was a very calm-looking man. He looked neither to the left nor the right and was approaching a balcony which hung out over the street. As he neared the balcony a woman suddenly appeared on it. She had a bucket in her hands and moved purposefully to the edge of the balcony.

When the man was almost directly beneath her, with a scream, she hurled the contents of the bucket all over him. The thick dust and rubbish, sweepings from her house, dropped firmly on the man passing below.

'She never forgets,' said somebody among the watchers.

'Never. You know why she does it?'

'No. Tell me.'

'Well, that man is called Muhammad (pbuh)[1]. Some people say he is a great prophet. He went to the mosque in the centre of town and threw out all the statues of gods. He says there is only one God.'

'But why did that bother the woman?'

'Ah well, lots of people think that if the gods are harmed a great disaster will befall Mecca and its people. This woman is just one of the people who want to get at Muhammad. He is very unpopular.'

The people went away; but exactly the same time the next day they were all there to see it happen again. Everybody knew when Muhammad went to pray and they knew the route he always took.

Then, one day, the woman was not there to throw down the rubbish. Nor was she there the next day, or the next.

Muhammad asked round. 'The woman who throws her rubbish down on me – where is she? I haven't seen her for three days.'

'Ah,' said one of the townspeople, 'she's ill, I think.'

So Muhammad went to the woman's house. After he had knocked for several minutes, a frail voice finally told him to come in.

'You're ill,' said Muhammad, looking at the woman as she lay pale and shaking on a chair. 'You must let me help you.'

The woman was too ill to say anything but she couldn't help wondering why this man whom she had treated so dreadfully had come to help her.

Muhammad cared for the sick woman – cleaning, cooking and making sure she had everything she needed. Slowly she recovered.

'Sir,' she said one day when she was feeling strong again, 'thank you for looking after me so well. Would you let me do something?'

'Of course,' replied Muhammad.

'May I come to the mosque with you and say a prayer too?'

So, by his actions, Muhammad had got the woman to believe his teaching.

Information for the teacher

1   The name of the prophet Muhammad is followed by the initials 'pbuh'; this is the written abbreviation of the words 'Peace be upon him', which are always spoken after Muhammad's name by Muslims, as a mark of respect.

2   To be considerate to others was one of Muhammad's basic teachings. Muslims consider the words of the Qur'an to be the words of God – as told to Muhammad by the angle Gabriel. There are many Muslim stories which emphasise caring for others.

3   Muhammad was born in Mecca (in about 570 AD Christian dates). Despite the presence of the famous shrine (the Ka'aba) in the city, Muhammad was concerned about its false gods. He and his followers suffered much abuse trying to establish that there was only one God.

   He left to live in Medina but returned to Mecca in 630 when the city became fully Muslim, the idols were finally removed and the Ka'aba took on its great significance for the religion.

   At least once in his or her lifetime every Muslim should take a pilgrimage (*hajj*) to Mecca.

4   A possible calendar link might be with other significant religious figures: Swami Vivekananda, the Hindu reformer, was born in 1862 on 12 January; Wilson Carlile who founded the Church Army was born in 1847 on the 14th.

Hymn suggestion

Come and Praise Vol 1 'Spirit of God' No 63

Prayer

In our prayer this morning, let us listen carefully to some words which were said by Muhammad. Let us then pause quietly for a minute to try and understand them.

'It is charity for any Muslim to plant a tree or cultivate land which provides food for a bird, animal or man.'

'Visit the sick, feed the hungry and free the captives.'

'Say part of your prayers at home so your houses do not become like graves.'

33 Avalanche!

Introduction

January is a month when we often get snow. Snow can be beautiful and fun to play in – but it can also be dangerous. Sometimes in Alpine areas snow sweeps down mountainsides crushing and burying everything in its path. These rushes of snow are called 'avalanches'.

Story

'*Danger of avalanches. Those people in threatened areas are strongly advised to leave their houses.*'

The Swiss Radio broadcast this warning over and over again in the winter of 1947. Listeners took it very seriously and moved away from homes in dangerous areas, but Hans Altschwank was worried. As the village schoolmaster in Urteli, he knew that a party of boys were staying in a hut high above the village. They were skiing during the day and would not have heard the warning.

'Come on, Werner,' said Hans to his fifteen-year-old son. 'We'd better go up there and get those lads to safety.'

So father and son set off, and reached the hut just as the group of boys were getting ready to go skiing.

'I'm glad we've caught you,' said Hans, 'and I'm glad you're all dressed for skiing. We've got to get out of here – and quick!'

'Why, what's the problem?' asked one of the boys.

When Hans told them about the threatened avalanches several of the boys exchanged frightened looks, and all hurried to follow Hans and Werner down the mountain. But they didn't quite make it.

As they began their descent, they heard the sinister 'whooshing' noise of snow rushing down the mountainside behind them. It filled the group with terror.

'Dodge from side to side!' shouted Hans, and the skiers swerved desperately to miss the rushing snow. It seemed that they had made it – until suddenly the last boy was swept off his feet and, in seconds, was buried under the snow. 'I know where he is,' shouted Werner, and the group rushed back to where he was pointing now that the snow had swept past. Digging feverishly, they sighed with relief when a hand suddenly poked up through the snow – and wiggled its fingers.

'Hang on, we'll soon have you out,' shouted Werner. He grabbed the hand of the missing boy, whose name was Paolo. 'We'll soon . . .'

But no sooner had Werner started to shout again, when 'Whoosh!' . . . a second avalanche began its rush down the mountain, as fast as an express train. Once again the group scattered, except for Werner who steadfastly held onto Paolo's hand.

Now Werner was buried too, but the others scrambled back once the danger was past and began digging again. Gradually they freed the two bruised and frozen boys, and the party skied down to the village below.

The group of boys were given beds in barns, and Hans and Werner went back to their own home. They were exhausted and fell asleep as soon as they had eaten. But the danger was not over.

While the village was asleep, a third avalanche swept down the mountainside, crushing and burying the houses at its foot. Troops from a nearly army barracks were rushed in to help with the rescue and soon almost everybody was accounted for. Only three people were missing – Hans Altschwank, his wife, and Werner.

When the party of boys heard this they refused to leave. 'We've got to find them,' said their leader. 'Come on, let's get digging.'

The story had a happy ending. Werner was discovered safe and sound fairly quickly, and finally, after fifty-seven hours, Hans and his wife too were found safe and alive.

This was a story of friendship, help and determination, and it filled the newspapers of the world.

Information for the teacher

1   Some poetic licence has been used with this story. Werner was discovered fairly quickly and evacuated to another village along with the other boys. It was there that they heard of the Altschwank parents' rescue and they were so inspired by this that they journeyed to another buried village, Valgretto, and rescued a girl who had been given up for dead.

2   The boys in the story were from the Pestalozzi Children's Village at Trogen, in Switzerland. The Pestalozzi Villages were set up after the war to care for the thousands of children who had been left homeless, friendless, and without relatives after the fighting in Europe.

Pestalozzi Villages still exist to teach skills to children from poorer countries so that they can return home and utilise their skills for the benefit of all.

Hymn suggestion

Come and Praise Vol 1 'He who would valiant be' No 44

Prayer

Let us give thanks this morning for those people whose quick thinking and determined courage save so many lives when disasters occur.

Let us learn from this example.

34 *The cut*

Introduction

'Help!' You just never know when you might have to use this word, and you can only hope that somebody will be able to give you the help you need. Fortunately, there are many people who help us in different ways.

Story

Sue was nine. Her dad called her 'Speedy'.

'She never walks anywhere, that girl,' he was always saying, 'always runs – upstairs, downstairs, to school, back home again – run, run, run.'

One day Sue was running downstairs as usual. She didn't notice that Liz, her sister, had left a doll on the stairs. Sue tripped over it.

At the bottom of the stairs was a radiator. Sue hit the radiator head first. She felt a sharp, stabbing pain in her head. When she put her hand up to feel it, her hand came away covered in blood.

'Help, help!' cried Sue. 'I'm hurt.'

Mum, Dad, Liz and Paul all heard Sue's shout and rushed to the bottom of the stairs.

'Her head,' shouted Mum shakily. 'Look at the blood.'

Dad got his handkerchief out and held it tightly over Sue's head. Sue was trying to be brave – but she did not like the blood.

'Get the car out,' said Dad. 'She'll have to go to hospital.'

Mum rushed out with the car keys.

'Hospital,' thought Sue. 'I've never been to hospital before. I'm scared!' She looked at Paul and Liz, and she could see that they were scared too.

Soon the family were on the way to the hospital. Sue lay on the back seat with her head on Mum's knee. She had a clean cloth on her head now, but there was still a lot of blood.

Swinging in at the hospital gates, Dad called out, 'We'll have to follow that sign,' as he pointed to a sign saying Casualty.

As they entered the building, a nurse saw them coming. 'follow me,' she said to Mum and Sue. Dad and the others stayed behind and Dad gave some details to another nurse.

Mum and Sue were shown into a small room where a doctor was washing his hands. 'Hmm,' he said, after looking at Sue's head. 'Nothing that a few stitches won't put right.'

'Stitches!' thought Sue. 'They'll hurt, for sure!'

Very carefully the doctor examined Sue's head. Then the nurse cut off some of Sue's hair and washed all round the large cut. Then she put some other stuff on and Sue thought it felt funny.

'Where's the machine?' she asked.

'What machine?' asked the nurse.

'You said you were going to do some stitching – don't you need a sewing machine for that?'

'Oh, you'll just have to put up with me doing it by hand,' smiled the doctor, who was already working very carefully on Sue's head. After a few minutes he finished what he was doing and came round and sat in front of her.

'You've been very brave, Sue,' he said. 'You might have a headache for a little while but you'll soon feel fit again.'

Dad, Paul and Liz were pleased to see Sue.

'Hi, Speedy,' said Dad.

Soon the family was back home.

'You've had a busy day,' said Mum.

'Yes,' said Sue, 'but I've learned a lot. Now I know exactly what happens when you hurt yourself.'

'That's when we need nurses and doctors and hospitals,' said Dad.

But Sue didn't hear him – she was already running upstairs!

Information for the teacher

1   A possible January calendar link for this story is with the 14th. On this date in 1875 one of the world's most famous doctors was born – Dr Albert Schweitzer.

2   Some useful addresses are as follows:

Royal Society for the Prevention of Accidents, Edgbaston Park, 353 Bristol Road, Edgbaston, Birmingham, B5 7ST, www.rospa.org.uk

Royal Association for Disability and Rehabilitation (RADAR), 12 City Forum, 250 City Road, London EC1V 8AF, www.radar.org.uk

Help the Aged, St James Walk, London EC1, www.helptheaged.org.uk

St John's Ambulance Brigade, 1 Grosvenor Crescent, London SW1X 7EF, www.sja.org.uk

3   The theme could be extended to consider some people who have lived outstanding lives of giving service and help. One of the most famous was Mother Teresa.
Mother Teresa was born in Yugoslavia in 1910. Originally she went to India in 1948 to be a teacher but she was so shocked by the suffering and poverty that she decided her life's work must be to help those people in desperate need.
Her work resulted in world fame and gifts of money and medicine from far and wide to help her mission. She was awarded the Nobel Peace Prize in 1979. Mother Teresa died on 5th September 1997 at the age of 87.

Hymn suggestion

Come and Praise Vol 1 'When I need a neighbour' No 65

Prayer

This morning we are concentrating our thoughts on a particular word – Help.

Let us think very carefully about the following words of a Hindu saying: 'He who does not help to turn the wheels of this great world lives a lost life.'

February

35 The recipe

Introduction

None of us likes people who are selfish. Listen carefully to this morning's story: it is about somebody who was selfish, and thought he was very clever.

Story

The king was hurt. As the king was the great lion, all the other animals were very concerned. The hare went to see him.

'My lord,' said the hare. 'That was a great battle you won, but you have been badly hurt. You must rest until your wounds have fully healed.'

'Rest? Rest?' snarled the lion. 'I must eat, mustn't I?'

'Don't worry about that,' replied the hare. 'All the other animals want their king to recover. They will help, and I will prepare good meals and look after you.'

The lion hesitated. He was more badly hurt than he had at first realised. It would be good to be looked after and rest until he was well again. But could he trust the hare? He would see.

'Very well,' he replied firmly. 'You may be my servant, Hare.'

So the long healing process began. The hare was as good as his word. He made the lion comfortable, got his meals ready, arranged the times for visitors. He was an excellent servant, but the lion was very slow in getting completely better.

As time went by, the hyena grew to envy the hare more and more. 'What a job he's got,' he thought. 'Everything provided for him and safe as houses in the home of the king. He must be the luckiest animal alive at the moment, I'd like his job, and I've got a pretty good idea of how to get it.'

So the hyena made an appointment to see the lion. The hare arranged it, greeted the hyena pleasantly, and then left him alone with the lion.

The hyena bowed low before the lion.

'My lord,' said the hyena, 'the animals are all very worried that you are not better by now.'

The lion gave a growl that could have meant anything.

'So they have sent me to be their spokesman,' went on the hyena. 'They don't think the hare is looking after you properly. They think

I could do a better job – especially as there is a recipe for a meal which I'm sure would make you feel much better. That hare is just too lazy to make it.'

Now while the hyena was saying this, the hare, who was just about to come into the room, heard everything. He stepped inside quickly and spoke at once to both the lion and the hyena.

'No, no,' he said. 'You're quite wrong there, friend Hyena. I've got everything ready for that special meal – I was only waiting until I could get the last ingredient which, as I'm sure you know, is hyena flesh.'

As the hyena listened to what the quick-witted hare was saying, a chill of fear ran through him.

The lion gave a snarl, and bared his huge teeth. Without another word, the hyena leapt up and fled as fast as he could.

(Adapted from an old African folk tale.)

Information for the teacher

1   A very useful date and story to link with this one are 1st February 1811 and the tale of Bell Rock Lighthouse. On 1st February 1811 the lighthouse was opened which warned shipping off the dangerous Inchcape Rock.

In earlier years a bell had been put on this rock to warn ships but a pirate named Ralph the Rover, in a mood of bravado, cut away the bell and it sank. Later on, returning from a voyage, his own ship hit this rock and sank, taking the pirate leader down with it.

Hymn suggestion

Come and Praise Vol 2 'You can build a wall' No 91

Prayer

Dear God,

Help us to avoid the sin of selfishness, and teach us to be aware that trying to trick people in order to gain things for ourselves often leads to unhappiness.

Help us to learn how to be content, thoughtful and modest. Amen.

36 Judy

Introduction

This morning's story is about a boy called Evan Davies. One thing you could certainly say about him is that he didn't give up easily.

Story

'Great, great, just what I wanted.'

Evan's eyes lit up with delight when he saw what his eleventh birthday present was. The 'present' looked pretty happy too – she was a mischievous Jack Russell puppy whom Evan promptly christened Judy.

Evan's birthday was in February and in the months that followed he and Judy became almost inseparable companions. When the summer holidays arrived, Evan looked forward to having even more time to spend with his pet.

'We're going to go on the longest walks ever,' said Evan to Judy, playfully tickling one of her ears. Judy wagged her tail fiercely.

Next morning the two of them were up early and off exploring the countryside round their home in Builth Wells, Mid Glamorgan.

'Judy . . . Judy . . . come on,' called Evan, when he realised it was time to get back home for dinner. Instead of the normal excited barking there was silence.

'Judy . . . Judy!'

This time a note of alarm crept into Evan's voice. Running back to where he had last seen Judy, Evan called out her name again and again. He whistled and shouted but there was no reply. Finally, with tears streaming down his face, Evan ran home.

'Well, it doesn't sound too good, I'm afraid,' said his mother when he told her. 'You know there are a lot of rabbit holes up there. Judy must have crawled into one, got stuck and couldn't get out. We'll go and have a look, but don't build your hopes up.'

So mother and son followed the path of the last walk, whistling and shouting and looking everywhere where the little dog might be trapped. Mrs Davies looked at the many rabbit holes, and felt that, sadly, they would never see Judy again.

'I know she is still alive somewhere,' said Evan, after the fruitless search. 'I just know it.'

So began a lonely routine for Evan. Every morning and evening he followed the now familiar path to where Judy had disappeared.

Once he reached the area of the rabbit holes he called her name for about five minutes, then made his weary way home.

Mrs Davies looked on with concern, but admired her son's determination. One week went by, then another. Day after day Evan went and returned, went and returned, his face set firmly.

Then, thirty-six days after Judy's disappearance, Evan and a friend were out calling when suddenly . . .

'I heard something.'

'You sure?'

'Definitely.'

'Well . . .'

'Listen, there it is again.'

'It's . . . it's . . . it's a bark! Faint, but definitely a bark.'

Events then moved quickly. On hearing the news, neighbours with spades rushed to the spot where the faint barking was heard and began digging. As they dug, the barking, although desperately weak, seemed to get nearer.

Finally the rescuers broke through a warren of rabbit holes and there was the long lost dog. Almost dead through lack of food and water. Judy was in a desperate condition – but it was nothing that love and care could not put right. And with Evan as a master it was certain she would get as much of that as she needed!

Information for the teacher

1   The happy conclusion to this story occurred in September 1990 but it is included here because Judy was a February birthday present. This in itself might be a useful starting point after ascertaining which children have birthdays – and what their presents were.

2   Animal – and particularly dog – stories are always popular with children. Useful sources for more material are:

The RSPCA, The Causeway, Horsham, West Sussex
RH12 1HG, www.rspca.org.uk

The Battersea Dogs' Home, 4 Battersea Park Road, London
SW8 4AA, www.dogshome.org

3   A useful comparison with this story, in this case a dog's devotion to its owner, is the story of Greyfriars Bobby. Bobby was a Skye terrier so devoted to his master that when the latter died the little dog 'guarded' his grave for fourteen years. In doing so he became one of the most famous and best-loved dogs in Edinburgh – and his fame ultimately spread much further.

Hymn suggestion

Come and Praise Vol 1 'Lost and found' No 57

Prayer

Let us bow our heads and think quietly about the message of this morning's story. Many people and creatures would not have survived without other people's determination to try and help as long as necessary. Let us pray that we might be given this kind of determination and dedication.

37 Patience

Introduction

One of the qualities we need in our lives is patience. We just can't get exactly *what* we want exactly *when* we want it – as this story reminds us.

Story

'I'm so hungry,' thought the crow as he flew along. 'What I wouldn't give for a . . . what's that?'

Out of the corner of his eye he had seen a rich, ripe mango hanging on a tree. Swooping down, he perched on a branch beside the mango.

'You're just what I've been looking for,' said the crow. 'I'm going to enjoy eating you so much.'

'Well, that's fine,' answered the mango. 'I'm ripe and I should be eaten. Before you eat me, though, you must wash your beak!'

The crow agreed to do this but could find no pot to get water from the well. Hurrying to a potter he asked the man to make him a pot.

'Certainly, certainly,' said the potter, 'if you bring me some clay.'

When the crow got to a field to get some clay the field told him that he needed to find a deer with a strong horn to dig up the clay. Getting very hot and flustered, the crow flew off and found a deer.

'Certainly, certainly,' answered the deer in reply to the crow's question. 'But first I will need some milk from a cow.'

The crow flew off again and soon found a cow. He explained to the cow what he needed and the cow said: 'Certainly, certainly, but before I can give you any milk I'll have to have some grass to eat.'

Back to the field flew the crow.

'Now I want some grass before I want some clay,' he gasped. 'Let me have some grass please, Field.'

'Aaah,' said the field, 'you can certainly have some grass – but you'll need a sickle to cut it with.'

Once again the crow flew off. This time he went to a blacksmith and explained what he needed.

'Certainly, certainly,' said the blacksmith. 'I'll give you a sickle but I'll have to sharpen it first or else it won't cut the grass.'

So the blacksmith put the sickle into a hot fire and sharpened it.

'Quickly, quickly,' said the crow, thinking of the beautiful mango.

'But it's too hot to carry yet,' said the blacksmith. 'You must wait until it cools down.'

'Nonsense,' said the crow, 'I haven't time for that. Put it on my back and let me be off.'

So the blacksmith put the sickle on the crow's back. Immediately there was a terrible smell of burning feathers and the crow, in great pain, found that now he couldn't even fly.

Meanwhile, back at the tree, the mango waited and waited and waited for the crow with the clean beak to come and eat. Finally it became so ripe that it could hang onto the tree no longer and it fell to the ground.

(Adapted from an Indian 'village story')

Information for the teacher

1 A useful February link for this story is the Hindu festival of Sarasvati Puja. Sarasvati is the Hindu goddess of learning, wisdom and knowledge. She would be the source of sound advice about life, and about foolish attitudes such as are portrayed in this story.

Hymn suggestion

Come and Praise Vol 2 'Time is a thing' No 104

Prayer

Let us bow our heads and think of patience.
Patience to bear with disappointment,
Patience to bear with hardship,
Patience to bear with dangers.
Lord, give us the strength to have this quality.
(Very loose adaptation from the Qur'an)

38 Rescue

Introduction

If you ever desperately need help then you should hope that it would come from a man like Patrick Sliney. This is his story.

Story

February 10th, 1936, brought with it some of the worst weather anybody could remember in the fishing village of Ballycotton in Ireland. Howling gales tore slates off roofs, people were blown over in the streets, and rocks were torn from the harbour wall.

It was in these conditions that Patrick Sliney, coxswain of the Ballycotton lifeboat, heard that the Daunt Rock lightship had broken loose from its moorings. It was now adrift in the tumultuous seas and the only hope for the eight men on board was – the Ballycotton lifeboat.

Patrick and the seven crew members boarded their boat and set out into the terrifying seas. By noon they had spotted the drifting lightship.

'We've got to get a wire hauser across to her and then we'll pull her into shore,' said Patrick.

For hours the seamen tried to get the two ships tied together. Every time they got the wire rope fixed, a terrible wave crashed the ships apart and the rope snapped. After twenty-four hours the lifeboat had to give up the attempt and put into the nearest port to refuel. None of the men on board had had any food during this time.

Snatching a quick rest and some food while their boat was being refuelled, the men gazed anxiously at the weather, hoping it might improve. It got worse.

Putting to sea again, the lifeboat tried again to get a tow rope on the lightship. When this failed Patrick decided more drastic action had to be taken.

'She's drifting towards Daunt Rock,' he told the lifeboat crew. 'If she hits that, all aboard are done for.'

'What can we do, Skip?' asked one of the crew.

'Well, the only way to get those lads off,' replied Patrick, 'is to get our boat close enough for them to jump.'

'But if they miss they'll be doomed for sure.'

Patrick's look told the seaman he already knew this. He gave orders for the lifeboat to be steered as near as possible to the bucking, rearing lightship.

On the first run there was enough time for only one man to jump safely aboard before the waves pushed the two boats apart. Time after time Patrick steered the lifeboat alongside with great skill. One by one the men managed to jump off the lightship until the lifeboat became damaged by the sea hurling the two ships together.

'There's only two of them left,' shouted one of the crew, above the shrieking gale.

'Yes, but look at them,' cried Patrick.

The two men left on the lightship were hanging outside the guard rail. They had climbed there ready to jump but were so exhausted they had no strength to climb back.

'They're too done for even to jump,' shouted Patrick. 'We'll have to get so close this time that they can be snatched off the side. Any volunteers to do the snatching?'

Every man on the crew volunteered and Patrick edged the lifeboat nearer once again. The waves pounded the ships and the gale tore frantically at the drenched and exhausted men. Nearer . . . nearer . . . nearer . . .

Finally, close enough to snatch the dangling men, the lifeboat crew seized them and dragged them to safety. Thankfully, Patrick turned the boat for home. Seventy-six hours after they had set out, he and the crew of the Ballycotton lifeboat had completed their task and eight men's lives had been saved.

Information for the teacher

1. Ballycotton is situated on the southern coast of Eire and is one of the 134 offshore lifeboat stations of the RNLI. This organisation was founded in 1824. Its address is:

   Royal National Lifeboat Institution, West Quay Road, Poole, Dorset D15 1HZ. www.rnli.org.uk

Hymn suggestion

Come and Praise Vol 1 'He who would valiant be' No 44

Prayer

Let us bow our heads and pray this morning for those men and women who work on ships of all shapes and sizes.

Let us pray that they may be kept safe in storms and dangerous weather.

Let us pray particularly for the crews of lifeboats whose work is to try to save others, often in very dangerous conditions.

39 Two's company

Introduction

Have you ever known anyone whom you really liked – but you couldn't understand why they behaved badly? If so, this morning's story will make you think.

Story

In all of Italy there was no more beautiful girl than Katharine. Sad to say, few people were as rude or as bad tempered either!

Petruchio was a lively and clever young man, and when he arrived in the town where Katharine lived, he soon heard of her reputation.

'I wonder why she behaves like that?' he thought. 'And I wonder if I can get her to change her ways?'

He went to visit her.

'Get out of here, you stupid oaf,' shouted Katharine when Petruchio called on her. 'Out – right now.'

'How kind of you to ask me to stay,' replied Petruchio. 'You are most generous.'

'Are you mad?' screeched Katharine. 'Are you deaf? I *don't* want you to stay. I want you to get out – NOW!'

'Please, please,' interrupted Petruchio. 'I don't really need any persuading to stay. Thank you again.'

Katharine was mystified. Every time she met this strange man again she hurled insults at him – and he treated them as if they were compliments!

Wherever she turned, Katharine seemed to bump into Petruchio. Meanwhile, he had come to like her very much. One day he staggered her by asking her to marry him.

'*Marry* you? Marry *you*?' screamed Katharine. 'Never. I'd sooner see you hanged than marry you.'

'Thank you, my dear!' exclaimed Petruchio. 'I'm so glad you've said yes. You've no idea how happy that makes me.'

Then, to the astonishment of Katharine, he told her that he had made all the arrangements for their wedding.

The day of the wedding soon arrived. Katharine, working herself up into one of her worst tempers, prepared to give Petruchio the worst possible time. Marry him, indeed!

But when Petruchio arrived Katharine got another shock. Instead of the neat, charming man she had got to know, Petruchio turned up dressed like a beggar and began to shout and insult everybody there except Katharine. She was so astonished and surprised by his behaviour that, before she knew what was happening, she was married and on the way home with her husband!

'You – get that door open quickly,' shouted Petruchio to a servant when they arrived. 'I hope my wife's food is ready – now get out!'

Petruchio led the dazed Katharine into a large dining room where a most beautiful feast was laid out. Despite her confused feelings Katharine suddenly realised she was absolutely starving. She moved hungrily towards the table.

'No!' shouted Petruchio. 'No, my sweet, that food is nothing like good enough for you. Servants, take it away!'

Before Katharine could take a bit the feast was removed. By now, exhausted, confused and speechless, she wanted nothing more than to go to bed. Telling her husband this she sank gratefully into a large and comfortable bed – only to find that within seconds Petruchio was beside the bed, hurling off the covers.

'No, no. You can't sleep here. This bed is nothing like good enough for you. Servants, you idle lot, take this bed away at once.'

This went on for days, until the couple paid a visit to Katharine's father's home. He was amazed to find his daughter quiet, polite and helpful!

For a day or two more, Petruchio played the part of the noisy bully. Then, seeing that Katharine was cured of her bad-tempered, rude ways, he became his charming, considerate self again. From that point on the pair were one of the happiest couples in the whole of Italy.

Information for the teacher

1 Teachers will recognise the characters and plot of Shakespeare's *The Taming of the Shrew*, or, in more modern Hollywood guise, *Kiss me, Kate*.
This seems an ideal story to use on St Valentine's Day, 14th February, with all its connotations.

2 The opportunity should not be lost to discuss something of the origins of St Valentine's Day. There were in fact two Valentines, both Italians: one a bishop and one a priest. Both were executed for refusing to give up their Christian faith but it is the priest, who was also a physician, around whom the most famous legend grew up.
Valentine, knowing full well that Christians should be handed over to the Romans, chose instead to hide them from their persecutors. He also broke a Roman law by marrying couples

although marriage was forbidden. He was caught and sent to prison to await execution. There he befriended one of the guards and restored the sight of his blind daughter. He was beheaded on 14th February 269.

Hymn suggestion

Come and Praise Vol 1 'A man for all the people' No 27

Prayer

Let us think this morning about showing how we care for other people. Let us learn to be kind, considerate and caring.

Let us remember how St Valentine showed all these qualities. Amen.

40 The plot

Introduction

This morning's story is about a man who was jealous of his cousin. This jealousy made him try to do a dreadful thing.

Story

Devadatta was a jealous man. He was a cousin of the Buddha, and as the Buddha's wisdom became more and more famous, so Devadatta's jealousy grew stronger.

'I'm sick of people flocking to listen to him,' thought the jealous cousin. 'But one day I'm going to have the chance to get him out of the way once and for all.'

Devadatta's chance came sooner than he expected.

He was preaching in a village one day when he noticed that hardly anybody was listening to him. They were all drifting off towards the other end of the village.

'Where are you going?' Devadatta called out.

'The great Buddha is coming,' shouted back the villagers. 'We are going to greet him.'

This made Devadatta angrier than ever. Soon he was alone in the village street with only some nearby elephants for company. As he looked at the peaceful creatures a plot came suddenly into his mind. Moving to a house behind the elephants, he found their keeper.

'Haven't you heard?' he said sharply to the man. 'The great Buddha is coming. He doesn't want to walk all the way. Let me have one of these elephants so that he can ride into the village.'

'Certainly,' replied the keeper. 'You're absolutely right. He must have the best elephant I've got.'

So Devadatta took the elephant and went with it quickly to where some monks lived.

'Quick,' he said to one of the monks, 'we're going to meet the great Buddha, but my elephant is thirsty, he needs some rice wine.'

Devadatta watched where the monk got the rice wine – and then, when he was alone with it, he fed the elephant several buckets of it. As it drank, the elephant got more and more agitated and angry. Finally, with a great trumpet, it lunged out into the main street of the village, as Devadatta had known it would.

The village street was full and when all the people saw the normally peaceful elephant lunging angrily and dangerously towards them they fled in terror.

Soon only two figures were left at the end of the street. These were the Buddha and his travelling companion, Ananda.

'My lord,' gasped Ananda anxiously, 'that animal is dangerous! We must get out of the way – quickly!'

The Buddha put a hand on Ananda's shoulder. 'No, my friend – we must stay.'

With all his wisdom the Buddha knew exactly what had happened. He watched the roaring, wild elephant's approach with a calm smile on his face.

When it had almost reached him and seemed more furious than ever, the Buddha slowly held up his hands. Amazingly, the elephant stopped at once, then gradually bent its front legs and lowered its head in front of the Buddha. The Buddha stroked its head and spoke to it in a calm voice.

So Devadatta's plot had failed. The villagers marvelled even more at the Buddha's calmness and wisdom and from that day on this elephant became famous and admired for miles around.

Information for the teacher

1   February 15th is the date on which Mahayana Buddhists celebrate Parinirvana. This is the festival commemorating the death of the Buddha, when he passed on to Nirvana.

2   There are interesting comparisons to be made with this story in the realms of both folk and religious stories. To choose two only,

Androcles and the lion, and St Francis of Assisi could be contrasted and compared.

3   There are other stories of the Buddha and an elephant. The *Jataka* tales are a vast source of Buddha stories.

Hymn suggestion

Come and Praise Vol 2 'All the animals' No 80

Prayer

Let us pray this morning that we can live our lives without feeling jealous or envious of anybody else.

Let us be grateful for what we have ourselves.

Let us try to act towards other people in exactly the way we would want them to act towards us.

Let us end our prayers with some words of the Buddha: 'Earn your living in a way which is good. Avoid evil thoughts and actions and work hard.'

41 A great discovery

Introduction

At this time each year the famous Cruft's Dog Show is held. You can see it every year on television when proud owners show their dogs. Today's story is about a dog.

Story

In 1916 the First World War had been raging for two years. Every day in the trenches men were killed or injured by flying bullets and exploding shells.

Meanwhile, far from the fighting, in England, France and Germany, doctors and nurses were working desperately to try and help wounded soldiers to recover from their awful experiences.

One doctor who was busy with this work was Klaus Rimmer. He lived in Germany and he had strong ideas about how the injured men should be treated.

'Apart from the right medicine we should try and give them peace in beautiful surroundings,' he said.

Of course, if the soldier had been blinded in the war he could never see such surroundings, and Klaus felt very sorry for one of his blind patients, a man called Captain Fleitel.

One day Klaus was sitting in his office writing up some notes. He paused and looked out of the window. There he saw the tall figure of Captain Fleitel, moving slowly and hesitantly across the huge, beautiful lawn. After every few steps Fleitel paused and took a deep breath. Then summoning up his courage and putting his arms out in front of him he edged slowly forward again. Dr. Rimmer sat admiring the courage of the poor soldier, when suddenly he felt a prick of alarm. Because the lawn was so big Fleitel had got more and more confident and was moving a little more quickly – straight towards a huge oak tree.

Klaus pushed open his window and was just about to shout a warning when a strange and marvellous thing happened. Frieda, Klaus's friendly Alsatian dog, had also seen the blind soldier making his worried way across the lawn. Sensing what was going to happen, the dog bounded over the grass, stopped beside Captain Fleitel and, rubbing its body against his legs, stood between him and the tree.

As the astonished doctor watched, the blind soldier reached down and gently took hold of the dog's collar. Frieda then moved slowly forward, led the man round the tree, and then up a narrow path between two flower beds.

From this marvellous event the wonderful idea of dogs guiding blind people was born.

Information for the teacher

1   The development of the use of guide dogs for the blind has obviously come a long way since this incident in 1916. The United States pursued the idea and in 1928 Morris Frank became the first guide dog owner in that country. The Guide Dogs for the Blind Association was established in Britain in 1934, and its address is:

Hillfields, Burghfield Common, Reading RG7 3YG,
www.gdba.org.uk

There are over 2,600 guide dog owners in Britain. Most of them own Labradors and the dogs need from six to eight months' training.

2   In many ways this is a heroic story and could cause some reflection on some words from the Bible: 'Let us sing the praises of ... the heroes of our nation's history ... Their lives will endure

for all time and their fame will never be blotted out ... and God's people will sing their praises.' (Ecclesiasticus 44, 1–2 and 13–15)

3 Some reflections on Cruft's Dog Show might be both interesting and provocative.

Hymn suggestion

Come and Praise Vol 2 'All the animals' No 80

Prayer

Let us give thanks this morning for dogs.

Let us be grateful for those dogs who help the blind, the deaf and the lonely.

Let us give thanks for those dogs who work for the police and the army and air force.

Let us hope that all dogs everywhere are valued and cared for as they deserve to be.

March

42 This month

Introduction

Out of doors, March is one of the most exciting months of the year. The days are starting to get longer and there is the feeling of things awakening on the land, in the air and in water.

Story

March is a good month for saying to somebody: 'Go outside, look and listen.'

Some of the things you could look for are hares. This is the time of year when male hares leap about, box each other and beat their hind legs on the ground. If you are lucky you could see them doing this – and the females looking on in the distance.

March is a good month to look out for birds and their nests. With many trees still bare it is easy to see that the birds – rooks in particular – are busy, noisy and fussy. Rooks nest in big trees and are notorious thieves who steal nest-building twigs whenever they get the chance.

For the careful watcher it is interesting to make a list of how birds differ in their approach to nest-building. Tawny owls, for instance, make only a very simple nest – a saucer-shaped thing made of bits of bark and the remains of owl pellets. These can be found in hollow trees. The peewit (lapwing) nests on open ground and its nest is little more than a hollow scraped in the ground. Sparrows work at building their nests in holes in walls and under the eaves of barns, sheds and houses. They use plenty of straw and feathers for their nests.

Other things to look out for in March include the activity in and around ponds. Duckweed plants start to spread over the ponds, and in and around the water frogs, toads and newts can be found. Butterflies can be seen trying their wings and in different places a variety of flowers start to appear.

Marsh marigolds bring a yellow pattern to the sides of streams; bluebells and anenomes start to show and, if it is warm, look out for the first star-white flowers of stitchwort.

So much for 'looking' in March; now what about 'listening'? The following are sounds you could expect to hear. The cock snipe swoops in flight at this time of year and when this happens the wind rushes through its wing- and tail-feathers – making a definite 'drumming' sound. Listen too for birds with 'whistles'. The peewit has a long whistle and to spot it you should look for a glossy brown and white bird who looks as if he is tumbling about when flying. The blackbird is another whistler and he is black with a yellow beak.

It is hard to miss the noisy and often angry 'cawing' of the rooks in March. Perhaps a more interesting sound is the quickfire 'rat-a-tat-tat' of the woodpecker at work.

The weather in March can change very quickly. Wind, rain, frost, snow and sun are all equally possible but it is cheering to remember the old saying: 'When March comes in like a lion it goes out like a lamb.'

Information for the teacher

1   In connection with an assembly like this some teachers may want to develop some symbolism as well: flowers like Lent lilies, for instance, supposedly symbolise betrayal when yellow and purity when white. The lungwort (*Pulmonaria officinalis*) is an early spring flower whose hanging bells are blue with a touch of red. Old traditions claim the blue represents Mary's robe, splashed with the blood of Jesus from when she stood beneath

the cross at his crucifixion. Other names for this flower are Soldiers and Sailors and Our Lady's Violets. Another flower symbolising Mary's blue robes is the anemone.

2   Another old traditional story which children enjoy hearing at this time of year concerns Lady Day (25th March). In Belgium it was believed that on this day God commanded the world to be silent. Everything obeyed his command – except the cuckoo. As a punishment, this bird was never allowed to have a nest of its own or to stay in any one place too long.

3   Notable feasts which often occur in March are: Mothering Sunday which is the fourth Sunday in Lent and was tradition-ally the day on which apprentices were given time off to visit their mothers; Passion Sunday which is the fifth Sunday in Lent and commemorates Christ's suffering in the Garden of Gethsemane; Palm Sunday, which commemorates Jesus's triumphal entry into Jerusalem.

Hymn suggestion

Come and Praise Vol 2 'Sing, people, sing' No 110

Prayer

Let us bow our heads and listen to the last verse of our hymn this morning:

> Sing, people, sing,
> And follow in a ring,
> Praise to God for all we do,
> Marching, seeing, hearing, too;
> Sing, people, sing,
> Sing, people, sing.
>
> (Traditional)

43 One hot Australian day

Introduction

Australia is a huge country. Away from the cities many of its roads are not good and driving lorries in intense heat is a hard, and sometimes dangerous, way of earning a living.

Story

Sandor Gubonyi came out of the hospital on that late March day feeling lucky, as well as glad to be alive. As he came down the steps he saw a group of people waiting for him. With them, and barking excitedly, was his dog Bimbo. As Sandor ruffled the dog's ears he thought of their first meeting weeks ago ...

The huge truck bounced and rattled over the potholed road in the West Australian outback. The heat was tremendous and Sandor constantly wiped the sweat from his brow as he fought to control the twisting, leaping steering wheel.

'Boy, will I be glad to finish this trip,' he muttered to himself, as another deep pothole sent a crushing shudder up his arms. Then it happened – the truck hit the deepest rut yet, swerved violently, and, with a scream of tearing metal, crashed on its side and slid sideways along the rough road surface.

When it finally stopped Sandor found himself trapped beneath part of the overturned lorry. 'I've got to get out of here,' he said aloud through gritted teeth. 'I've got to.'

The pain in his injured back was terrible but, inch by inch, the driver edged his way out from under the lorry. Finally, he could move no farther. Then he realised that he had more serious problems.

'The water carrier,' muttered Sandor. The crash had taken care of it and without water he knew he would not survive long in the intense heat.

'Maybe I won't have to wait that long,' Sandor thought as he looked upwards. Blackening the sky above him was a huge flight of swirling, cawing crows. Alerted by the crash and with the sight of easy prey on the ground, they began to swoop lower and lower. Their hideous cries and savage beaks were terrifying and Sandor buried his head in his hands and waited for the first strike.

Then, a new noise rose above the cries of the birds. A dog was barking. Cautiously, Sandor opened his eyes and peered over a protective arm. Leaping and barking at the diving crows was a dog. It was the sort of dog that many local cattlemen used and it looked as dusty and worn as Sandor felt.

'Go on, chum, good on you,' muttered the driver encouragingly.

Again and again the dog fought off the birds until at last, with their meal now taking too much effort, the crows flew off to find other prey. When they had gone the dog came and lay beside Sandor and gently licked his face.

'If we ever get out of this you and I are never going to be parted,' said the driver, 'and I'm going to call you Bimbo.'

The story had a happy ending. Before too long a helicopter found the overturned lorry, and driver and dog were airlifted to hospital. When Bimbo's story was told he became famous. Not only was his courage written about in all the newspapers but he was awarded the Australian Dogs' Victoria Cross. Now, instead of being a stray in the bush, he was a celebrity!

Sure enough, when Sandor came out of hospital the two were reunited. 'After all, I wouldn't be here without him,' said the driver, now fully recovered.

Information for the teacher

1   Driving long-distance lorries in Australia remains a very tough job. Enormous distances, a demanding climate, lack of dual carriageways and a sparse population all contribute to this.

2   'Journeys' is a theme which could be expanded from this story. Joseph's journey with Mary prior to the first Christmas is a very famous Biblical one. Another from the same source is the Israelites' journey from Egypt. This could begin with Moses's instructions at the burning bush (Exodus 3) right through the ten plagues (Exodus 8) to the crossing of the Red Sea (Exodus 14) and the journey on into the desert (Exodus 16).

One of the most remarkable journeys of both ancient and modern times is the Muslim *hajj*. This is the journey to Mecca which Muslims have been making for over thirteen centuries. From all over the Muslim world, up to two million pilgrims make this journey annually. Before arriving at Mecca all put on the simple *ihram* costume. For men this is two pieces of unsewn white cloth; for women it is a simple gown with the face unveiled. These costumes, worn by everyone regardless of how rich or poor, important or humble, emphasise the fact that everyone is of equal importance in the eyes of Allah.

Hymn suggestion

Come and Praise Vol 2 'The sun burns hot' No 77

Prayer

Let us think this morning about journeys. Let us pray for those whose work causes them to make long and difficult journeys. May they be kept safe and well until they return to their homes and families. Amen.

44 Tell the truth

Introduction

This morning's story is a very old one. It describes how, when people want to do something which is very wrong, they are sometimes stopped in mysterious ways.

Story

The farmer was very busy sowing wheat when he saw the little group moving towards him. As they got nearer he saw a man, a woman with what looked like a tiny baby, and a donkey. The farmer was a friendly man so he called out to the strangers.

'Hello there! You look tired and hot. Why not rest here in the shade awhile? You're welcome to share some of my food and drink.'

The couple stopped.

'That's very kind of you,' said the man. 'My name is Joseph. This is my wife Mary and this is our baby son.'

'Well,' said the farmer, 'I'm pleased to meet you – but, if you don't mind my asking, why are you trying to make such haste in the heat of the day?'

Mary looked at her husband as if to say, 'Why don't you tell him?'

Joseph looked at the farmer's honest face and then he told him that soldiers were trying to kill Jesus and that this could give the farmer trouble later on.

'Why,' said the farmer, 'that's absolutely terrible. You must get away! What a dreadful thing.'

'Thank you again,' said Joseph. 'We will get on our way now. But I must warn you that Herod's soldiers are everywhere. It's quite likely that they'll come here and ask if you've seen us.'

'Oh dear,' said the farmer. 'I'm no good at telling lies. What on earth will I say?'

'Well,' replied Joseph, 'you must tell them the truth – but tell them what you were doing when you saw us.'

As the couple and child went on their way the farmer got back to sowing his wheat. When he had finished he went home to bed.

The next morning the farmer could hardly believe his eyes when he awoke. There in the field in which he had been working was a mass of tall, ripe wheat just ready for harvesting!

'But that's impossible, it can't be . . .'

He was still looking out in amazement when, at the edge of the field, he noticed a group of soldiers urging their horses on cruelly.

Within minutes they had reached his house and were hammering on the door.

'Now you,' snarled the leader of the soldiers when the farmer had opened the door. 'We've got some questions for you, and it will be a very bad job for you if you don't tell the truth. We're looking for some people.'

The soldier gave a very good description of Joseph and Mary. When he had done this he asked, 'Have you seen these people?'

'Oh yes,' said the farmer, 'I have certainly seen them.'

'Ah,' said the soldier, 'at last! Now then, man, when did you see them?'

'Oh, it was the day I was sowing wheat seeds in this field,' answered the farmer truthfully.

The soldier turned to look at the field of ripe wheat, then he looked again at the farmer.

'The day you sowed the wheat, why that must have been . . .' With a snort of disgust the soldier stormed away. 'They can't be anywhere near here!' he called out to his men.

Information for the teacher

1   The three wise men went originally to Jerusalem. Having seen the star in the sky as the sign of the birth of a king, and knowing that the royal palace was at Jerusalem, they thought they would find the new king there.

Herod received them and, wondering who this new king of the Jews could be, he questioned them carefully. He then told them that when they did find the new king they should let him know where he was so he could go to worship him too. Having found Jesus in Bethlehem, however, they were told by God in a dream that they should not give Herod this information. By the same means Joseph was told to take Mary and Jesus away.

Herod was furious when the wise men did not report back to him. When he heard of the birth in Bethlehem he ordered the death of all baby boys under two years old who lived there, or nearby. (Matthew 2 is useful for source material.)

2   The calendar link for this day is that early spring is the time when crops start to appear.

Hymn suggestion

Come and Praise Vol 2 'And ev'ryone beneath the vine' No 149

Prayer

Let us think of the many mysteries in life which we don't understand. Let us remember the words of a very old saying: 'God moves in mysterious ways, his wonders to perform.'

45 A cause for concern

Introduction

Sometimes we need to find out why people behave as they do in certain circumstances. This morning's true story tells us a lot about life today.

Story

John and Rachid were sitting in their car outside a block of flats in a busy city on a cold March day. They were waiting for their friend Ivor.

'I wish he would hurry up,' said John.

'Yes,' replied Rachid, 'if he doesn't get a move on we'll miss the beginning of the picture.'

'Hmm. It will take us at least ten minutes to reach that car park next to the cinema.'

The two men sat chatting. It was dark outside and there were very few people about. Suddenly John noticed an old lady walking along the pavement in front of the flats. At first she was walking quite briskly but, as she got nearer, she seemed to go slower and slower. It was almost as if she was walking in thick sand.

Now Rachid was watching her too. As she got alongside the car, her knees gave way and she sank slowly to the ground.

'She's ill!' called John. 'Quick, let's go and help her.'

The two men jumped out of the car and hurried over to where the old lady sat gasping on the pavement.

'Can we help?' asked John anxiously.

'No . . . leave me alone, please,' gasped the old lady. 'I'll be all right in a minute.'

'I don't think we can do that,' replied Rachid. 'Let us get you home and call a doctor.'

'No, really, I sometimes get these breathless spells,' went on the old lady. 'Just leave me alone.'

'Certainly not,' went on John. 'We've got a car here – we'll take you straight home, or to hospital if you like.'

'What's your address?' asked Rachid.

For a moment or two the old lady looked as if she would ask them to leave again. Then, with a sigh and a sad look on her face, she said, '21, Eastville Close.'

'Oh, that's quite near,' replied John.

He and Rachid then helped the old lady into the car. She seemed much better – but very worried. Within a few minutes they were holding her and knocking on the front door of 21 Eastville Close.

'Mum!' cried the young woman who opened the door.

Soon they were all inside, and while the young woman put her mother to bed, John and Rachid waited to see if there was anything else they could do.

When the daughter came back they asked her.

'No, I don't think so,' she said. 'I've called the doctor from the bedroom telephone and he'll be round in a few minutes.'

'Oh, that's good,' said John.

'But I would like to say,' went on the young woman, 'how much I appreciate you bringing Mum home. It really was very kind of you.'

'It's the least we could do,' said Rachid. 'But, you know, it was ages before she would tell us where she lived.'

'I know,' replied the daughter. 'You see, she was frightened that if she gave her address it would be easy for you to come and rob the place when you brought her here.'

John and Rachid were shocked.

'You mean ... she really thought we would do that?' gasped John. 'How awful.'

Information for the teacher

1   Although the names have been changed, this story happened exactly as described. As such it can stimulate a great deal of discussion with upper juniors, ranging over a wide variety of themes from 'trust' to 'our society today'.

2   All religions advocate helping one's neighbour without reservation. They do so in a variety of words:

'Out of the cotton of comparison spin a thread of contentment.' (Guru Nanak)

'There is only one race – the human race.' (Guru Gobind Singh)

'If you shut your ears when people cry for help, When you cry for help, no one will hear you.' (Proverbs 21, 13)

'May God keep us safe;
May He protect us.
Let us all work together;
Let Him enlighten our minds.
Let us not dislike each other.'

(From the Hindu *Upanishads*)

Hymn suggestion

Come and Praise Vol 2 'Sad, puzzled eyes' No 74

Prayer

Dear God,

Help us to behave in a way which will allow people to rely on us and trust us.

Let us pray also for those who seek to rob and cheat other people. We pray that they may be shown how to behave with kindness and trust too. Amen.

46 Fame

Introduction

When we are young we sometimes dream that we will be famous one day. But being a famous person can have its worries too ...

Story

Nellie Melba tore open the envelope and read the words which were written on the sheet of paper inside it.

The letter was dated March, 1893, and it said, 'Twenty minutes after the curtain rises and you make your first appearance on stage, you will be dead.'

Now, you might think Nellie had done something dreadful to deserve this threat, but you would be wrong. In 1893 Nellie Melba was probably the most famous singer in the world and the letter was sent to her by a music lover in Milan, in Italy, because he was annoyed that she had won her fame in other cities before coming to sing in Milan!

The worst thing that happened when she finally began to sing in the Milan Opera House, however, was that a man tried to throw a bunch of flowers to her.

Nellie's fame was hard-earned and she had no easy start to life. She spent her childhood in Australia where her father was an unsuccessful goldminer. She hated school and stayed away whenever she could – but she loved music and singing.

When she was six years old she appeared in her first concert in Melbourne. She sang an old Scottish song called 'Comin' Through the Rye' and this made her determined that more than anything in life she wanted to be a singer.

Saving desperately hard, she eventually had enough money to catch a ship to Paris where she hoped to take singing lessons. Once she got there she made an appointment with a famous singing teacher called Madam Marchesi.

Madame Marchesi looked at the keen Australian girl and decided that she had better prepare her for disappointment.

'Now look here, young lady,' she said. 'I hardly take anybody for singing lessons because they're just not good enough. In fact, you could say I've turned down more people than there are sheep in Australia, so you can't say I haven't warned you. Now, sing.'

When Nellie began to sing, however, Madame Marchesi was enthralled. The young singer had hardly finished before the teacher leaped to her feet to say, 'You're going to be a star!'

For years after that Nellie sang in the great cities of the world giving pleasure to thousands of people. No matter how famous or how busy she became, she always had time for little kindnesses to ordinary people.

In 1894 she was singing in London. She so enjoyed the food in the hotel in which she was staying that she gave the chef two very expensive, and hard-to-get, tickets for one of her shows.

'That's fantastic,' said the chef. 'Such kindness deserves a special Thank You. I'm going to make up a new sweet and call it after you, madame.'

The chef disappeared into the kitchen. There he peeled some peaches and put them in a vanilla sauce. Next he lay the peaches on a layer of vanilla ice cream and then covered the whole thing with a raspberry sauce.

Now, if you ever ask for a Peach Melba, you will know how it got its name.

Information for the teacher

1 The calendar anniversary for this story was the March occasion of the Milanese threats. These were taken very seriously at the time and the theatre was packed with both uniformed and plain-clothed policemen.

Nellie Melba was born Nellie Mitchell. Other significant dates in her life were: her birth in May 1861 in Melbourne, Australia; her death in the same place in 1930.

2   There are several themes which can be drawn from this story. Two are: the determination which is needed to succeed; and the pleasure and enjoyment we get from seeing and hearing a brilliant artist perform.
There is a most appropriate Bible reference here:

'I know that there is nothing good for a man except to be happy and live the best life he can while he is alive. Moreover, that a man should eat and drink and enjoy himself, in return for all his labours, is a gift of God. A merry heart keeps a man alive, and joy lengthens the span of his days.' (Ecclesiasticus 30, 21–22)

For those who want to follow this up with an appropriate 'linking' Biblical story, 2 Samuel 6, 12–22, tells of the celebrations when the Ark of the Covenant was brought to the city of Jerusalem.

Hymn suggestion

Come and Praise Vol 2 'Let the world rejoice together' No 148

Prayer

Let us give thanks this morning for all those who bring so much pleasure to our lives by their skill and talent in entertaining us. Let us give thanks for singers, actors and actresses, artists, writers and sportsmen and women. Amen.

47 Thanks, driver!

Introduction

Sometimes in our day-to-day lives something dangerous happens. If it does we should hope that there is somebody around like John Robson. This is his story.

Story

Thursday, March 15th, was just like another normal working day. John Robson left his home in Bruce Castle Road, Tottenham, and went off to work – to drive an Underground train in London's hustle and bustle.

By the afternoon he was driving a train along the Piccadilly line in the rush hour. This meant that the carriages on his train were packed full with seven hundred people.

'You'd wonder where all these people came from,' thought John to himself, as he eased down the speed of his train to stop at a red light in a tunnel at King's Cross. 'Still, I'll soon be finished and off home for my tea.'

John's thoughts topped abruptly, his eyes opened wide and the hair on the back of his neck began to prickle with fright. Round a bend in front of him, another train had suddenly appeared. Its headlights shone in his eyes and the train was heading straight for him.

'Oh no!' gasped John. A terrible crash seemed absolutely certain.

Then John leapt into action. Flinging back his driver's door, he reached out and grabbed two wires which ran along the side of the Underground tunnel. Brushing the dust off them and ignoring the mild shock the wires were sending through his hands, he slowly brought the two ends of the wires together.

'Work, please work!' begged John as he held the wires together.

Like a charging monster, the oncoming train raced towards him. Its lights glistened like angry eyes as it rocked and swayed in the noisy tunnel. Then, painfully slowly, it began to lose speed. John held his breath as the train got nearer, and nearer, and then slowed to a stop just a few yards in front of his own train.

John slumped down in his seat and, for a moment, put his head in his hands to calm himself. Another few seconds and over a thousand people would have been involved in a terrible accident.

Later, London Transport praised Mr Robson's brave, quick-thinking action. One of their officers said, 'By using the low-voltage wires as he did, Mr Robson switched off the current from the track and turned on the tunnel's emergency lighting. There's no doubt he was a hero and there are plenty of people to say, "Thanks, driver".'

Information for the teacher

1   This incident took place on 15th March 1990. Special signals to prevent this sort of thing happening had been installed in many areas following recommendations made in 1988. A major inquiry followed this incident.

The low-voltage line-side wires are specially designed to switch the current from the track and light up the tunnel. All the Underground train drivers are taught how to use these low-voltage wires to cut off the power.

2 A useful web site address in connection with this story is:

www.detr.gov.uk (The Department of the Environment, Transport and the Regions)

3 This story could be one of a series where ordinary people perform extraordinary actions which save lives. Such a series can be constantly kept up-to-date and fresh by stockpiling newspaper stories.

Hymn suggestion

Come and Praise Vol 1 'He who would valiant be' No 44

Prayer

Dear God,
Let us give thanks this morning for ordinary people who, so often, by their quick thinking, bravery and determination, save the lives of others. Thank you for your guidance. Amen.

48 The lost sheep

Introduction

None of us likes to lose anything. In this morning's story something is lost – and then found again. It is a story to make us think.

Story

Benjamin was a shepherd. Whatever the weather, his long cloak protected him against sun, wind and rain. His bag of food was always well filled because he was not sure when he could refill it. With bread, cheese, olives and raisins bouncing against his hip, and money and small stones in the girdle round his waist, Benjamin quite happily trudged the lonely miles behind his sheep.

'Soon be time for a rest,' he said to himself as the sunset turned the sky into a brilliant red. As he spoke, his fingers felt the reed pipes which he played after eating his supper, before going to sleep.

Ahead the shepherd saw the sheepfold into which he would gather his flock for the night. Here, surrounded by brick walls and with himself sleeping in the doorway, his sheep would be safe from wolves and any other kind of prowler.

'Come on, my beauties,' said Benjamin quietly. 'In we go.'

Matching his actions with his words, the shepherd poked and prodded his sheep to guide them into the safety of the sheepfold. As he did so he counted each one as it passed through the small entranceway.

Knowing that he had exactly one hundred sheep, Benjamin was disturbed when ninety-nine had passed into the sheepfold – and there were no others to be seen.

'Oh no,' muttered Benjamin. 'One of them must have got lost on that rocky path near the mountains.'

Putting rocks across the entrance to keep the sheep in, Benjamin then turned and began the long walk back to where the path had been flanked by rock-strewn cracks and crevices. All the while he whistled softly through his teeth, partly to make the lost sheep feel better. He knew that alone, and in danger from its enemies, it would be nervous and afraid.

With darkness falling, his feet ached as he reclimbed the rocky footpath, looking on either side as he did so. Half an hour passed before he saw a sudden movement in a crevice off to the right of the path. It was the missing sheep, terrified and motionless.

Soothingly, Benjamin called to it as he stretched his hand into the crevice. Then, with his long staff, he helped it back up onto the path. The sheep was still shaking with fear and weakness. Bending down, Benjamin took its forelegs in one hand and its hindlegs in the other. With a mighty lift he swung it astride his shoulders and began the long walk back to the sheepfold.

Weary but satisfied, Benjamin began to whistle again – pausing only to mutter to himself, 'Ninety-nine, one hundred – now they're *all* safe again.'

Information for the teacher

1   The text refers to the shepherd's girdle containing 'money and small stones'. The small stones were thrown to attract the sheep's attention. The shepherd's reed pipes and horn were Israel's earliest musical instruments.

Sheepfolds were stone enclosures and shepherds often slept across the entrance when the sheep were all safely inside for the night.

2   The good shepherd is obviously a symbolic Biblical figure. His characteristics include faithfulness, diligence, tenderness and

the readiness to risk his own life to look after his charges. There are many Bible references extolling such virtues: John 10, 11; Ezekiel 34, 11–16; Psalm 78, 70–72.

3   References for this particular story are Matthew 18, 11–14; Luke 15, 4–7.

4   From a calendar point of view this story could be used to lead up to assembly and/or RE work on Easter.

Hymn suggestion

Come and Praise Vol 1 'The Lord's my shepherd' No 56

Prayer

Dear God,
    Help us to understand the meaning of this morning's story. Teach us to remember that every single person is important.
    Help us to remember that everyone has hopes, worries, fears, joys and disappointments, just as we do. Amen.

49 Hero Wong

Introduction

We often hear stories of dogs coming to the rescue of their masters or mistresses. Cats, however, are another matter – or are they?

Story

'Oh, she'll be all right on the lawn for a minute or two.' So said Mrs Viviers as she looked out into the sunshine and saw her daughter Wanda, playing happily with her toys. It was a beautiful day and everything was calm and peaceful in the Johannesburg street where the Viviers lived.
    'Right,' replied Mr Viviers. 'It will only take us a few minutes to rearrange this furniture. Then we'll go out on the lawn too and have our tea.'
    Meanwhile, four-year-old Wanda was quite happy as she stepped in and out of her paddling pool, singing as she did so. She could hear her mum and dad talking in the house and somewhere in the distance a radio played softly. Then, suddenly, she heard a new and strange noise. It was a sort of slithering . . .

'I wonder what that can be?' thought Wanda to herself. Then she turned – and felt a chill of absolute terror run right through her.

Sliding towards her over the lawn was a huge snake. Its five-foot-long body hissed over the grass and its hooded head swayed horribly towards her.

Wanda screamed – but another wild, screeching noise was even louder. Suddenly, there was a flash of hurling, spitting fur and Wong, Wanda's Siamese cat, threw himself in front of her. As the snake's head swayed threateningly, Wong scratched defensively at the long body. For what seemed a lifetime the air was alive with hissing and howling as again and again the little cat attacked the dangerous invader.

By now Mr and Mrs Viviers had heard the noise and were racing down the lawn. In her fear, Wanda had not moved, and Wong was still darting and leaping to protect her. Suddenly the snake had had enough. Sliding away as quickly as it had arrived, it was chased all the way by the cat.

Mrs Viviers had now reached her daughter and swept Wanda up into her arms. 'Are you all right? Wanda! Speak to me!'

'All right, all right, Mummy,' gasped the little girl.

'Thanks to Wong!' murmured Mr Viviers, bending down to stroke the panting, trembling little Siamese cat.

Information for the teacher

1   Many of the children will be aware that very few animals are prepared to attack a snake – the armadillo and the mongoose being two of those who do. For a cat to do so is very rare – particularly in this instance when the creature was a five-foot-long Ringhalls snake.

2   Not surprisingly, this story appeared in newspapers throughout the world and in London the PDSA awarded Wong a silver medal for his life-saving bravery.

3   As a calendar reference, 20th March is one possibility. This is St Cuthbert's Day – among his many other accomplishments, Cuthbert was supposed to have a remarkable affinity with animals.
    On another 'animal' theme, 17th March was considered in mediaeval times to be the day on which Noah entered the Ark.

Hymn suggestion

Come and Praise Vol 2 'All the animals' No 80

Prayer

Let us think this morning about the word 'Thanks'. Do we say it as often as we should? Do we think enough about all the people to whom we should be grateful for looking after us and helping us in our daily lives?

Let us spend a quiet minute thinking about all that we should be thankful for.

April

50 A good joke

Introduction

If we enjoy a joke with our friends then laughing together is fun. To laugh *with* somebody is good, to laugh *at* somebody can often be cruel.

Today's story is about a good April Fools' Day joke which everybody enjoyed.

Story

Most of us enjoy watching television – particularly when programmes make us laugh. Some years ago the producers of a TV programme called *Panorama* decided that they would play a joke on the whole of Britain.

'We've got a programme due to go out on April 1st,' said the chief producer. 'We're going to use it for a great joke. Now, this is what we are going to do . . .'

After he had finished explaining, writers, camera operators and all the other programme staff prepared themselves for spending a few days in Switzerland. They were very excited about the idea.

'What a joke! Do you think anybody will believe it?'

'I think they will if we do it well enough.'

'So it'll have to be well done.'

'I can't wait to see the finished programme.'

Soon all the programme's staff arrived in Switzerland. Once there, they went to a little village near Lake Lugano. Their next job was to unpack some special material they had brought with them – this was over twenty tons of cooked spaghetti!

Once they had unpacked the spaghetti they got a number of ladders. Climbing these, they began to hang the spaghetti from the branches of a group of trees in the village. Soon the trees were completely covered with spaghetti draped all over them. Now it was time for the next step!

'Now we've got to get the Swiss people living in the village to help us,' explained the chief producer. 'We'll get them all to wear farm workers' clothes and they can collect the spaghetti from the trees and pack it in large baskets. While they're doing this the cameras will shoot them from lots of angles. Then the writers will write the script to go with the film.'

Soon everyone was having fun as the 'spaghetti harvest' was collected in. Then, when all the films had been successfully taken, the programme staff packed up and returned to England.

It soon came round to April 1st and all over Britain people switched their television sets on to watch *Panorama*.

'Good evening, ladies and gentlemen,' said a voice, as the pictures on the screen showed the Swiss countryside flashing by.

'Today we are visiting a small village in Switzerland where the local people grow an unusual crop. We will watch them harvesting their produce.'

So the words went on, and as they did the pictures showed the trees, heavy with their 'spaghetti crop'. Then there were lots more pictures of the people harvesting the crop.

The joke was a great success. Millions of people, realising the date, and watching spaghetti 'growing' on trees, had a really good laugh at the programme. A few didn't realise it was a joke and rang up the BBC to ask where they could buy spaghetti trees!

Information for the teacher

1   The theme of 'laughing with' rather than 'laughing at' (in the sense of derision, etc) is a very important one with young children and can stand a fair amount of repetition. This April 1st story provides a starting point for its development via further discussion.

2   The origin of April Fools' Day is obscure. Indeed, *Poor Robin's Almanac* of 1760 said:

> The First of April, some do say
> Is set apart for All Fools' Day;

But why the people call it so,
Not I, nor they themselves, do know.

One suggestion had been that it is the aftermath of a festival celebrating the Celtic god of Mirth; another is that it was traditionally a day of frivolity to celebrate the end of winter and the coming of spring.

This is a time of year when 'fooling' goes on not only in English-speaking countries and Europe, but also in India when the great spring festival of Holi involves a lot of fun with throwing coloured water and powder.

Hymn suggestion

Come and Praise Vol 2 'You shall go out with joy' No 98

Prayer

This is an occasion for using a well-known and very good prayer. It is the anonymous offering found in Chester cathedral:

> Give me a good digestion, Lord,
> And always something to digest;
> Give me a healthy body, Lord,
> With sense to keep it at its best.
>
> Give me healthy eyes, good Lord,
> To keep the good and pure in sight,
> Which seeing sin is not appalled
> But finds a way to set it right.
>
> Give me a mind that is not bored,
> That does not whimper, whine or sigh;
> Don't let me worry overmuch
> About the fussy thing called I.
>
> Give me a sense of humour, Lord,
> Give me the grace to see a joke,
> To get some happiness from life
> And pass it on to other folk.

51 The second chance

Introduction

I expect most of you have heard an adult say at some time: 'Oh, I wish I had worked harder at school.' This morning's story makes us think about that.

Story

The boy didn't like school. He didn't work very hard there and, when he got the chance, he stayed away. So he fell further and further behind in his work. He didn't mind though, it didn't matter – he was going to be a famous singer.

In the big city where he lived there was a great opera house. Most of the world's most famous singers performed there. Whenever the boy got the chance he went to the opera house. Day after day, week after week, he could be seen there.

The musicians and singers got used to seeing him – and talking to him.

'Why do you hang around here, boy?'

'I'm going to be a great opera singer.'

'Have you had any training?'

'No.'

'You're wasting your time then – you'll never make it.'

But the boy kept coming. One day the singers and musicians got together.

'Perhaps this lad's a genius.'

'He's certainly determined.'

'Let's give him a chance.'

So one day when the boy arrived at the opera house the musicians were waiting for him.

'Come on,' they said, 'we've set aside ten minutes to hear you sing.'

The boy wasn't at all nervous. After all, a singer was what he was going to be.

The musicians got ready. The boy began to sing. For a minute or two there was absolute silence. Then, someone began to laugh. Within seconds all the singers and musicians were roaring with laughter. The boy was *awful* – the very worst singer any of them had heard.

One of the ladies in the group, however, felt sorry for him. 'Come on,' she said, 'you'll never make a singer because you haven't got the voice for it. But you must be good at something – and we've still got five minutes left. What else can you do?'

'Well,' said the disappointed boy, 'people say I'm good at telling stories.' And he began to tell one.

Soon there was again silence, but it was not followed by laughter. The boy's story was marvellous, his audience were entranced. When he'd finished they burst into applause.

'That was wonderful,' said the lady. 'Write that story down. I think the king should know about your talent.'

So, excitedly, the boy went home – to disappointment and frustration. Because he had paid no attention at school he couldn't write very well and his spelling was very bad indeed. Eventually, after hours of work, he got the story written and took it to the lady.

When the king read the story he stroked his chin and then spoke to all the people waiting expectantly round him. 'The story is great,' he said, 'but the writing and spelling are dreadful. Send this fellow back to school so he can learn to do these things properly and send the bill to me. Then I want to see his next story.'

So the boy went back to school and this time he worked hard and paid attention. After some time he found he could not only tell stories well, but write them well too. The king was impressed and asked for more and more stories. Other people did too. Soon the stories were being published in books. People all over the boy's country were reading them. Soon they were translated into other languages and eventually the whole world was enjoying them – it still is. Oh yes – the boy's name, if you haven't already guessed it, was Hans Christian Andersen.

Information for the teacher

1 Hans Christian Andersen was born on 2nd April 1805 in Odense, Denmark. The son of a poor shoemaker, he sought to start his singing career at the Copenhagen Opera House. The king who paid for his schooling was Frederick IV – although just when this was is not altogether clear.

Andersen died in 1875 having already become world famous. 'The Emperor's New Clothes' is arguably his most famous story, and certainly one which primary school children enjoy.

Hymn suggestion

Come and Praise Vol 1 'The best gift' No 59

Prayer

First of all this morning we can listen to some words from the Bible: 'Let us now sing the praises of famous men.' (Ecclesiasticus 44)

Let us give thanks for those people who write stories and books which give us so much pleasure.

Let us give thanks for all those people whose special talents make our lives so much more interesting and enjoyable. Amen.

52 Mother Samwell

Introduction

One of the things that annoys all of us is being accused of doing something wrong which we haven't done. 'It's not fair,' we say straight away. Unfortunately, for many people hundreds of years ago, life was far from fair – as we can hear in this morning's story of Mother Samwell.

Story

The courtroom was crowded and the jury listened carefully as one witness after another told his or her story.

'Well, it was like this . . .' started a tall, burly man with a round red face.

'Yes – go on,' said the judge.

'Well, I was out riding one day and that . . . that . . . person was walking along a path in front of me.'

As he said this the burly man nodded his head in the direction of a frail, rather bent and tired-looking old woman who stood in the dock reserved for prisoners on trial. The woman was known as Mother Samwell.

'She was slow to get out of the way as we galloped towards her – so I shouted to her.'

'What did you say?'

'Well . . . I said . . . I mean . . . I said, "Get out of the way, you old witch."'

'And what happened?'

'Nothing, at the time, and after our usual hard ride I stabled my horse. Next morning when I went for him – there he was lying dead on the ground. Now – it's obvious, isn't it? she put a curse on him, she did. She's a witch all right – and this proves it.'

So the trial went on. More and more stories like this one were told. Parents told of their children being ill after calling rude names at Mother Samwell. Then there was the case of the old lady's badly burned arm. When she had first been accused of being a witch a group of local people had set about proving her innocence. 'It's quite straightforward,' said one of them. 'All you do is put one of her arms in boiling water. If it heals up in a week she's innocent, if not . . .'

When Mother Samwell's arm had been plunged into the boiling water she had fainted with the pain of it – and the arm was still swollen and blistered.

'Agnes Samwell, you have been found guilty of witchcraft. You, your husband and daughter will all be hanged.'

With a pitifully weak cry old Mother Samwell sank to the floor. Through her tears she protested her complete innocence. It was no use – she, her husband and daughter were duly hanged.

Information for the teacher

1   The trial of Agnes Samwell took place in Huntingdon on the 4th April 1593. The last 'witch' to be executed in Britain was Janet Horne in 1727.

2   'It's not fair' and the evils of superstition can both lead on to a comparison of life 'then and now'. Such a comparison shows the unreasoning cruelty of times past in situations like this.

3   There are several other examples of unreasonable behaviour and unfair situations from the past. Early aboriginal women in Australia settled arguments by hitting each other with sticks. They took it in turn to land a blow and the one who survived longest was 'right'. In Nigeria an accused thief was only considered innocent if a duck's feather could be stuck through his tongue and come out without sticking.
A similar test to the 'arm in boiling water/healing in seven days' test of this story was making the accused walk on red-hot ploughshares. Again innocence was 'proved' if the feet were completely healed in seven days.

Hymn suggestion

Come and Praise Vol 1 'From the darkness came light' No 29

Prayer

Let us give thanks this morning that in Britain today people are no longer punished because of fearful superstitions. Let us give thanks for our schools where we can learn to be fair and kind to other people. Amen.

53 Don't leave it too late

Introduction

There are lots of times when we look back and say, 'I *wish* I'd done that.' This morning's story makes us think even more about this.

Story

It was April weather at its wettest. There was a freezing cold wind blowing, and heavy rain blanketed the whole market place in an atmosphere of gloom. The stall holders huddled under cover and looked round for the few customers who were about.

'What a day!'

'We'll be lucky to sell anything today.'

'Nobody's going to turn out in this.'

'Have you seen him – over there?'

The stall holders looked over to a place in the market where old Bill Johnson's stall had stood for years. He had been dead for a long time now and no one had ever put up a new stall there. Today, however, a man was standing on the very spot where the stall had stood for so long. He wasn't looking round, or trying to shelter from the downpour. He wore no hat and his clothes were black with rain. His unmoving feet were set firmly in a large puddle.

'Who is he?'

'I've never seen him before.'

'He's not a customer . . .'

'. . . and he's certainly not a stall holder.'

'Just a minute, just a minute – it's old Bill Johnson's son, I'm sure of it.'

'What's he doing down here? He never came near the place when his father was alive. What's he doing here now?'

'There's only one way to find out. Let's ask him.'

The curious stall holders left their shelter and gathered round the drenched figure.

'Samuel – isn't it?' said one of them.

'Yes,' replied Samuel Johnson. 'I know you'll be wondering what I'm doing here, so I'll tell you.

'Years ago my father was sick and he couldn't look after his stall for a few days. He asked me to help. I wasn't working at the time and I could easily have done it. But I was far too proud to look after a market stall – I thought it was beneath me.

'Now my father is dead and I can't tell him how sorry I am that I let him down. The next best thing seemed to be to come down here and stand in the rain – perhaps somehow he'll know I'm trying to say sorry.'

The stall holders looked at each other without speaking. Then one of them said, 'You're very welcome to come and shelter with us.'

Information for the teacher

1   Dr Samuel Johnson (1709–84) was born in Lichfield, the son of a poor market bookseller. Johnson was acutely conscious of his poverty when he went up to Oxford. On one occasion a benefactor left a pair of new shoes at his door after having seen the appalling state of the shoes Johnson was wearing. The new pair was angrily returned. He moved to London 'with twopence half-penny in my pocket'.

   In later life Dr Johnson was renowned for his kindness to the poor and the destitute.

   He owes his immortality to James Boswell's *Life of Johnson*, published 1791.

2   The theme of this story is always contemporary and could lead on to discussion among the children about their own experiences.

3   A Bible story with sufficient points of similarity and comparison is, of course, the Prodigal Son (Luke 15, 11–32).

Hymn suggestion

Come and Praise Vol 2 'When your Father' No 73

Prayer

Let us pray this morning about the mistakes we make in the way we behave.

Let us try always to see the other person's point of view as well as our own.

Let us remember that every job is worth doing well and that even though it is sometimes hard, we should be prepared to help wherever and whoever we can. Amen.

54 Learning a lesson

Introduction

At some time or other we have all done something we wish we hadn't. This morning's story is quite a funny one but it helps to remind us that a guilty conscience is not something we want.

Story

'This way we'll get rid of him forever,' said Brer Rabbit.

'Well . . .' muttered Brer Bear.

'Of course, don't you see?' went on Brer Rabbit. 'We set fire to his house, nobody will know we've done it, and we'll be rid of him forever.'

So the plotters decided to get rid of their arch enemy, Brer Anansi.

That night they crept through the woods to his house. Making sure nobody was about, they piled dry branches round the trunk of the tree and set the whole thing on fire. The flames shot skywards, smoke billowed through the wood and within a very short time the tree in which Anansi had his home was just a blackened stump.

'That's the end of him,' smirked Brer Rabbit. 'Let's go and celebrate.'

Next morning the plotters met together to have a feast. At last they had got rid of that pest Anansi. Soon the pots were boiling and Brer Rabbit bent over them smelling the delicious food. Brer Bear dozed nearby. Then a third figure appeared in the clearing – Anansi.

He had of course not been in his house when it burnt down. On returning from spending the night with a friend, he had found the wreckage of his home and assumed that it had been destroyed by lightning. Now he was collecting a large piece of wood to build a new house. He had been on his way to do this when the lovely smell had tempted him to the clearing.

He was just about to speak when Brer Rabbit turned from his pots. Seeing Anansi he gave a terrified gasp, dropped everything and fled into the forest.

'Strange,' thought Anansi. 'What peculiar behaviour.'

At that moment Brer Bear saw Anansi coming towards him with a large piece of wood.

'Aaaaah,' cried Brer Bear, 'he's come back to take his revenge!'

With that, he leaped onto a donkey and fled. A piece of wood at the end of the donkey's tether kept hitting Brer Bear and he was sure that the ghost of Anansi was in pursuit, beating him with the stick.

So the two plotters fled and did not return for weeks. Meanwhile Anansi thoroughly enjoyed their feast.

Information for the teacher

1   Stories of Anansi the trickster abound. Originally a West African legendary figure and reputed creator of the world, he has achieved a more international status while remaining a cultural hero. Only with the Wax Girl does he meet his match.

2   The early reference to fires in this story could direct things to a different and more serious tack if the teacher wishes. The danger of fires might be linked with fire brigades in a 'people who help us' theme.

3   A possible calendar link here is that on 13th April 1695, Jean de la Fontaine, one of the most famous of all fable writers, died in France. In similar vein Hans Christian Andersen was born on 2nd April 1805.

Hymn suggestion

Come and Praise Vol 1 'God knows me' No 15

Prayer

Dear God,

We pray that you may give us the wisdom to think before we act. In this way, may we be free from doing something about which we will be very sorry later. Amen.

55 The tooth

Introduction

Do you remember when you started school – how lonely and worried you felt? Of course, lots of other children felt the same and you probably soon made friends. It's a bit different when you change schools and everybody knows everyone else – except you.

Story

Assundra kept her eyes down on the book's page. She wasn't reading it though, she was listening.

'Are you going to Brownies tonight?'

'Yes – it's going to be something special, Brown Owl says.'

'Jackie Bence's big brother's got a new colour telly in his bedroom.'

'My mum says I can stay up as late as I like if I'm working on my computer.'

So it went on. Everybody chatting, everybody saying something – except Assundra. Nobody said anything to her, so she didn't dare interrupt and say anything herself.

Worriedly, she poked her teeth with her tongue again. Then, suddenly, she was no longer aware of what the voices were saying. Her tooth! It began wobbling backwards and forwards, and then, with a sort of little click, it came away from her gum. She put up a hand and took it from her mouth. Around her the voices stopped for a minute, and then they all started again, as if at once.

'Assundra – your tooth's come out!'

'You lucky thing – put it under your pillow tonight.'

'The tooth fairy left me 50p when mine came out last week.'

'Doesn't it feel funny where the tooth used to be, 'Sundra?'

'Here, let's have a look.'

Assundra felt herself go hot and cold. She had forgotten all about the tooth.

'They're talking to me,' she thought. 'And they're calling me by my name.'

She felt a warm feeling spread over her.

'Think I'll see if there's any more loose,' she said, pressing her teeth with her finger.

There was a burst of laughter from the other girls.

'Oh – she's going to be rich, this girl,' one of them joked.

Information for the teacher

1   Guru Nanak, the founder of the Sikh religion, was someone who advocated kindness and consideration to all. Several stories about him illustrate this, and he was born on 15th April 1469. Thus this calendar link could be integrated into the story and provide the following thought-provoking quotation. Guru Nanak was once criticised by a Muslim because he slept with his feet towards Mecca. He replied, 'If you think it is wrong for me to point my feet towards the house of God, show me some direction in which God does not dwell.'

2   This assembly could easily lead on to others of a similar nature, devised by the children themselves. 'How I made friends' could yield a selection of true incidents which would make good assembly material – and provoke useful discussion afterwards.

Hymn suggestion

Come and Praise Vol 1 'When I needed a neighbour' No 65

Prayer

Dear God,

Help us to be aware of everyone's needs for friendship. Let us not wait for others to be kind to children who are new and lonely. Teach us to be welcoming and generous. Amen.

56 Jonah

Introduction

All of us know the feeling that there is something we should do – but don't want to. This morning's story is a very old one. It is about a man who had a job to do but tried to get out of it. He certainly learned his lesson as a result!

Story

Jonah was God's messenger. One day God said to him, 'Go to the city of Nineveh and tell the people there to change their evil ways.'

Jonah was shocked. Nineveh was the capital of the great empire of Assyria and Jonah was frightened about what might happen to him if he went to do this job.

'They're cruel people there,' he thought. 'They won't listen to me and they could throw me in prison or even kill me. I'll just pretend to go.'

So Jonah went to the docks, but instead of boarding a ship to take him to Nineveh he got on one which was going in the opposite direction.

'God will never know where I have gone,' he thought to himself.

He was wrong. A day out of port, the ship ran into a terrible storm. Huge waves crashed over it, tearing away the rigging and threatening to capsize the ship at any second. The sailors worked like madmen. In the screaming wind, they fought with what was left of the sails and they even hurled some of the cargo overboard to lighten the ship. Nothing made any difference. The wind blew with ever-increasing force and the waves rose higher and higher. The captain asked Jonah to pray to his God, but of course this made no difference.

'It's no good,' said Jonah. 'I think this is all happening because of me. You see, I was supposed to go and do a job and . . . well . . . I've tried to get out of it.'

He then told the captain the whole story. When he had finished, he asked the captain to throw him overboard.

'I can't do that!' gasped the captain. 'What we'll do is row the ship into the shore and let you off.'

So the sailors tried to do this. The mast and sails were now all gone and the ship could only be kept under control by being rowed. Still the storm raged all round it.

'Don't worry, Jonah, we'll soon have you safe!' called one of the sailors as the waters streamed down his tired face.

He was wrong. As soon as the ship headed towards the shore the storm got even worse. Oars snapped like matchsticks and the crew were knee-deep in the water which thundered over the sides of the boat.

'You've got to throw me overboard – now!' yelled Jonah above the tumult. Reluctantly, the terrified sailors took his arms and legs and hurled him into the raging sea.

As Jonah hit the water, two things happened. The storm died at once and the ship settled calmly. Secondly, a passing whale opened its huge mouth and swallowed Jonah, despite his struggles. By a miracle, however, he survived and was eventually washed up safely on the shore. There, exhausted and wiser, he lay recovering his strength.

'How foolish I've been,' he thought. 'I should have known I could never run away from what God wants me to do.'

So he began to prepare for his journey to Nineveh.

Information for the teacher

1   The consequences of 'not doing what we know we should do' offer plenty of opportunity for supplementary material for this assembly – the mechanic who doesn't service a car properly, the builder who builds a sub-standard house, the teacher who doesn't prepare a lesson, etc, etc.

2   For those who wish to refer in more detail to the Biblical source of this story, the reference is Jonah 1, 1–17.
    It is interesting that in some symbolic interpretations of this story the sea stands for 'world politics!'

3   Another feature which this story emphasises is the courage and determination of sailors in the most extreme danger. This is another topic which could be followed up with plenty of more modern examples which are well documented.

4   There are plenty of sea-related April calendar anniversaries to which this story could be linked. Isambard Kingdom Brunel, building of the *Great Western* (the first ship to provide a regular transatlantic service, in 1843) and the *Great Eastern* (the largest ship to be built up to that time, in 1858) was born on 9th April 1806. Robert Watson-Watt, the Scottish inventor of RADAR, was born on the 13th, in 1892. The *Titanic* sank on the 15th, in 1912. John Franklin, discoverer of the North West Passage, was born on the 16th, in 1786. Joshua Slocum set sail from Boston, USA, on 24th April 1895 to make the first single-handed voyage round the world in the nine-ton sloop *Spray*; it took him three and a quarter years.

Hymn suggestion

Come and Praise Vol 2 'Make us worthy' No 94

Prayer

Dear God,
    Give us the strength that we may do those things which we know we should do. Help us to avoid laziness, carelessness and fear and guide us so that we always do a job as well as we possibly can. Amen.

57 Trust in Allah

Introduction

This morning's story is about the adventures of three men. Two of them were dissatisfied and wanted more; the third was a man who was grateful for what he had. This is what happened to them . . .

Story

The three friends had been on a long, tiring journey. They were desperate for a rest.

'Look,' said Haroun, 'there's a garden. It looks inviting and quiet. Let's camp there for the night.'

'An excellent idea,' agreed Anim.

Abdul, the third of the friends, was already looking for a spot where he could light a fire to cook the evening meal.

An hour later, the fire was blazing merrily. The friends had eaten well and were relaxing and talking before they went to bed.

Now, what they did not know was that this garden belonged to a king, and his palace overlooked the garden. Some time ago the king had told his gardener that he didn't want any more fires lit in the garden. Now, looking out of his palace windows, he saw the flickering firelight.

'That gardener,' he muttered furiously to himself. 'How dare he light a fire and disobey my orders.'

Stopping only to wrap himself in a long cloak, the king left the palace and hurried to the garden. As he got near to the fire he saw the three friends. Intrigued, he stopped, hid behind a tree and listened to what they were saying.

'Money – that's what life is all about,' Haroun said. 'If you are rich, life's no problem. I wish, above all else, that I was rich.'

'No, no,' replied Anim. 'What you want is a wife to look after you. Then you've got no worries – you've got good food and a comfortable house. I'm fed up of life the way it is. I wish I had a woman to look after me.'

Abdul smiled.

'You're too discontented, my friends,' he said. 'Allah provides everything we need. We have to thank him for everything.'

The other two continued to moan and grumble in the same way.

Meanwhile, the king listened carefully, and then, as quietly as he had come, he slipped back to the palace.

116

Early next morning he had the three men arrested and brought before him.

'Last night you trespassed in my garden.'

'We didn't know, Your Majesty,' said the three frightened friends.

'What's more,' went on the king, 'I know every word you said. Tell me your words. If you speak the truth I will reward you; if you lie I will have you executed.'

Terrified, the three friends repeated their conversation.

'Right,' said the king, pointing to Haroun. 'You shall have the treasure you desire so much.'

So saying, he clapped his hands, and Haroun was given a huge sack of treasure.

'And you,' went on the king, indicating Anim, 'shall have my daughter as your wife.'

At this a princess bowed low, and joined the astonished Anim.

'And as for you,' snapped the king, pointing at Abdul, 'you can just carry on waiting to see how your God looks after you.'

Two hours later, the friends were on their way again. They still hadn't recovered from their surprise – but Haroun was already moaning again.

'This bag is so heavy,' he grumbled. 'Abdul, will you carry it a while for me?'

'Of course,' replied Abdul, heaving the sack of treasure onto his shoulders.

Just at that moment a group of the king's soldiers appeared behind the friends. Being a strange man, the king had been unsettled by the calm contentment of Abdul. So he had said to the soldiers, 'Go after the three and kill the one who carries neither money nor wife.'

When Haroun saw the soldiers heading for him, he fled, and no one knows what happened to him.

Meanwhile, Anim, Abdul and the princess carried on their way. Eventually they reached a fast-flowing river.

'It's hard enough to get myself over here,' grumbled Anim. 'Here – you help her.'

So saying, he pushed the princess towards Abdul.

The heavy sack anchored Abdul safely as he crossed the river, and he held firmly onto the princess's hand. Anim was not so lucky. The current swept him away and he was never seen again.

Later, as Abdul and the princess ate a splendid meal in a pleasant village, he smiled at her.

'You know, my dear,' he said, 'there's a lot to be said for being content.'   *(A very free adaptation of an old Iranian folk tale.)*

Information for the teacher

1   Middle Eastern folk tales are a rich source of material for assemblies. Whilst many involve fantastic happenings, princes and princesses, the significance of Allah is often apparent.

2   A Biblical quotation which is appropriate for this story is: 'Happy is the man who has God as his helper, whose hope is in God.' (Psalm 146, 5)

3   A possible calendar link for this story is with St George's Day on 23rd April. The legendary St George, confident in his Christian faith, captured the child-eating dragon outside the Middle Eastern town of Sylene. He then took the captive beast into the town saying that he would kill it if the king would be baptised. The king, and fifteen thousand of the town's people, thus became baptised.

Hymn suggestion

Come and Praise Vol 2 'God in his love' No 76

Prayer

Dear God,
   Teach us the value of contentment and give us the strength to resist feelings of envy, dissatisfaction, discontent, greed and jealousy.
   Help us to be people whose company others enjoy. Amen.

58 I don't like you

Introduction

All of us like some people more than we do others. It's a strange thing, though, that when we really get to know somebody who we thought we didn't like, they usually seem much nicer!

Story

The mouse did not like the crow.
   'I don't like you,' he used to say to himself, when he saw the black shape of the crow flying overhead in the sky. He was always very careful not to let the crow see him – after all, he didn't want to be the bird's dinner!

One day the mouse was scurrying about his business as usual when he heard a terrible noise. It was as if a thousand birds were all shouting at the same time. Heading for where the noise came from, the mouse came upon a terrible sight.

A huge net lay on the ground, and trapped inside it was a complete flock of doves. The mouse was horrified, and didn't hesitate for a minute.

'I'm coming!' he shouted, and scuffed up to the net as quickly as he could. 'No hunter is going to get you, my friends – not if I can help it.'

At once he began to gnaw the net with his small sharp teeth. His jaws ached and his body trembled with the effort, but slowly and surely he began to work through the net. Finally, with a sharp twang, it parted and the relieved doves swept away upwards to the sky. Their leader paused.

'Thank you, my friend,' he said. 'Thank you.'

High above, the crow had watched all that had taken place.

'That mouse,' he said to himself, 'is really some fellow. I'd like to be his friend.'

Later that day, the crow swooped down and perched outside the mouse's hole.

'Mouse!' he called out. 'That was a great deed you did today. I saw you rescue all those doves. I'd like us to be friends.'

Inside his hole the mouse was tired out. He'd been asleep until the crow's voice had wakened him.

'I don't like you,' he thought, as he listened to what the crow had to say. 'I'm sure this is a trick and if I go up there he'll eat me.'

So, no matter what the crow said, the mouse didn't answer. Finally the crow got tired of talking to himself.

'Are you still asleep in there, mouse? I know you must be tired after your rescue. I'll come back tomorrow and talk to you again.'

So saying, the crow flew off.

Next day the crow came again, and the day after, and the day after. Eventually the mouse could stand it no longer.

'Such nice things he says,' thought the mouse. 'Perhaps he really does want to be my friend.'

Cautiously he poked his nose out of his hole.

'Mouse!' cried the crow. 'How delighted I am to see you. We have so much to talk about.'

And so the mouse and the crow became the very best of friends. Sometime afterwards, there was a terrible shortage of water near their homes, and the crow carried his little friend to another place where there was plenty. Here they lived very happily.

Information for the teacher

1 This story is an adaptation of one of the many tales in the *Panchatantra*. This book of Indian stories, reputedly told by the great storyteller Pandit Vishnu Sharma, is a very useful source of assembly material.

2 As one of the main protagonists in this story is a crow, there is a useful, and unusual, calendar reference which could be used here. John Audubon was born on 26th April 1785. As a boy in Paris he became an avid drawer of birds. Later as a businessman, he went to the United States, where he kept up this hobby. The end result was four volumes of hand-coloured drawings of all the known species of birds in North America: *The Birds of America*.

3 For those who would like a different kind of calendar link, the second half of April is unusually rich in literary associations with 'storytellers'. It is thought that Shakespeare was born on the 23rd in 1564. Daniel Defoe (author of *Robinson Crusoe*) died on the 24th in 1731, and Charlotte Brontë was born on the 21st in 1816.

Hymn suggestion

Come and Praise Vol 1 'The Family of Man' No 69

Prayer

Dear God,
   Help us to be more sensible and caring people. Teach us that it is so much better to say to ourselves, 'I'd like to get to know you better,' than 'I don't like you,' when we meet others.
   Guide us too in our own behaviour so that others feel we can always be trusted and relied on. Amen.

May

59 The move

Introduction

Think for a minute about your bedroom. Are any of your favourite toys in it? Have you got a special bedspread? Is yours a comfortable bed? Now listen to this morning's story.

Story

Jessica could remember when Mum and Dad first talked about it.

'We'll certainly be better off there,' Dad had said. 'There are more rooms for the kids, the garden's bigger and I can get to work in half the time.'

'I don't know, Jack,' Mum had said doubtfully. 'We're so settled here.'

'It'll be all right, you'll see,' Dad went on. 'I think – Harry, stop moving that food about.'

Harry was Jessica's eighteen-month-old brother who was far too young to know what anybody was talking about. But Jessica kept hearing Mum and Dad talking about this 'moving'. And then one day it really happened.

'Well, we've moving on Wednesday,' said Mum. 'After school on Monday you'd better start packing the things in your bedroom.'

'Mum,' said Jessica in a small voice, 'I don't want to move. I like it here.'

'Our new house is really nice,' answered Mum with a smile. 'You'll like it there even more.'

Jessica was miserable at school. She kept thinking of her bedroom – all her toys in their special places, her warm, comfortable bed with the Snoopy bedspread, the window where she could look out at next door's cat sneaking across the lawn. She didn't want to move!

Wednesday came all too soon. Mum had arranged for Jessica to have the day off school and when she woke and looked at the packed crates and curtainless window she felt more miserable than ever. The removal men arrived and everything was soon in a frenzy. Men with boxes clattered up and down stairs, the cat hid in the meter cupboard, Mum and Dad were tetchy – only Harry seemed to enjoy it.

Finally the house was empty and the family got into their car and set off, following the removal van. When they reached the new house, the dashing about started all over again. While Jessica was standing miserably holding Harry's hand Mum had a quiet word with Dad.

'Jack, I'm going to get Jessica's room ready first to try and cheer her up. Why don't you drive back to the old house and make sure we haven't left anything? Take Jessica with you. My mother's coming over to look after Harry.'

'Good idea,' said Dad. 'Come on, Jessica,' he called.

Soon the two of them were making the trip back to the old house. As they turned into the familiar street Jessica felt tears prick her eyes. This was home and it always would be – why did they have to move? Soon they were parked and Dad was stomping through the house. While he did so, Jessica went up to her old room. It looked so cold and bare and even . . . unfriendly. She felt confused – she didn't seem to belong here any more.

Dad found a couple of books they'd overlooked and soon they were back in the car again. The new street had a couple of nice trees in it and when they reached their new house Mum was waving out of an upstairs window.

'Jessica – I've got your room ready. Come on up and have a look!'

Dutifully Jessica plodded up the stairs. How could it ever be as good as her old bedroom – just how *could* it? Mum stepped aside and Jessica went in.

There were her toys lined up just like they'd always been. Snoopy grinned up from the bed and everything seemed a bit bigger. Some new flowered curtains blew in a cool breeze from the open window. It looked . . . well . . . it looked . . . nice . . . really very . . .

'Jessica!' Dad's voice sounded from downstairs. 'There's some-body here to see you.'

When Jessica got downstairs again, a girl of about her own age, with the brightest ginger hair she had ever seen, was standing next to Dad.

'Hi,' said the girl. 'My name's Natasha and I live next door. I thought you might like to come round while your Mum and Dad are sorting the house out.'

'Oh . . . thanks,' murmured Jessica.

'Come on, then,' said Natasha cheerfully. 'Moving's rotten, isn't it? But this is a great place to live, you know. There's a smashing stream, and woods just a couple of minutes away. And Dalia lives just two doors away and . . .'

As Natasha chattered away, Jessica felt a smile creeping over her face. It was going to be all right here. Yes, there was no doubt about it – it was going to be all right.

Information for the teacher

1   The themes of changes, uncertainty, welcomes, etc, could be discussed before the assembly, or developed in post-assembly discussions. If appropriate, one or two children could speak of their personal experiences during the assembly presentation, after the story.

2   A bit of thought and preparation could go into music to accom-pany this assembly. 'Home' is a powerful theme in popular music

– 'Keep the home fires burning', 'Show me the way to go home', 'Pasadena', 'Home on the Range', etc.

3   The following is a famous quotation from a child of refugee parents: 'Yes we have a home, but no house to put round it.'

4   An unusual, and stimulating, calendar reference could be with 5th May. It was on this date in 1944 that tools used by people of the Old Stone Age (250,000 years ago) were discovered forty miles from Nairobi in Kenya.

Hymn suggestion

Come and Praise Vol 1 'O Lord, all the world belongs to you' No 39

Prayer

Dear God,

Let us give thanks for our homes and all who make them so precious to us. Let us pray too for those unfortunate people who have no home. Please give them hope for the future. Amen.

60 It's not fair

Introduction

None of us can do anything about how we look – we were just born this way! Sometimes, though, the way a person or creature looks or moves makes others dislike him or her. How unfair this is. Many people feel this way about spiders, but old stories show them in a very different light.

Story

There are a lot of spiders around – in Britain alone there are many more than two hundred thousand billion of them! Although lots of people say they are frightened of spiders, there are some old stories about them which are very interesting.

For instance, it was said that, at the first Christmas when Jesus was born in the stable, one of the first creatures to appear was a spider. Lowering itself down from the roof, it began busily to spin a web over the manger containing the newborn baby. This was to protect him.

There is another spider story about the birth of Jesus: when King Herod ordered his soldiers to kill all newborn baby boys because of his fear of the 'new King', Joseph and Mary took Jesus and fled before the soldiers could find them. On their journey they stopped one night and hid in a cave. While they slept, a party of soldiers reached the cave and were about to look inside when they saw that a spider's web completely covered the entrance.

'Waste of time looking in there,' they said to each other. 'Nobody can have gone in there recently, not with that spider's web over the entrance.'

Then there is the story of Robert I, known as Robert the Bruce, who was crowned King of Scotland in 1306. At this time his country was full of English invaders and in trying to drive them out his army lost a great battle and he had to flee for his life.

Hiding out on Rathlin Island, he watched a spider spinning its web. Time and time again it ran into difficulties and time and time again it started again and would not give up.

'What a marvellous example,' said Robert to himself. 'We should be like the spider and learn how important it is to keep on trying at whatever we are doing.' Robert got his army together again and led them in successfully driving the English out of Scotland.

Information for the teacher

1   Probably the most famous spider legend concerns Athena and Arachne. Arachne was a Greek girl who was so good at weaving that she challenged the goddess Athena to see who could produce the best piece of work. Arachne duly won, but Athena was so angry that she tore up Arachne's work and turned the girl into a spider.

2   Anansi, or 'Mr Spider', the great trickster of West African origin and fame, was originally thought to have created the world. There are dozens of stories about him and his popularity is now worldwide.

3   There are several Biblical quotations which could be used in connection with this material:

> Countless Kings are made by your hand,
> And the earth is full of your creatures.
>
> (Psalm 104)

> Do not overrate one man for his good looks or be
>   repelled by another man's appearance.

The bee is small among the winged creatures,
Yet her perfume takes first place for sweetness.
(Ecclesiasticus 11, 2–3)

As opportunity offers, let us work for the good of all.
(Galatians 6, 9–10)

4 A possible calendar link for this material is 3rd May. On this date Columbus 'discovered' Jamaica – one of the areas where Anansi has become most famous.

Hymn suggestion

Come and Praise Vol 1 'All creatures of our God and King' No 7

Prayer

Let us think this morning of all the many living creatures in the world. Let us learn not to judge them, or human beings, by their appearance.

Let us always remember the needs of those creatures who are our pets, and care for them with love and attention.

61 Enough is enough

Introduction

Perhaps you complain when you are told it is bedtime. Perhaps you want a little extra cake when Mum says you have had enough. It is tempting to want a little more, but this is sometimes not fair on the people we share our lives with.

This morning's story is about a man who had great good fortune – but still wanted a little more ... and a little more ...

Story

The moon shone down on the icy, snow-covered countryside. Suddenly, through the still night air, came the jolly sound of a fiddle being played. There, skating across the iced-up river, was Janek. Janek was a herdsman who loved playing the fiddle. He had been playing at a party and was going home.

Reaching the other side of the river, he set off homewards, and was just about to pass a small hill when, to his absolute astonishment, a door in the hill opened and a beautiful lady stepped out.

Janek thought he was seeing a ghost and was about to run away when she spoke.

'Don't be afraid,' called out the lady. 'Your music was so lovely I just had to find out where it came from.'

Janek stood as if rooted to the spot as the lady told him her story.

Long ago she had been a queen of Poland and every night between eleven o'clock and midnight she was allowed to come back to the land she loved.

'Now,' she went on, 'play a tune for me. If there is anything you ever want you can find me here at the hour I have mentioned.'

With trembling fingers Janek played once again. As he finished, a distant clock began striking midnight and the queen disappeared into the hillside again.

Now, Janek was a wonderful fiddler but he was not so good as a herdsman. He spent a lot of time daydreaming. One day he lost one of his farmer's cows. His master was furious. The cow couldn't be found and Janek was told he must pay for it. He had no money and was desperately thinking what he might do, when - he remembered the mysterious queen.

That night he went back to the hillside and played a tune. Immediately the secret door opened and the queen appeared.

'Welcome, Janek,' she said. 'Please play for me.'

Janek did this, and then told her his troubles.

'You may go into my hill,' said the queen, 'but take only the ten gold pieces you need to pay for the lost cow.'

Janek went into the hill and gasped. There at the bottom of a flight of steps, and lit by flickering light, was a fabulous hoard of treasure. Remembering what the queen had said, the fiddler took only ten pieces of gold and returned to the outside of the hill.

Another night, Janek came back to ask the queen for help again. He wanted to marry a young woman called Margaret, but Margaret did not love him. The queen told him about the touch of a secret fork which would make Margaret love him. Now all seemed well, until Margaret's father refused to let his daughter marry Janek because he was such a poor man.

So Janek returned to the secret hillside once again.

'Play for me, Janek,' said the queen, and when he had finished she listened to his latest story.

'I know that I can be a good farmer,' said Janek. 'All I need is enough money to buy a piece of land which I know is for sale.'

'How much is it?' asked the queen.

'Four hundred gold pieces,' replied Janek.

'Very well,' said the queen. 'Go into the hill, down the steps and take only the four hundred pieces you need.'

'Thank you, thank you,' said Janek.

'But,' the queen went on, 'remember it is nearly midnight and when the clock strikes, the door will disappear and if you are still inside you will be trapped in the hill.'

'Oh, I'll be quick and only take exactly what I need,' said Janek. He hurried into the hill.

Hurriedly, he counted out the four hundred pieces and then, as he was going back up the stairs, he saw them. Standing on the floor in a corner was a magnificent pair of bright red boots. Janek stopped.

'It can't do any harm to try them,' he thought to himself. Putting down his gold, Janek slid on the boots. They were a perfect fit! The soft leather warmed his ankles and he looked to where he had lain his own tattered old boots.

'If only . . .' he thought. Then, in the distance, he heard the clock begin to strike midnight. Desperately, he seized the gold, raced up the steps and flung himself through the hillside door before he was trapped.

'Safe!' he gasped as he burst out into the night air. Then he remembered the queen's words, 'Take only what you need.'

No sooner had these words come into his head than - his feet were burning! Tearing at the boots with his hands, Janek tried again and again to pull them off. All the time the heat grew hotter and hotter . . .

The next morning, passing travellers saw something lying by the roadside. What had obviously been a good pair of boots lay smouldering on the grass, the smoke still rising. As for Janek - he was never ever seen again.

Information for the teacher

1   This is an assembly which could be presented with a judicious mixture of readings and mime.

2   There are possibilities for linking it with the Bible story centred on the saying: 'It is easier for a camel to go through the eye of a needle than for a rich man to enter the Kingdom of God.' This story of man's desire for riches on earth can be found in Luke 18, 18-26.

3   A possible calendar link here is with 9th May 1671, the date on which Colonel Blood stole the Crown Jewels from the Tower of London. Alternatively, 23rd May 1701 was the date on which Captain Kidd, the infamous pirate, was hanged.

Come and Praise Vol 1 'The best gift' No 59

Prayer

Let us think this morning about sharing the good things of our lives and being thankful for what we have. Let us remember that to want more is often to get less.

62 Christian Aid week

Introduction

Every May there is a week when we think about Christian aid to people all over the world who are less fortunate than we are, and need as much help as they can be given.

Story

This morning we are going to hear about two of the sort of people who are given help by the Christian Aid organisation. Listening to their stories makes us think about the many things we take for granted.

First of all, let's think about water. How much do we use each day – to wash ourselves, drink, use to flush the toilet, and so on. Whenever we need it, whatever we need it for, it always seems to be there.

This is not the case for a lady called Tazunda who lives in a wooden hut in a tiny village in Africa. This is a very dry part of the world and the nearest water for Tazunda comes from a muddy hole which is ten minutes' walk away from her hut.

Twice every morning and twice every afternoon, Tazunda walks barefoot from her hut to this water hole. When she gets there she has to scoop water from the dirty iron drum sunk into the water hole. She does this with a jug and pours the water into a rusty old 23-litre bucket. Then she carries the jug and the bucket back home.

Every single day Tazunda must do this. This water must do for her family of four and the amount she gets every day is only the same amount as we use when we flush the toilet twice.

Sanja is much younger than Tazunda and she lives in Nepal, in the shadow of Mount Everest and the other great Himalayan mountains. Sanja was born with a disease called polio and for the first ten years of her life she could only crawl. At first this wasn't too bad because her mother could carry her, but when she was ten years old and her mother had to go to market Sanja could only crawl round behind her in the dirt, dust, noise and bustle. Nobody thought that she would ever be able to walk.

One day, however, a worker from the Save the Children organisation saw Sanja crawling round in the market. Soon help was being offered to her and her mother. Sanja was taken to a health centre in a village called Chautara and after a year's exercises on parallel bars, and with the help of crutches, she has learned to walk.

> (These stories were adapted from
> Save The Children information.)

Information for the teacher

1   Most primary schools are circulated with information, photographs and very helpful assembly material by the Christian Aid Organisation for their week in early May. Their web site address is www.christian-aid.org.uk

Save the Children is another organisation which does an excellent job, and it also provides first-class material for schools. A useful contact is:

The Education Unit, Save the Children Fund,
Mary Datchelor House, 17 Grove Lane, London SE5 8RD.
www.oneworld.org/scf

2   Tazunda comes from Western Zimbabwe. In Africa as a whole, thirty to fifty per cent of child deaths under five are caused by contaminated water.

3   To illustrate that concern for others is a feeling which pervades all religions, two quotations might be useful:

He who does not help to turn the rolling wheels of this great world lives a lost life. (Hindu)

A man should treat everybody and everything in the world as he himself would like to be treated. (Jain)

4   For information on water provision in the UK, to make comparisons with Third World problems, contacts with local Water Board Authorities could be useful.

Hymn suggestion

Come and Praise Vol 2 'Water of Life' No 2

Prayer

Let us think this morning of all those people, all over the world, whose lives are desperately hard and who are often suffering terribly.

Let us give thanks to the workers everywhere who are helping, and let us pray that the kindness of others will continue to raise money to support the work that is being done to help.

63 The grave

Introduction

Have you ever noticed how much attention we pay to the way other people behave? Listen to this morning's story . . .

Story

'I am going to travel and see something of the world,' Abdul said to himself.

So he set off, with his donkey as his only companion. For twelve years he travelled through deserts and mountains, staying in many different places and meeting many different people. He became a much wiser man.

One day he was travelling through the mountains of Kashmir.

'This is one of the most difficult trips yet,' Abdul muttered to his faithful donkey as they toiled higher and higher up into the thin air.

'Come on my . . .' Abdul stopped speaking. His donkey was suddenly slowing down. 'What is . . .'

This time, before Abdul could finish what he was going to say, the donkey slipped quietly to the ground, and there it died. It had finally become exhausted with old age and ceaseless travel.

Abdul was heartbroken. In all the years of his journeys the donkey had been his faithful companion and friend. Now he was dead.

After a while, the traveller looked up from his tears. Seeing the beautiful scenery around him he found he had lost his desire to travel further.

'This will be my home,' he said aloud.

He set about burying the donkey and, when he had done so, he marked the grave with a simple mound of earth. Then he began making a home for himself nearby.

As the days and weeks went by, he made sure that the donkey's grave was always beautifully looked after.

Now, the path Abdul had been following was a busy one and many travellers passed by there. They noticed the grave, and the man who cared for it so lovingly, and they talked about this.

'That must have been a dear friend who lies buried there.'

'How carefully that man cares for the grave.'

'I think it must belong to somebody who was really important.'

So the tales went on. Abdul said nothing. One day a very rich man came by. He had heard all the stories about the man who lived on the mountain.

'Now sir,' he said to Abdul, 'I've heard about the way you care for your lost friend. I'd like to help.'

So the rich man built a shrine over the donkey's grave. In order that there would always be money to keep it in good repair, he had terraces cut into the hillside, where the villagers could grow crops to sell. This helped the villagers grow more prosperous, and the whole community cared for each other.

One day Abdul stood on the hill beside the donkey's grave and looked at the happy village spread before him.

'Now my dear friend,' he said, 'look what a simple donkey has achieved.'

Information for the teacher

1   Although this is an adaptation of an old folk tale which has no link with Christianity, there are many Christian associations with donkeys.

When St Anthony of Padua was seeking to convert a group of people he lost patience and said that it would be easier to make a wild donkey kneel down than it would be to persuade them to listen to him. At this point a nearby donkey knelt, the unbelievers listened and were converted to Christianity.

St Jerome's monastery was built thanks to the donkey who carried all the wood.

The donkey also features in Nativity scenes ('the ox and the ass') and in Jesus's entry into Jerusalem.

2   In times gone by in the Middle East, and elsewhere, the ass was of enormous importance to its owner. It ate only a quarter of the barley which a horse ate, it was particularly sure-footed in seeking out desert paths, and it could be used for hauling and ploughing.

3   One possible calendar link could be with 8th May. This was the day, in 1828, on which the Swiss philanthropist Jean Henri Dunant was born. As a traveller he was an eyewitness to the terrible battle of Solferino on 24th June 1859. He was appalled at the high number of casualties – forty thousand – and organised emergency help for French and Austrian wounded alike. He ultimately founded the International Red Cross and was the first to be awarded the Nobel Peace Prize, in 1901. (He shared the award with Frédéric Passy.)

Hymn suggestion

Come and Praise Vol 1 'Travel on' No 42

Prayer

Let us think this morning about some words Jesus said: 'If you want to be a leader you must be a servant.'

Let us pray that we may have the strength to behave in a way which is both a help and an example to other people. Amen.

64 *This month*

Introduction

In May there is a real feeling that summer is coming and there are plenty of messages to tell us this.

Story

A man who spent his lifetime studying the English countryside said that it reached its most beautiful on 18th May every year. This man's name was W H Hudson and if we look around on this date we can certainly see what he means.

Let's start with trees. It is very strange that things as large as trees have very small flowers and seeds. By 18th May these flowers and seeds look their most beautiful. The hawthorn and horse chestnut are in blossom, the greenish-yellow flowers of the sycamore dangle in big clusters, and there are tiny white flowers on holly and catkins on oaks.

If you visit a wood, looking down is as exciting as looking up at this time of year. There is often a 'carpet' of blue, where masses of bluebells are growing. These contrast with the red of red campions. On roadsides leading to woods, cow parsley seems to grow taller almost by the minute and great heads of blossom appear on it. Watch out, too, for buttercups and forget-me-nots. White dead-nettles take a bit more finding but it is worth having a search for them and then seeing if you agree with their old country name – 'white archangels'.

Of course, this is a time when everything grows – and that means some difficulties for people too. Along country lanes weeds and grass start to grow to a height which creates danger for traffic, and have to be cut down.

In the fields weeds start to grow as fast as the corn and the fields may have to be treated with sprays. These are often fitted to the back of tractors and they kill the weeds while letting the corn continue to grow.

In times gone by the dew on the grass in the early morning in May was thought to make girls more beautiful. So it was not unusual to see them 'washing their faces' in the grass.

People liked to enjoy themselves in May in other ways, too. There was dancing round the maypole on the first of the month and great celebrations on 29th May. This is 'Oak Apple Day' when King Charles II rode into London as the new king in 1660. Before this the Puritans had ruled and the reason people gave this day its name was because the king had hidden from the Puritan army in an oak tree after the Battle of Worcester.

So May is a month to take a deep breath and enjoy all that the countryside has to offer. An old rhyme reminds us of this:

> Here we come a-piping
> In Springtime and in May,
> Green fruit a-ripening,
> And winter fled away.

Information for the teacher

1   The word 'May' reportedly comes from Maia, mother of the god Mercury. The Anglo-Saxons had a more descriptive name for this month – 'Tri-Milchi', denoting the fact that the ideal grassy conditions meant that cattle could now be milked three times a day.

2   The Puritans denounced maypoles and maypole dancing (in 1644). On the restoration of the monarchy, Charles II reintroduced May Day in style by erecting an 134-foot-high maypole in the Strand.

3 The hawthorn has symbolic associations with the return of summer. Hung outside a cowshed, it was believed to guarantee good milk; placed in the rafters of a house, it was believed to keep evil spirits away.

4 The start of growth begins with a mean daily temperature of 43°F (6°C).

Hymn suggestion

Come and Praise Vol 1 'For the beauty of the earth' No 11

Prayer

Dear God,

Thank you for the beauty of the month of May. Thank you for our senses of sight, smell and hearing which help us to enjoy it so much.

We pray for your help to make sure that people do nothing to destroy the beautiful flowers, trees, woods and fields which look so lovely at this time of year. Amen.

65 Once too often

Introduction

'You've tried that trick once too often!' You might have heard a parent say that to a child who has been naughty. Your Mum or Dad might even have said it to you! This morning's story shows exactly what this comment means.

Story

Jake was excited.

'Maria,' he said to his wife, 'we'll definitely be able to earn more money if we do this. Then we'll have enough to mend the roof.'

'What are you talking about?' asked his wife.

'Well,' Jake went on, 'I've heard that you can buy salt really cheaply at the seaside. I'll go and buy a load, bring it back and sell it for a good profit at the market.'

'But how will you get it here?'

'That's easy – that's what I've got old Oscar for.'

Now, Oscar was the family ass. He did all the fetching and carrying to and from market. To tell the truth, he was a lazy creature and would do anything he could to get out of work.

The next day Jake set off with Oscar to the seaside where the salt was cheap. When they got there Jake bought the salt and loaded it in sacks which he strapped on Oscar's back.

'This is terrible!' thought Oscar. 'These are heavy and I've got to walk all the way home with them. What a life!'

The two set off on the return journey. At one point they had to walk along a steep and slippery path which ran alongside a fast-flowing stream. The grumbling and weary Oscar wasn't watching where he put his feet and with a sudden clatter he fell into the stream.

Concerned, Jake pulled him out. 'What a rotten fall,' he said, stroking the ass's head. 'I hope you're all right.'

Oscar kept his eyes fixed on the ground – he had made a wonderful discovery. When he had been in the water a terrific amount of the salt in the sacks had dissolved, and his burden wasn't even half as heavy now!

Next day, Jake took Oscar back to the seaside again so that they could get another load of salt. Trying to make good his loss, he got an extra sack this time. Oscar responded in his usual awkward way – until they reached the slippery path again. Then, with a great show of panic, he pretended to slip again and fell into the stream.

The same thing happened as before. Jake pulled him out, dried him off and consoled him. Meanwhile, Oscar smirked to himself and walked on with hardly any burden at all.

Next day they were off back to the seaside again. Jake busied himself buying and filling sacks. Oscar stood quietly, sure that he knew how to get the best out of this situation now.

'Rightho Oscar, off we go then.'

Jake had finished loading the sacks onto the ass's back and they were moving off along the familiar path home.

'That's funny,' thought Oscar, 'these sacks are much lighter than they were before. Maybe he's feeling sorry for me and just got a lesser load. Anyway, by the time I fall in the stream again it'll seem as if I'm carrying nothing.'

The journey went on until they reached the slippery path again. Once more Oscar managed to slip and splattered down into the water. Once more, Jake dragged him out and consoled him. But there was a difference: Oscar's load now seemed to weight about ten times more than before he had fallen into the water.

'This is ... this is terrible,' muttered the ass to himself as he laboured homewards with the heaviest load he had ever had to carry.

That night Jake and Maria were talking again.

'Did you solve the problem?' asked Maria.

'Oh yes,' replied Jake. 'I bought a load of sponges today and after he had fallen deliberately into the water his load was much, much heavier. I think our Oscar has learned his lesson – he tried his trick once too often.'

(Adapted from an old fable)

Information for the teacher

1   There are two possibilities for a calendar link with this story. It could be used on the anniversary of the French writer Charles Perrault, who died on 18th May 1703. He was a father in old age and published his children's tales ('Mother Goose', 'Blue-beard', 'Tom Thumb', 'Cinderella', 'Red Riding Hood' and 'The Sleeping Beauty') under his son's name.
    Another possibility is to link this story of 'trickery' with the date on which Jonathan Wild was executed – 24th May 1725. Jonathan Wild was acknowledged as a masterly tutor of thieves, tricksters, pickpockets and the like.

2   Another fable with a rather similar theme is 'Cry Wolf' which could be used for comparison with this one.

3   Any book of Aesop's fables is a useful resource for assemblies. Aesop lived in Greece about three thousand years ago. He was a slave whose stories of animals reflected both the virtues and frailties of people. Such was his skill as a storyteller that he was given his freedom from slavery.

Hymn suggestion

Come and Praise Vol 1 'God knows me' No 15

Prayer

Let us think this morning about how we often try to make our lives easier by tricks and excuses. Let us learn to be straightforward in our dealings with people so that we are not embarrassed when our tricks and excuses are discovered. Let us pray that we always have a clear, and not a guilty, conscience.

June

66 Down and out?

Introduction

There is an old saying: 'Beauty is in the eye of the beholder.' For instance, some people may see a chair as just something to sit on, others may think it is a beautiful piece of furniture. A teapot might be a precious ornament to one person – just something to make tea in to another. This morning's story makes us think about this.

Story

The German village was a very smart one. It was in the Alps and people came to ski there in the winter, and walk in the summer. The shops were fashionable and expensive – all except one.

Emma's shop was on the corner of two streets in one of the busiest parts of the village. It had been there for over a hundred years and Emma didn't like changes – everybody in the village called it *'Tante Emmas Laden'* – 'Aunt Emma's shop'.

'You never know,' said Emma to anybody who asked, 'something in this shop window might be just what somebody wants – or what somebody else thinks is really beautiful.'

Whomever Emma said this to always looked very doubtful when they saw what was in the shop window. It was piled high with old-fashioned record players, careworn musical instruments, ragged books, badly injured dolls, and so on.

For several weeks, high up in the right-hand corner of the shop window had been an old violin. The strings were tangled up and the wood was scarred. It didn't look as if it were worth much and it was impossible to think that it had once made music.

It was about this time that there came to the village a visitor quite unlike the smart crowd who were usually there. It was winter and, among the brightly coloured anoraks and the expensive coats, the threadbare overcoat and thin shoes of this visitor looked very out of place.

He stayed in the cheapest place he could find and seemed only to walk slowly through the streets for daily exercise. Usually he stared at the ground but, on this particular day when passing *Tante Emmas Laden*, he happened to glance in the window.

It was as if he had seen something magical there. His head came up, a new and almost youthful look came into his eyes and he began to clasp and unclasp his hands eagerly. He went into the shop.

'Good morning,' said Emma.

'Good morning,' replied the visitor, 'I ... I ... could I have a look at the violin?'

Smiling, Emma reached over the piles of junk and got down the violin.

'Might have been quite good once,' she said.

But the stranger wasn't listening. With his head bent over the old instrument he was running a forefinger round the edging of the wood. Then, with finger and thumb he began plucking and gently tugging one of the strings.

Emma watched quietly. Seeing how captivated the old man was with the violin she began to get on with other jobs and left him alone. For more than an hour he stood there caressing and adjusting the old instrument. Then he spoke.

'Excuse me, but you don't happen to have a bow, do you?'

'One here somewhere,' said Emma, going on another rummage through the shop and coming up with a dusty-looking violin bow.

Slowly and carefully the old man tucked the violin under his chin and began to play. At once notes of clear calm beauty began to fill the shop. Emma stopped what she was doing and sat down. The music was beautiful.

After a few minutes the man stopped playing.

'Who are you?' asked Emma.

'Nobody,' replied the man. 'But when I was young I worked in Mittenwald where some of the world's best violins are made. When I looked in the window I was sure that this was one I had made many years ago – and I was right.'

He gently stroked the wood of the violin.

'Would you like it?' said Emma.

'Oh I couldn't afford it,' said the man. 'I've been ill for a long time and I have no money. The doctor told me to come here for a few days for my health.'

At this moment the doorbell rang as another person entered the shop. It was Otto Lehrer, quite famous in the village and leader of the town orchestra which played, winter and summer, for visitors.

'Emma!' said Otto. 'I just heard the most fantastic violin playing coming from this shop – fantastic ...'

Emma didn't speak, but just nodded her head towards the old man.

'Oh ... well ...' he began to mutter.

'So it was you, sir. Well, a talent like yours doesn't come our way very often and we're looking for a lead violinist for the orchestra. The money's not bad and there's a tiny flat with the job – are you interested?'

'Well . . . it's wonderful . . . but, you see, the violin doesn't belong to me.'

'It does now,' said Emma, 'and thank you for paying for it with that wonderful music.'

Information for the teacher

1   There are many folk and traditional stories similar to this where violins, trumpets and other musical instruments come to life in the hands of a 'mysterious stranger'. Mittenwald, near the German border with Austria, is traditionally a great centre of violin-making. Craftsmen here have to serve a long and demanding apprenticeship in the art.

2   A useful calendar link with this story is 3rd May. It was on this date in 1899 that Johann Strauss, the Viennese 'King of the Waltz', died. This provides an excellent opportunity to introduce and end the story with some sweeping waltzes in which violins are so heavily featured.

3   Beauty – 'any of those qualities of objects, sounds, emotional or intellectual concepts that gratify the aesthetic nature' (Funk and Wagnall) – is certainly something which could be followed up either in the assembly or later.

4   Among the many quotations regarding beauty, one which seems particularly apt for this story is by Robert Bridges: 'Beauty, being the best of all we know, sums up the unsearchable and secret aims of nature'.

Hymn suggestion

Come and Praise Vol 1 'For the beauty of the earth' No 11

Prayer

Let us give thanks this morning for the sights and sounds which give us so much pleasure. Let us be grateful to artists and musicians who help us to enjoy these things.

67 A wise man

Introduction

This morning's story is about a man who was clever, funny and popular. Because of this three other men tried to 'catch him out'. This is what happened.

Story

When Nasr-ud-Din took his pupils to the mosque he always rode backwards on his donkey.

'Why do you do that?' asked one of his pupils.

'To keep an eye on you as you are behind me,' replied Nasr-ud-Din, 'and to make sure I am still leading you.'

Now, as it happened, three other men who fancied themselves as very wise, but who were not Muslims, saw Nasr-ud-Din riding backwards like this.

'How can anybody think this man is wise?' said the first man,

' "Stupid" would be my description of him,' said the second.

'Why don't we show him up for what he is?' went on the third.

So the three men went to the Sultan of Turkey and said that they wished to test the wisdom of this so called wise man, Nasr-ud-Din.

Now the sultan knew what a wit and joker Nasr-ud-Din was so he didn't quite know what to expect when he summoned his old friend to the palace. There the sultan ordered the three men to ask their questions.

'Tell me, sir,' said the first man, 'exactly where is the centre of the earth?'

Nasr-ud-Din smiled. 'That's an easy question to answer, my friend. The centre of the earth is exactly under the spot where my donkey has his right foot at the moment.'

The questioner gasped. 'But how can you know that?' he queried.

'It's quite simple,' replied Nasr-ud-Din. 'But of course if you want to prove it, get a tape measure and measure the earth. If you think my calculations are wrong, please come and see me again.'

The first man sat down in confusion, and the second stood up.

'My question is – how many stars are there in the sky?'

'Easy, my friend,' replied Nasr-ud-Din immediately. 'The same number as the hairs on my donkey.'

The questioner was taken aback by the speed of Nasr-ud-Din's answer. 'But you can't prove that.'

'I don't need to, my friend, but perhaps you do. Would you like to count both and see if I'm right?'

So the second man sat down, confused and embarrassed by all the smiling faces at the court.

The third man had watched all these goings-on with interest. He was determined not to be caught out in the same way. He stood up and with a wide, but false, smile, he said, 'Sir, may I call you "Hodja"?'

'Certainly. Most people do,' replied Nasr-ud-Din.

'Now, it's true you don't know me, isn't it?'

'Never seen you before in my life,' answered Nasr-ud-Din.

'Well then, tell me how many hairs I've got in my beard.'

'Oh that,' replied Nasr-ud-Din instantly. 'You've got as many hairs in your beard as my donkey has in his tail.'

This time, the third man smiled more widely. 'I'm going to ask you to prove that,' he said.

'Well that won't be difficult,' went on Nasr-ud-Din. 'What we'll do is this – we'll pull out a hair from the donkey's tail, then we'll pull a hair out of your beard and we'll count them as we go along We'd better start straight away though – you've got a very big beard.'

Suddenly the third man didn't seem so keen to have the point proved or disproved in this way!

After Nasr-ud-Din had gone the three men were so impressed with his quick-thinking that they told the sultan that from now on they would become Muslims.

(Adapted from an old Turkish story)

Information for the teacher

1 Nasr-ud-Din is a great folk hero of the Middle East and the Balkans. Known for his quick-thinking, ready answers and wit, it is possible that this legendary figure lived between the fourteenth and fifteenth centuries.

Nasr-ud-Din was given the honorary title of *Hodja*, which means a scholar who is particularly knowledgeable about the Qur'an. The Hodja would act as a preacher in the mosque (Khatib), a prayer leader (Iman) or a magistrate (Cadi).

2 A most useful calendar anniversary to link with this story is 8th June. It was on this date in 632 that the Prophet and founder of Islam, Muhammad (pbuh), died. There are many Muslim stories concerning Muhammad. One of the most succinct tells of his dealings with people who were always complaining. When

a man was bemoaning the fact that he had no shoes, Muhammad pointed out a man kneeling in the mosque – who had no feet.

4   It is useful and interesting to compare 'Hodja' tales with others where a 'message' is often transmitted with wit and style. Stories of Anansi, Brer Rabbit, and tales by Aesop and La Fontaine provide suitable material.

Hymn suggestion

Come and Praise Vol 1 'I listen and I listen' No 60

Prayer

Dear God,
   Help us to value good advice and the wisdom of others. Help us to be good listeners when something worthwhile is being said. Amen.

68 Getting over a bad start

Introduction

Many people do very worthwhile things in life after making a bad start. This morning's story is about a man called Columba and he certainly knew about trouble!

Story

The fight which had taken place had left several men bruised and battered. There were more than a few black eyes and bleeding noses.
   The king was furious. Surrounded by his courtiers he glared angrily at the man who stood in front of him. 'This is all your fault – and you know it. Look at the trouble you have caused!'
   'Yes, Your Majesty,' said the man bowing his head. His name was Columba.
   'When you borrowed that beautiful manuscript of the Bible you promised you only wanted to look at it,' the king went on.
   'Yes, Your Majesty.'
   'But that wasn't enough, was it? Oh no – you had to try and make a secret copy of it and when the owner found out he was very angry – and rightly so.'
   'Yes, Your Majesty.'

'And as if that weren't enough, when he complained, you and your families started this . . . this quarrel . . . this fight!'

'Yes, Your Majesty.'

'Well, I've had enough of you, Columba. This is the last straw. Get your things packed and leave Ireland within the next two days. You are expelled!'

So Columba was expelled from his native Ireland.

With a group of his followers he got a boat and set sail for Scotland, landing on the island of Iona in the year 563.

'I've made enough mistakes in my life,' said Columba to his friends. 'I've got the chance of a new start here and I'm going to make sure I take it.'

So, as the months passed, Columba and the rest of the group built first of all a monastery, and then a cathedral. As they prayed in these, Columba realised that it was not enough to help people on the island; he must go across to Scotland and northern England and tell people there about Christianity.

So he sailed backwards and forwards to the mainland, helping people to be good neighbours, to care about each other, to be unselfish, and to remember that, even if they had made a bad start in life, it was never too late to change and do good.

Information for the teacher

1   Columba died in 597 and his feast day is 9th June. He is credited with spreading Christianity over the northern part of England as well as Scotland. The island of Iona eventually became a famous place of pilgrimage.

2   A further interesting piece of 'hearsay' concerning Columba is that a stone was supposed to mark his birthplace in Garton, Donegal. When Irish emigrants were about to leave the country, tradition had it that they went and slept a night on this stone, thus curing themselves of any incipient homesickness.

3   The idea of Columba's determination and persistence to get over the difficulties of being expelled from his native land could be conveyed in the following quotation from the Bible: 'Bless the Lord, my immovable rock – he gives me strength and skill'. (Psalm 144, 1)

Hymn suggestion

Come and Praise Vol 1 'The journey of life' No 45

Prayer

Dear God,

We all make mistakes but please give us the wisdom to learn from them. Teach us that it is never too late to make new starts. Help us to have the determination to do what we know is right, and resist the temptation of laziness. Amen.

69 Peace is best

Introduction

This morning's story is about something which took place in a war long ago. The war was between the Greeks and the Persians and what you are going to hear took place four hundred and eighty years before Jesus was born.

Story

'We could defend this pass for ten years,' said the first soldier.

'I agree,' said the other.

'We've got all the food we need in the village behind us and this is the only way into Greece.'

Hearing his soldiers talk like this, Leonidas, commander of the Greek army, was very pleased. The huge Persian army, which had swept all before it, was advancing fast, but Leonidas knew that here, at the mountain pass of Thermopylae, he could stop the advance.

The pass was so narrow that only a few soldiers at a time could charge into it. The steep sides meant that the enemies' arrows wouldn't be much good and Leonidas knew that the Spartan soldiers he had at the front of the pass were the best in the world.

'We'll hold out here until the Persians get tired and go home,' he said to his men.

Soon the mighty Persian army arrived. It numbered over a million men and as well as foot soldiers there were bowmen, horsemen and chariots. Xerxes, the Persian commander spoke to his men.

'Once we are through this pass we will be on our way to Athens, Corinth and Sparta,' he said. 'The world will be ours. Now, they've got only a few thousand men holding this pass, so let's get on with it.'

The great battle started, but the Persians got nowhere. Every time they attacked the narrow opening of the pass they were driven back.

They couldn't go round it and the sides were so steep they couldn't get more men in. Xerxes got more frustrated and angry as each day went on.

After one particularly bad day, he sat in his tent eating his evening meal. Suddenly there was a commotion outside.

'What is it?' the commander called out.

Two soldiers entered. 'We've got a Greek outside, sir. He says he must see you – and it will be worth your while.'

For a moment Xerxes was tempted to have the Greek taken away as a prisoner but then he thought, 'What have I got to lose by seeing him?'

'Bring him in,' he said to the guard.

Twisting out of the guard's rough grip, the Greek came into the tent. He had a furtive, greedy look in his eye and Xerxes took an instant dislike to him. 'Well?'

The Greek didn't waste time. 'I know how you can win this battle.'

'Indeed? And how is that?'

'There's a secret path through the mountains which comes out at the other end of the pass. Leonidas has his poorest troops stationed there. For a small consideration I can lead a party of your troops along this secret path. Then they can attack the Greeks from behind while you attack from the front.'

Xerxes looked with contempt at this traitor – but he thought about how this would be the solution to his problem.

'Right,' he said, 'let's go into this in more detail.'

Two nights later, Ephialtes, the traitor, led some of the Persians' best soldiers through the stony, dangerous mountain path which led to the other end of the pass at Thermopylae. They reached the far end of the pass just as dawn was breaking. Just as Ephialtes had said, this was where the poorest soldiers in the Greek army were stationed. When they saw the approaching Persians they were so shocked that they ran away without putting up a fight.

Thanks to careful planning, the Persians now made a frontal attack on the pass. The confident Greeks were then horrified to find that there were Persians behind them as well. They could no longer hold out and in a short time the Persians had won the battle and were on their way to Athens.

Information for the teacher

1   Greece and Persia were at war in 490 BC but neither side could gain a conclusive victory. As a result both spent the next ten

years preparing for the next clash. The Persian army's invasion began with the crossing of the strait known as the Hellespont (now called the Dardanelles). Two thousand six hundred ships were lashed together to form a bridge over which the great army crossed.

The Persian victory at Thermopylae yielded them little. Within a year Pausanias, Leonidas's successor, defeated them at Thebes. Xerxes was killed and the Persians fled.

2   This kind of betrayal and treachery can be reflected in religious sources by the story of Judas Iscariot (Matthew 26, 14–16) and also that of Devadatta who was a cousin of the Buddha, jealous of his wisdom and therefore ever ready to harm him.

3   Another possible link for this story is the tale of the Greek siege of Troy, and their eventual victory through concealment in the Wooden Horse. A calendar link is provided by 21st June. On this date in 546 BC the Greek philosopher and advocate of peace, Thales, died.

Hymn suggestion

Come and Praise Vol 2 'Spirit of Peace' No 85

Prayer

Let us pray this morning for peace throughout the world. Let us pray that those responsible for the terrible things which happen in war are helped to see peaceful solutions to their problems. Amen.

70 Gehazi's story

Introduction

When you do somebody a good turn you don't expect something in return – or do you? Listen to this morning's story.

Story

Many years ago there lived a man called Elisha. He was a special person who told others how God wanted them to behave.

Elisha was famous and one of those who had heard of his work was the chief of the Syrian army. This chief was called Naaman.

He was a great soldier and an honest and reliable man, but he suffered from a terrible disease called leprosy.

One day his wife told him that one of her maids had said to her that there was a man in Israel who could cure his leprosy. At once Naaman set off to see this man, who was of course Elisha. When Naaman arrived, Elisha sent one of his servants to him with a message.

'My master says that you must dip yourself seven times in the River Jordan,' said the servant. 'If you do this you will be cured of your leprosy.'

'What a strange cure,' thought Naaman. However, he did as he had been told and, to his astonishment and delight, he found himself cured of the disease. He couldn't wait to get to see Elisha to thank him.

'Sir,' said Naaman to Elisha when they met, 'I cannot thank you enough for your help. I would like to take some of the soil of Israel back with me to remind me of the God you worship, and I would like to give you these gifts as my personal thanks to you.'

As he said this Naaman pointed to where his servants held donkeys laden with gold, silver and fine clothes.

'No, no thank you,' replied Elisha with a smile. 'I try to do God's work, that is reward enough. Please take your gold, silver and fine clothes back with you. I am sure there are many people in need of help in your country.'

Naaman thanked Elisha again and marvelled at what a kind and honourable man he was. 'As you wish,' he said. 'But thank you again.'

And so he set off to return to Syria.

Now, while this conversation between Elisha and Naaman had been taking place, Gehazi, Elisha's servant, had been listening and watching very carefully.

'My master might not want all those magnificent things,' he thought, 'but if I could get my hands on them I'd be rich for life – no more money worries, ever.'

So, allowing Naaman to get an hour or two on his way, Gehazi then went after the Syrian chief at great speed. He soon caught up with the little procession.

'Sir, sir,' called out Gehazi.

'Why, it's Elisha's servant. What can I do for you?' asked Naaman. 'Is something wrong?'

'No, no, sir, nothing is wrong . . . but it's like this. Two men have just arrived at my master's house and he wants to give them gifts. Well, he has nothing to give them and then he thought of you . . . and . . .'

'Of course,' said Naaman. 'I quite understand. It will be my pleasure. Please, take what you will and once again give your master my good wishes.'

So by this lie Gehazi got some of the treasure for himself and when he returned home he hid it away carefully.

But Elisha had missed him and it was not long before he found out what had happened. He sent for Gehazi.

'That was a terrible thing to do,' he said, 'you did not need Naaman's gifts. Now you have lost all you had.' And he sent Gehazi away with nothing.

Information for the teacher

1   This is an adaptation of the story of Elisha, Naaman and Gehazi which can be found in II Kings 5, 15–27.

2   This assembly could focus on the real 'treasure' of life – family, friends, health, etc, as opposed to material possessions. A useful quotation in this context is the often 'misquoted quote' which should read: '*The love of* money is the root of all evil.' (I Timothy 6, 10)

3   Leprosy can now be cured by treatment. The Hebrew word *zara'ath* was translated in the Bible as 'leprosy'. The description of the disease in Leviticus 13 implies however that several diseases were covered by the word *zara'ath*, and these included various fungus type infections, and possibly things like psoriasis.

Hymn suggestion

Come and Praise Vol 2 'I come like a beggar' No 90

Prayer

Father, we thank you for the night
And for the pleasant morning light,
For rest and food and loving care,
And all that makes the world so fair.
Help us to do the things we should,
To be to others kind and good,
In all we do, in all we say
To grow more loving every day.
   Amen.

71 The disappointment

Introduction

This morning's story is a true one about someone who is an old man now. He has had a very happy life and done lots of interesting things – but he has never forgotten what happened once when he was a schoolboy, as you will hear.

Story

John loved cricket. Whenever he had the chance he watched adults play and he practised as hard as he could every summer. The trouble was, he was not a really good player and although he had good days he was never given a chance in the school team . . . until one day.

Before every Thursday afternoon's match the list of boys in the team was pinned up on the school noticeboard. Every Thursday morning playtime, John went along and read the names in the team. Although he went to every practice his name was never there.

On one lovely June morning John knew that there was a home match for the team that afternoon.

I'm sure I won't be playing – but I'll go and have a look anyway.'

The noticeboard was in a particularly dark part of the school and people had to get close to read what was on it. When John reached it at playtime he found the usual crowd jostling round. As one boy broke away from it, he called out to John.

See you're playing this afternoon.'

John thought this was some sort of nasty joke but when he had edged into the crush so that he could see the board, there it was – in the middle of the batting order – his name!

For the rest of the morning John could hardly concentrate on his work. His greatest dream had come true. It didn't matter that he had got his place because some of the regulars were on a school trip. He was in the team! What's more, he had a feeling that all that practice was going to pay off. Yes, he felt he was going to score some runs today.

Dinnertime passed in a haze. A couple of his friends said how pleased they were for him and he smiled his thanks. Most of the afternoon before the match was spent doing art. Every five minutes or so John looked out of the windows at the pitch. At about a quarter to two the caretaker came out, put the stumps in place and marked out the pitch.

It must have been about ten past two when the first raindrop hit the window. It was followed by another, larger one and soon the window streamed as the tears of rain ran down. As John peered anxiously out, the outline of the stumps blurred and the sky darkened by the minute.

It was near to half past when there was a knock on the door and a messenger came in.

'Please, Miss, Mr Clarke's sent me to say that this afternoon's cricket match is off.'

As John peered through the streaming windows he saw the rain-coated caretaker re-appear and yank out the stumps. He could feel his disappointment almost like a pain. He was never chosen for the school team again.

Information for the teacher

1   This morning's story is a true one and although it happened to the subject almost fifty years ago it remains a very clear memory. Usually children receive this story very attentively and thoughtfully and it is a useful and relevant way of reminding them that all lives have disappointments in them. The next point – for discussion and reflection – is how one reacts to disappointments.

2   A useful follow-on to this story, or indeed an addition which might be made to the assembly, is for the children to relate at first-hand some disappointments they have suffered. In these days of such social upheaval some sensitive awareness and tact on the part of the teacher may be called upon here.

3   The assembly might be enhanced by some taped cricket radio commentary being played, or some videoed TV test match coverage. Some bats, stumps, balls, etc, could also be on display.

Hymn suggestion

Come and Praise Vol 2 'It's a new day' No 106

Prayer

Dear God,

Please help us to treat the ups and downs of our lives with cheerfulness and patience. Let us not fall into the trap of boasting about our successes and moaning about our disappointments.

Please help us to be the sort of people who can help and encourage others at all times. Amen.

72 Trees

Introduction

June is a month when it is lighter than at any other time of the year in the British Isles. This means we can spend more time outside looking at things – trees, for instance.

Story

A poet, who is not very well known, once wrote two lines which have become very well known. They are:

> Poems are made by fools like me,
> But only God can make a tree.
>
> (Joyce Kilmer)

June is a good month not only for looking at trees, but also for learning about some of the more famous ones in the British Isles. For instance, some of them act as sort of signposts in our history.

Yew trees are often found in churchyards. One of the reasons for this is that their foliage is poisonous to cattle, so they were planted to keep cows from straying among the graves. The oldest yew trees in England are supposed to surround the small church in Westbourne, Sussex. These were planted by the Earl of Arundel in 1544, which is almost half a century before the great battle with the Spanish Armada.

If you go to Richmond Park, near London, you can see some of the oldest oak trees in England. Five of them were already there when Charles I first made this a park in 1637. Another very famous oak tree is at Boscabel. It was in this tree, after the Battle of Worcester, that Charles II hid from the Parliamentarian army. When he eventually returned to be king, people celebrated by carrying round oak tree branches to remind themselves of how he was once saved.

One of the most dreadful things ever to happen in England was the Great Plague in 1665. This caused many people to die, but one group supported each other by meeting under a tree. This tree was a sycamore tree near Mapperton in Dorset and a plaque was put up there which said: 'In 1665 when the Great Plague reached its peak, the parishioners gathered under this tree holding posies of flowers and herbs to ward off the disease.'

Then there is the famous Holy Thorn tree at Glastonbury Abbey. This blooms every Christmas and there is an old story that the first tree grew when St Joseph visited the spot and stuck his staff into the ground.

Although only God can make a tree, we should remember that if we are to go on enjoying the beauty of our trees it is up to us to take care of them and protect them. Here is a short poem to remind us of this:

Woodman, spare that tree!
Touch not a single bough!
In youth it sheltered me,
And I'll protect it now.
                                 (G P Morris)

Information for the teacher

1   The information contained here could be used to 'flesh out' a fuller assembly in which conservation is the wider theme. This could bring in things like acid rain, the destruction of too many trees, and issues which many children are both familiar with and concerned about.

2   Another direction in which this assembly might go is to look at local trees if this is appropriate. There may be a local park in which trees have been planted as memorials to local or well-known people, for example. Useful work could stem from a situation like this.

3   Useful addresses are:

Council for Protection of Rural England, Warwick House, 25 Buckingham Palace Road, London SW1W 0PP. www.greenchannel.com/cpre/

The Countryside Commission, John Dower House, Crescent Place, Cheltenham GL50 3RA. www.countryside.gov.uk

4   Trees are significant factors in the Bible – beginning with the one of such influence in the Garden of Eden (Genesis 2, 9; 3, 22–4).
In the arid deserts of Palestine trees were at one time considered sacred and have always been treasured.
In Christian art and tradition various trees have differing symbolic meanings: the almond symbolises the Virgin Mary; the leaves of the aspen are supposed to tremble continually because it was the only tree which failed to bow in sorrow when Jesus died on the cross.
The cedar symbolises Jesus; the elm represents the faith of good Christians; the oak is one of several trees looked upon as the

source of Christ's cross; the palm symbolises victory, and is particularly associated with Jesus' entry into Jerusalem; the olive is associated with peace.

Hymn suggestion

Come and Praise Vol 1 'For the beauty of the earth' No 11

Prayer

Dear God,

Thank you for the trees which grow in our countryside, parks and gardens. Help us to admire their beauty and to make sure that we care for them as well as we can. Amen.

73 An early hero

Introduction

Imagine this morning that a radio reporter has entered a time/space capsule. He has been taken back to a town in England called Verulamium and the time is between two and three hundred years after Jesus was born.

Story

'Good morning, listeners. I've been sent here this morning on a Time/Space mission to find out more about an event which happened hundreds of years ago.

'I must admit I've been very impressed with this town. The Romans have really made a good job here – it's a busy place with some splendid buildings and there are plenty of theatres, temples, houses and shops.

'Ah – but this is what I have come to report on. As I speak, there's a huge crowd of people heading towards the river. There's a group of Roman soldiers in the lead and in front of them they are pushing a man who has obviously been badly treated. Behind are lots of people of the town. I'm going to try and have a few words with one of these . . .

'Excuse me, sir, can you tell me what's happening here?'

'Well, as much as I know, yes. That poor fellow who is getting pushed around up there is called Alban and he's being taken to the river to be executed.'

'That's terrible! But what has he done?'

'On the one hand, not much, on the other a great deal. You see, just a few days ago he was just an ordinary citizen of the town, like me. Now in this town there is a group of people who call themselves Christians. Naturally the Roman magistrate wants to get rid of these people because he thinks they are troublemakers.

'Well, last week one of these Christians was on the run from some soldiers and the only place he could find to hide was Alban's house.

'Apparently the two men talked long into the night and by the time they had finished Alban had become a Christian too.'

'What happened next?'

'The soldiers finally tracked down the only place the Christian could be and it was then that Alban made his fatal move. He disguised himself as the Christian so that the other fellow could get away.

'Well, you can imagine how furious the magistrate was when he found out that his troops had arrested the wrong man. But, to be fair to him, he told Alban he could go free if he apologised and gave up his Christianity there and then.'

'But Alban wouldn't.'

'No, he certainly would not. So, to set an example, the magistrate ordered that he be taken out and executed – and so here we are.'

'Thank you, sir. Well, listeners, you heard that. I am now moving along with this procession and I can tell you there is a very strange feeling in the air. The soldiers don't seem very happy and the crowd are very quiet.

'A few minutes ago we came to the river and it seemed far too deep to cross, yet when Alban stepped into it there was no problem.

'I am afraid the execution is now taking place and . . . and again the strangest things are happening. Several of the soldiers are kneeling down and . . . and hundreds in the crowd are doing the same. I'm going to try and have a word with the man I spoke to before – he's kneeling too.

'Excuse me, sir. Why are people behaving like this?'

'If Christianity can give Alban the courage to behave in the way he did then I want to be a Christian too. I imagine all these other people feel the same way.'

'Thank you. Well, listeners, now you have my report on what happened to Alban. We know from living in our time what an example he set for other Christians. We know too that the town he lived in eventually became St Albans and a magnificent church now stands on the place where these events happened.'

Information for the teacher

1 St Alban's Day is celebrated on 22nd June but details of his life are extremely vague. There are no contemporary records of his life and the first written accounts of him did not appear until at least two hundred years after his death. The date of his death, however, is not fixed with any certainty. Many accounts depict it as 'about 209' but one source has it as late as 303.

2 The various accounts of St Alban's martyrdom are also very disparate. He is credited with 'parting the waters' of the river. One story also said that this feat converted the first executioner to Christianity and a replacement had to be found.

3 This story could be linked with those of others who have suffered for their Christian faith. Included in this group could be other saints and, of course, many Biblical figures. St Paul is one obvious choice, with his journeys and imprisonments, leading up to his execution in AD 65 (Acts 13–28).

Hymn suggestion

Come and Praise Vol 1 'He who would valiant be' No 44

Prayer

Dear God,
    Let us pray this morning that we can learn from those people who always behave in the way they believe they should. Let us remember Alban's kindness to the man who was frightened and being chased by others. Let us pray for a world where people are kinder to each other. Amen.

July

74 You can't make bricks without straw

Introduction

There are lots of sayings which we use as little reminders. We say: 'More haste, less speed'; 'Don't count your chickens before they're hatched'; 'Look before you leap.' (The teacher might comment on those.)
    This morning's story is about a saying: 'You can't make bricks without straw'.

Story

Moses and Aaron, the leaders of the Hebrews who lived in Egypt, were worried.

'To think we were once honoured guests here,' said Moses.

'Yes,' replied Aaron. 'When Joseph was alive he was the second most important man in the country after the Pharaoh.'

'And now we are just slaves,' Moses went on. 'We must go to the Pharaoh and tell him we want to leave to worship God in the desert.'

So Moses and Aaron went to see the Pharaoh, the king of Egypt, and told him what they wanted for their people. The Pharaoh was furious. If the Hebrew slaves left, his own people would have to do all the hard labour.

'I will not let you leave,' he said to Moses and Aaron. 'In fact, as a punishment for your asking, your people will now have to make all the bricks and collect the straw to go in them.'

Moses and Aaron were astounded: This would make the Hebrews' work almost unbearable. For years they had made all the bricks used by the Egyptians, but the Egyptians had collected the straw for them. The Hebrews had gathered mud from the valley of the River Nile, then mixed this mud with chopped straw collected by the Egyptians, and then put the mud and straw mixture into moulds to make bricks.

'The Pharaoh wants us to make the same number of bricks,' said Moses to the people.

'But to do so we will have to work twice as hard because now we have to collect and chop the straw as well,' Aaron continued.

'We must go,' said the people.

'Yes, we'll have to leave, no matter what.'

'Then the Egyptians will have to do everything themselves.'

So the Hebrews decided then and there that they must leave Egypt. Later, with God's help, they did. His foolish judgement finally cost the Pharaoh all his workers.

Information for the teacher

1   The Biblical reference for this famous incident is Exodus 5, 10: 'Thus saith Pharaoh, "I will not give you straw. Go yourselves, get your straw wherever you can find it; but your work will not be lessened in the least." '

2   Further discussion can take place on the folly of trying to complete something without an essential ingredient. In this context, without the scattering of straw in the brick moulds it

was almost impossible to turn them cleanly and cut them free when they were dry.

3 The idea of sage advice derived from sayings could be followed up with more examples.

4 The story ends with the brief phrase that eventually the Hebrews left Egypt. This of course is a long and dramatic story in itself and for teachers who want to use it the Biblical reference is Exodus 5–14.

5 As this story contains the point which led the Hebrews to seek and gain independence, it could be linked to several other Independence anniversaries which take place this month. For instance, 4th July is the date on which the USA celebrates its Declaration of Independence in 1776. Other countries which celebrate similar occasions during the month are Venezuela (1811) and Algeria (1962) on 5th July; Argentina (1816) on 9th July; Belgium (1831) on 21st July.

Hymn suggestion

Come and Praise Vol 2 'What about being old Moses?' No 81

Prayer

Let us think this morning about how important it is to have all the right qualities to be a complete person. Let us remember that it is not enough to be kind and thoughtful just some of the time. Let us learn to be always reliable.

75 Rich as Rockefeller

Introduction

If somebody has a lot of money an old saying claims that they are as 'rich as Rockefeller'. This is because John D Rockefeller was one of the richest men the world has ever known – but he was also one of the kindest.

Story

'It's a boy!' William Rockefeller looked at the newborn baby in his wife Eliza's arms and shouted with delight.

'Yes,' smiled Eliza, 'let's call him John.'

The date was 8th July 1839 and the Rockefellers lived in a small village near New York in the United States of America.

When John was a young man, the family moved to Cleveland and he borrowed some money from his father to set up a business selling salt and meat. From that moment on John moved into more and more businesses and made more and more money. He started to refine oil, he bought forests so that he could use the timber to make barrels, he made paints, paraffin and dyes.

'It seems that no matter what I do, I make money,' thought John to himself, 'so I must help others who don't have enough.'

So John continued to give away money – something he had done since he was a very young man with very little of his own. He gave money to universities in Chicago, London, Oxford, Edinburgh and Bristol. He paid for a foundation which worked to cure terrible diseases in the world, like malaria and yellow fever. He rescued Mexico from starvation when all its crops failed, and helped people all over the world as different as farmers and ballet dancers.

To have some idea of what sort of man John Rockefeller was, however, is to remember something that happened in Cleveland when he was a young man. At this time many people in America, whose ancestors had been brought from Africa, were still slaves. One day a man came to see John.

'Sir,' said the man, 'some friends of mine have told me that you are against slavery – and that you are a very kind man.'

'Well,' replied John, 'I don't think that any human being should be a slave for another human being. As for being kind – it's nice of you to say so, but I just try to give a little help where I can.'

'I have come to you for help, sir,' the man went on. 'Because I lost my job I couldn't pay a debt. As a result my wife was taken away from me and made a slave to the person to whom I owe money. I can only get her back and free if . . .'

John held up his hand. 'Say no more, my friend,' he said. 'Just tell me how much you need.'

Information for the teacher

1   John D Rockefeller was born in 1839 and died in 1937, aged ninety-seven. Nobody has even been able to calculate just how much money he gave away – but to Chicago University alone he gave one hundred million pounds during his lifetime. While being an incredible philanthropist, he lived very frugally and worked hard.

2   The adaptation of some words from Ecclesiasticus 4 are very
    appropriate for use with the life of Rockefeller: 'Don't refuse to
    help the poor, deny the hungry, be mean to those who need
    money and avoid people you think poorer than you.'
    There are other useful quotations along the same themes: 'Give
    all you can' (John Wesley); 'Give and do not count the cost' (St
    Ignatius); 'What really counts is man' (Ghanaian proverb); and
    'Be worthy of a reputation' (Confucius).

3   For those who want to extend this theme, two other men could
    be linked with Rockefeller. John Wellcome was an American who
    became a British subject in 1910. Immensely wealthy, he created
    the Wellcome Foundation which gives financial help to every
    form of medical research. He died on 26th July 1936.
    William Morris (Lord Nuffield) made a fortune from car manu-
    facture and formed the Nuffield Foundation with a gift of ten
    million pounds. He once put a cheque for £100,000 in a Red
    Cross collection box. He died in August 1963.

Hymn suggestion

Come and Praise Vol 2 'Bread for the world' No 75

Prayer

Dear God,
    We give thanks this morning for those people who can always
find time and effort to help others. Amen.

76 The traveller's gift

Introduction

This morning we hear first about a lovely idea – and then the
strange story which started it off.

Story

For many years travellers on the Pacific Ocean have practised a
thoughtful custom. Whenever they are making a sea journey they
throw coconuts overboard. The story which follows tells how this
custom came about.

Sina was a beautiful girl who lived on one of the islands in the Pacific. One day she was walking near a pool on the island when she saw a huge eel swimming in it. Going nearer to the pool she was astonished when the eel suddenly changed into a handsome young man.

'Do not be frightened of me, Sina,' said the young man. 'I am the protector of all eels, but I so much wanted to talk to you that I changed myself into human form.'

Sina was astonished to hear this, but soon she and the young man became great friends. At their meetings he changed into a human being, and when she left he went back to being an eel.

Then one day the young man had some very sad news. 'I am going to leave this place,' he said, 'and I will never see you again. I would like to give you a wonderful present before I go, so this is what you must do.'

The young man then told Sina exactly what she had to do during the next day.

Well, next day, because of what the young man had said to her, Sina was not surprised when a terrible storm broke out. The river bubbled and surged up out of the valley and, sitting in her house on the hill, Sina watched the water get higher and higher. Then, out of the water, leapt an eel which landed on Sina's doorstep.

Remembering her instructions, Sina immediately cut off the eel's head and buried it on the hillside near her house. The flood water went down and every day after that the beautiful girl went to look at the spot where the eel's head was buried.

Time passed and then she noticed a tall green shoot growing. Soon it grew more strongly until eventually it was a magnificent tree. Then it came into flower and finally large bunches of nuts hung from the branches.

Sina and all her family and friends were delighted with the tree. It was indeed a wonderful present – the coconuts not only provided food, but drink as well; the leaves could be woven to make mats and canoe sails, and could be used to thatch huts.

So the custom came about. Anybody sailing from one island to another in the Pacific threw a coconut overboard. This was because they thought it was a wonderful present which might save the life of a shipwrecked sailor, or reach another island and start to grow there.

Information for the teacher

1   This idea of 'help for the traveller' is a strongly held Islamic tradition; Muhammad's (pbuh) concern for beasts of transport such as camels is illustrated by several stories. Christianity has a patron saint of travellers (St Christopher) and the Bible is full of stories of journeys where help is needed: Jacob (Genesis 27–35); Joseph (Genesis 37–45); the crossing of the Red Sea (Exodus 14, 21–2); the Promised Land (Joshua 6); the good Samaritan (Luke 10); and St Paul's journey (Acts 13–28).

2   There are some useful travel anniversaries which can be linked to this story. On 8th July 1978 Naomi James completed her journey having sailed round the world single-handed; on the 16th, in 1963 Valentina Tereshkova, as the first woman in space, circled the earth in her space craft *Vostok 6*; on the 22nd in 1964 Sir Francis Chichester set a new record for sailing single-handed across the Atlantic in under thirty days.

Hymn suggestion

Come and Praise Vol 1 'Travel on' No 42

Prayer

Let us give thanks this morning for all those who by their care, thoughtfulness, concern and wisdom help all who travel by sea, air or land. Amen.

77 This month

Introduction

July is a good month for using our senses of sight, smell, hearing and touch out of doors. There is plenty to look at – but you may need to listen a bit more carefully.

Story

There is a sense of peace about the countryside in July. The excitement and activity of spring is over and things seem to be relaxing before preparing for autumn.

Birds are a lot quieter. By the middle of the month the cuckoo will have left for warmer climates and birds like song thrushes and song warblers won't be singing any more. Sparrows are still likely to be noisy and fussy and can be seen swarming round cornfields.

There are, however, other noises to listen out for, although careful listening is necessary. You are not likely to hear the scuffling of field mice and moles, but you may hear the squeaking of shrews hunting about for insects in the woods. This is the time when bats are about at night, too.

The hot weather brings out lizards, which dodge about looking for spiders and flies. Grass snakes are about near ponds, looking for food like frogs and newts. On the drier ground of heath and moor adders lie out in the sun. They are easily recognised by the zigzag markings on their backs and they should be left well alone!

There are hundreds of flowers in bloom in July. Watch out particularly for the light-blue heads of scabious, which look like pincushions; the blue nettleflowers which looks like wild Canterbury bells; the tall pink rosebay willow herb and the wild clematis which grows over hedges.

Keep an eye out too for butterflies – the purple hairstreak, warbled white and the rarer but beautiful purple emperor. At night there is the magic of tiny pricks of light which show that glow worms are about.

Another of the senses you will use in July is the feel of heat and humidity, and of the sudden threat of heavy rain. If you are caught in a thunderstorm, remember to check how far away from you its centre is. To do this, start counting the seconds between the flash of lightning and the clap of thunder. Every five seconds equals one mile.

Information for the teacher

1   July was the month of Julius Caesar's birth. The Anglo-Saxons called it 'Hey Monath' – the time of hay harvesting.

2   Rain and storms are significant in connection with St. Swithin's Day on the 15th, but there are other notable 'wet' happenings in the month, too. The Spanish Armada which was seen approaching England on 19th July 1588, was almost totally devastated by a tremendous storm after its clash with the English fleet. In 1945 a freak storm off Resguill, County Donegal, deposited shoals of fish in the streets!

Nevertheless, rain was a valued commodity in rural England:

> A show of rain in July
> When the corn begins to fill,
> Is worth a plough of oxen,
> And all belongs these till.

Prayer

Dear God,
    We thank you for giving us the beauty of the world around us, and the senses with which we can enjoy it. Amen.

78 Stick together!

Introduction

This morning's story reminds us that we all need friends. If we choose to be the sort of person who is disagreeable and unfriendly then we might find ourselves alone. Once we are alone, well . . . listen to the story.

Story

The lion stood looking down at the field which lay baking in the sun. How hungry he felt! Even more so as he looked at the four well-fed bulls who grazed in the field.

'All I've got to do is to get one of them away from the others – and I've got my dinner!' thought the lion.

Stealthily he crept down to the field. Soon he was in position to leap onto one of the bulls. At that moment, however, one of the other bulls saw the lion, gave a loud snort and galloped over. He was quickly followed by the other two bulls.

The lion snarled in dismay. As long as the four bulls were grouped together like this, he couldn't attack. He would have to go hungry. But he was a patient animal.

Finding what food he could elsewhere, he returned to the field every day to look at the bulls.

Meanwhile, the bulls kept a look out for each other and grouped together at the first sign of trouble. That is, until the day they had the argument.

Nobody could remember how it started, but it ended with the bulls no longer speaking to each other and storming off – each one to a corner of the field.

This was just the opportunity the lion had been waiting for. That night he killed one of the bulls and by the end of the week he had killed them all.

'How could those bulls have been so foolish?' he thought to himself as he stared down at the now empty field.

Information for the teacher

1   This adaptation of the well-known fable by Aesop could be used as a starting point to link with several others which not only have a 'message', but also have the lion as a central character. Any collection of Aesop's fables will probably contain stories such as 'The donkey in the lion's skin'; 'The man and the lion'; 'The stag at the pool'; 'The donkey, the rooster and the lion'; 'The lion and the boar'; 'The wolf, the lion and the lamb'; 'The lion and the mouse' and 'The sick lion'.

2   The lion is a very significant creature in Biblical writings. Although now extinct there, lions were common in the Jordan Valley of Old Testament times, and were also found in the mountains of Judea and Samaria.

They were infamous for killing men (I Kings 13,24) and sheep (I Samuel 17,34). It was a tribute to a man's courage and strength to kill a lion (Judges 14,5; I Samuel 17, 34–7). The famous story of Daniel in the lion's den is in Daniel 6, 16–23.

Artists have used the lion to symbolise St Mark. Perhaps this is because his gospel is 'the voice of one crying in the wilderness'. Old Testament writers regularly wrote about the roar of the lion in the country around.

Hymn suggestion

Come and Praise Vol 2 'All the animals' No 80

Prayer

Let us think this morning about how much we can learn from stories. So many stories have been written by wise people with a lot to teach us. Let us learn to be good listeners.

79 Locked in

Introduction

This morning's story is a true one which happened a few years ago. None of the people in the story is famous and what happened might well have happened to you some time.

Story

It was a usual sort of morning for the Simpson family. Mum and Dad were eating breakfast, baby Sue was getting more food on her face than in her mouth and three-year-old Paul was whizzing his cars about the floor.

The family lived in a bungalow in a hot country and all the windows and doors were wide open to let in some breeze.

Paul suddenly stood up and walked down the corridor to the bathroom. Nobody else paid much attention – not even when they heard the click of the bolt being locked on the other side of the door. Everybody paid attention about five minutes later, however . . .

'Help! I'm locked in!'

Paul's voice carried from the bathroom, along with sounds of banging on the door.

'Oh no,' said Mum, hurrying down the corridor. 'Push the bolt back, Paul – push it with your fingers.'

'I can't, Mum. I've tried and tried but I can't move it.'

'Well keep trying – push hard.'

By now Dad had left the breakfast table and joined Mum outside the bathroom door.

'He's never going to be able to move that bolt.'

'Well what can we do? This door's as solid as a rock.'

'I'll have to go round and get in through the window.'

Now, this wasn't as easy as it sounds. Although the window was obviously on the ground floor because the building was a bungalow, it was covered by a huge steel grill. This was to keep burglars out when the windows were left open at night.

'You'll be late for work, Geoff,' Mum called out to Dad.

'No, I won't. Anyway, we can't leave him in there all day!'

'No!' cried a tearful voice from the bathroom.

So Dad got his tools out and began to take out the screws which held the massive steel frame in place. Ten minutes later he eased the frame down onto the ground, and hauled himself up, through the window, and into the bathroom.

'Hello, Dad,' said Paul with a pleased smile.

Information for the teacher

1 This incident took place in Singapore before air conditioning was commonplace.

2 The main theme which could be developed from this story is one of feeling safe and protected in the care of those who love us. Minor problems are just that when family help is at hand.

3 An appropriate Shakespearean quotation might be: 'It is a wise father that knows his own child.' (*The Merchant of Venice*)

Hymn suggestion

Come and Praise Vol 2 'When your Father' No 73

Prayer

Dear God,
    We thank you this morning for those who care for us, who help us in difficulty and protect us when we are young. Amen.

80 The Sultan's gift

Introduction

Have you noticed how really kind people always have time – to listen to problems, to help out where they can, to give advice if it is asked for? This morning's story is about such a man.

Story

Abdul was desperate. After years of struggling to keep themselves alive, he and his wife now had nothing left.

    'There's only one thing to do,' said Mehnaz, Abdul's wife, 'we'll have to ask for help.'

    'But we've lived out here in the desert all our lives,' replied Abdul. 'Nobody out here has anything either. Who can we ask who is not desperately poor too?'

    'We must ask the richest man we know of – the sultan of the great city.'

    'Ha,' said Abdul. 'You must be mad! Why should the Sultan listen too a nobody like me?'

'I've heard he is a kind and fair man,' said Mehnaz. 'After all, we have nothing to lose. No . . . you must go and see him and take him a gift of the best thing we can offer.'

Abdul didn't need to ask what this was. Everybody who lived in the desert looked upon water as the most precious thing there was. So Abdul took a cup of their precious water supply, covered it tightly with a cloth and set out on the long journey to the city.

For several days the old man travelled. Desperate for food, his ragged clothing barely enough to keep off the hot sun, he was almost exhausted when he reached the city. As one who had lived all his life in the country he was amazed at the sights and sounds of the great city.

Finally, he came to the sultan's palace – and there he saw a sight which horrified him. Running through the gardens outside the palace banks on either side of it was – a river! The water looked clear and fresh and bubbled over the stones in the riverbed.

'Water,' gasped Abdul. 'Water – gallons and gallons of it, clear and fresh and plentiful. How can my pitiful little cup of ditchwater be any good now? I may as well go straight back home and give up.'

Now one of the sultan's servants had been watching Abdul, and seeing what a poor state he was in, he came up to the old man.

'Can I help you?' he said kindly.

'Oh – you startled me,' replied Abdul. 'No, I don't think you can, thanks. You see, I came to see the sultan. I brought him a gift and I wanted to ask his help . . .' Abdul's voice tailed off as he looked miserably down at the pathetic covered cup in his hand. The servant, seeing that the old man was at the end of his tether, put an arm round his shoulders and said, 'Come with me.'

A few minutes later Abdul stood in front of the sultan. All the things he had been going to say had vanished from his head. He felt an old fool. The sultan smiled.

'Many people come to see me, my friend, but my servant tells me you have come a very long way and have brought a gift.'

Still unable to speak Abdul shamefacedly held out the cup, covered with its old and dusty cloth. A servant took it, cut away the cloth and handed it to the sultan.

Without a moment's pause the sultan lifted the cup to his mouth and drank every drop of water. When he had done so he smacked his lips and held up the cup in his hand.

'Wonderful!' he said. 'That is some of the very best water I have ever tasted. It must have been very precious to you – and I thank you for letting me have some. Now, one gift deserves another.

Servant – fill this cup with jewels, cover it carefully and then see that my friend here is escorted through the city on his way home.'

Abdul managed to stutter a Thank You to the sultan and then he found himself once more outside the palace. He couldn't get over the sultan's thoughtfulness and kindness.

'For a man to value such a small gift that he didn't even need, and to reward it with such kindness . . . that surely is a great man.'

Information for the teacher

1 This story is an adaptation of an Islamic one from a thirteenth-century writer called Sumi.

2 As water features so strongly in this story it could be linked with one of Christianity's most famous July anniversaries. This is St Swithin's Day on 15th July. St Swithin, Bishop of Winchester and renowned for his humility and kindness, died in 862 and, at his request, was buried in the churchyard. In 891 a group of monks felt that it was inappropriate for such a distinguished man to languish outside the church so, on 15th July of that year, they set about removing his remains to put them inside the church. Torrential rain began immediately, and continued for forty days – until the remains were returned to the church-yard grave.

Hymn suggestion

Come and Praise Vol 2 'It's the spring' No 82

Prayer

Dear God,

We thank you this morning for the kindness of so many people: those who listen to us when we are in difficulties and for whom it is never too much trouble to help in any way they can. Amen.

Anniversaries, facts, fancies, anecdotes and religious notes

Many assemblies can be developed from the fertile ground suggested by the above title. This section aims to provide a selection of such starting material.

Introduction

Much of the information here will serve as source material for locally-developed assemblies. Where a particular event can be linked to an assembly (or assemblies) already detailed in this book, then there is an appropriate reference to aid teacher planning.

A note about the various calendars which govern the festivals of different faiths is important. *The Gregorian calendar*, which is solar-based and used in most western countries, enables most festivals related to this to be fixed. An exception is Easter, which is a movable feast. *The Jewish calendar* is lunar-based and to adjust it to the solar year an extra (embolismic) month is added seven times in each nineteen-year period. *The Islamic calendar* is lunar-based without adjustment, which means that Muslim festivals advance by some eleven to twelve days each year. More than one calendar has been in use in India.

The impact for teachers of these calendar fluctuations is that an annual plan of great religious festivals can only be accurately made by reference to the relevant current calendars. Otherwise it is a question of moving source material about as appropriate.

September

1st   Feast Day of St Giles, patron saint of handicapped people. A day remembered in Ireland for the death of Patrick O'Bryen (1806). At 8 feet 5 inches in height, he was one of the tallest men who ever lived.

Edgar Rice Burroughs, creator of Tarzan, was born in 1875.

2nd   On this date in 1752 Britain adopted the Gregorian calendar. The Great Fire of London began in the bakery belonging to a man called Farryner, who lived in Pudding Lane. (*Link – Assembly 2*)

3rd   Because the Gregorian calendar was adopted, eleven days were 'removed' from the calendar. This caused riots because people thought eleven days were being taken from their lives.

Louis Sullivan, the architect who designed skyscrapers, was born in 1856.

Sinking of the 'Delaware' in 1863.

4th   In 1567 Queen Elizabeth I allowed two Flemish merchants to work in England, and teach Englishmen their skill of glass-making.

In 1909 the first Boy Scout Rally was held in London.

5th   Count Barowloski died near Durham in 1837. He was ninety-six years old and had never grown to three feet high.

St Laurence Justinian, the patron saint of Venice, died in 1455.

6th   The 'Mayflower' sailed from Plymouth in 1620. Seventy-four men and twenty-eight women were on board.

7th   In 1533 Henry VIII's wife Anne Boleyn gave birth to a daughter – Elizabeth.

8th   In 695 a monk supposedly heard angels singing and when he asked why they were celebrating he was told that this was the anniversary of the birth of Mary, mother of Jesus.

9th   In 1835 the 'sport' of bear baiting was banned by parliament.

In 1754 William Bligh, Captain of the 'Bounty', was born.

10th   William The Conqueror died in 1087.

Scape Goat Day: a traditional Jewish custom was that a goat was let lose in the desert on this day. This was the 'scape goat' and it carried with it all the sins of the people.

11th   Death of Roger Crab in 1680.

A famous quotation was supposedly written by Benjamin Franklin on this day in 1773: 'There was never a good war or a bad peace.'

12th   John Alden, the last of the 'Mayflower' Pilgrim Fathers, died in 1687.

13th   The *Catholic Annual* of this date in 1830 carried a health warning about eating only ripe, and moderate quantities of autumnal fruit at this time of the year.

14th   Holy Rood Day. *Rood* is another word for *cross* and traditionally on this day children were freed from school and work so that they could gather nuts.

The actual cross on which Jesus was crucified was supposedly found by St Helena. To commemorate this, her son,

Constantine, built a great church in Jerusalem and it was opened on this date in 335 with the ceremony of the Exaltation of the Holy Cross. The annual custom has endured.

Robert Raikes, founder of Sunday Schools, was born in 1735.

15th The Liverpool–Manchester railway was opened in 1830.

This was the date in ancient Rome when the Circensian Games were held annually. An imitation of the Greek Olympic Games, the main event was the pentathlon – leaping, wrestling, throwing, boxing and racing on foot and by chariot.

Battle of Britain Day, commemorating the RAF's victory in 1940.

16th The German inventor of the thermometer, Gabriel Fahrenheit, died in 1736.

17th The first person ever to be killed in an aeroplane accident died in 1908. This happened in America and his name was Thomas Selfridge.

Sir Francis Chichester, solo round-the-world sailor, was born in 1901. (*Link – Assembly 4*)

18th Peter Sellers, one of Britain's funniest actors, was born in 1925.

The Emperor Domitian was a ruler of such cruelty that he had polished stones planted on all his walks. These acted like mirrors so that he could see if his many enemies were about to attack him. He was killed by his 'friends' on this date.

Dr Johnson was born in 1709. (*Link – Assembly 6*)

19th Dr Barnardo died in 1905. (*Link – Assembly 1*)

Mickey Mouse featured in his first cartoon in 1928.

An old Derbyshire belief is that a storm on this date means that the winter will be mild.

George Cadbury, chocolate maker and philanthropist, was born in 1839.

20th Eton School was founded by Henry VI in 1440.

Muhammad (pbuh) changed the name of the city of Yathrib to Medina.

Rahere, court jester and founder of St Bartholomew's hospital in London, died in 1144.

Jacob Grimm, fairytale writer, died in 1863.

21st This is St Matthew's Day. An ex-tax collector and disciple of Jesus, he died in the first century. By the time of his death his writings had become more prolific than any other gospel chronicle. It was said he used an angel's feather to write the first gospel, and his name is linked to many old sayings, for example, 'St Matthew's Day sends sap into the tree.' (*Link – Assembly 5*)

22nd This is the date on which, in 286, the Emperor Maximian ordered the death of one of his generals and an entire section of his army because they refused to give up their Christian beliefs. So died St Maurice and six thousand, six hundred soldiers. (*Link – Assembly 3*)

Michael Faraday, the scientist who invented the first dynamo to make electricity, was born in 1791.

23rd Today is St Thecla's Day. For refusing to give up her Christian belief, she was sentenced to be killed by wild beasts. They became calm in her presence, however, and wouldn't do her any injury. She died peacefully during the first century.

24th Traditionally this was the day on which harvesting began in medieval England:

> Harvest home, harvest home,
> We have ploughed, we have sowed,
> We have reaped, we have mowed
> We have brought home every load,
> Hip, hip, hip, harvest home, hurrah!

25th Samuel Pepys wrote in his diary in 1660 that this was the date on which he drank his first ever cup of tea. (*Link – Assembly 2*)

26th In 1580 Sir Francis Drake and his fleet returned to England after taking great treasure from Spain.

The 'Queen Mary', then the world's greatest ship, was launched at Clydebank in 1934. A crowd of 200,000 watched King George V and Queen Mary perform the launching ceremony.

27th A woman was arrested for smoking a cigarette in a car in New York in 1905.

The world's first passenger railway (from Stockton to Darlington) opened in 1825.

28th Louis Pasteur died in 1885. He was the French scientist who introduced 'pasteurisation'.

This date is Michaelmas Eve, a time of nut-cracking amongst medieval church congregations, and one of those rare occasions when master and men were considered equal.

29th St Michael's Day, or Michaelmas Day. The Archangel Michael killed Lucifer the traitor angel and his feast day was very significant in the England of former years.

On this day rents were due and for those who couldn't pay, geese were often sent to landlords as presents in the hope that longer credit could be obtained.

There are many old sayings associated with the day, for example:

'The Michaelmas Daisy among dead weeds
Blooms for St Michael's valorous deeds.'

30th This was the date agricultural labourers (after 1351 and the Statute of Labourers) sought new jobs for the following year at market town fairs.

The foundation stone of Nelson's Column was laid in 1840.

In 1846 the first tooth extraction under anaesthetic was performed.

Religious notes

Harvest Festival is usually celebrated in schools at the end of September and work in this book is aimed at this time.

September is also the month when the Hindu festival of Janam Ashtami could be considered. This festival celebrates the birth of Lord Krishna. The day before is one of fasting and prayer and a time when special sweets are put in images of Lord Krishna as a baby in a cradle.

Because of the many sides to Krishna's character – hero, people's champion, enjoyer of life – he is a very popular Hindu figure. As well as prayers, there are songs and plays about the great adventures of his life. The latter are told in the epic story, the *Mahabharata*.

The teachings of Lord Krishna are recorded in the *Bhagavad Gita*, which means 'Song of the Blessed Lord'. An example is:

'He who offers to me with devotion only a loaf, or a flower, or a fruit, or even a little water, this I accept from that yearning soul, because with a pure heart it was offered with love.'

(9:26)

Jews observe Succoth, the Feast of the Tabernacles, at this time of the year. Similar to the Christian Harvest Festival, it is a time of family celebration in specially-created temporary buildings, usually set in gardens.

The Old Testament sets the guidelines for this festival:

'Thou shalt observe the Feast of the Tabernacles seven days after thou hast gathered in thy corn and wine – and thou shalt rejoice in thy feast, thou, and thy son, and thy daughter, and thy manservant, and thy maidservant, and the stranger.'

October

1st Traditionally this was the date on which the English pudding season started. These were filled with steak, leeks, mushrooms, spices and some were cooked for as long as sixteen hours.

Paul Dukas ('The Sorcerer's Apprentice') was born in 1865.

Lord Shaftesbury, social reformer, died in 1885.

2nd Mahatma Gandhi, Indian leader, was born in 1869.

Aristotle died in 322 BC.

A curious custom takes place at Braughing in Hertfordshire on this date. Church bells are rung initially in a solemn manner, and then joyfully.

This is to commemorate Matthew Wall, a sixteenth-century farmer who was on the way to his funeral when the coffin was dropped. Wall, who had been mistaken for dead, recovered consciousness in the fall, and was released from the coffin.

3rd In 1754, a French nobleman won a wager that he could ride from Fontainebleau to Paris in less than two hours. He completed the forty-two mile journey in just over one-and-a-half hours, but the horses he used died from overexertion.

4th St Francis of Assisi died in 1226. Up to the age of twenty-five Francis was a wastrel. A serious illness changed this. He became a Christian and, much to the annoyance of his rich father, gave away large sums of money to the needy. He wore only the poorest of clothes and lived frugally. Impressed by his devotion, many people became followers. Known as Franciscans, they too practised self-denial.

5th In 1930 the great British airship R101 crashed into a hillside at Beauvais, in France.

6th Thor Heyerdahl, explorer and leader of the Kon-Tiki expedition, was born in 1914.

W K Kellogg, inventor of corn flakes, died in 1951.

7th This was the date on which the famous diarist John Evelyn recorded a significant visit in 1644. This was to a galley in the harbour at Marseilles. Here he saw galley slaves double-chained about their waist and legs, in couples, and made fast to their seats '. . . commanded by cruel and imperious seamen'.

8th In 622 the prophet Muhammad (pbuh) entered Medina on a camel.

A strange duel took place in Paris on this date in 1361. A man called Macaire was suspected of having murdered another man called de Montidier. Unfortunately the only witness was de Montidier's dog. The king decided that a duel should be fought between dog and suspected murderer. During the course of this, so determined was the dog to seek retribution for its master's death, that Macaire confessed to the murder. (Link – Assembly 7)

9th The famous district of Montmartre in Paris is particularly significant today. In 272 St Denis, patron saint of France and first Bishop of Paris, was beheaded for his beliefs. He is said to have carried his own head after the execution. The place where this occurred was called the 'mountain of the martyrs', or Montmartre.

Camille Saint-Saëns (composer of 'Carnival of the Animals') was born in 1835.

10th Lord Nuffield, car manufacturer and philanthropist, was born in 1877.

11th Sir George William, founder of the YMCA, was born in 1821.

This is the day after which it is supposedly unlucky to gather blackberries. Thrown out of heaven by St Michael, Satan fell in a blackberry bush on 11th October and put a curse on the bush.

12th Elizabeth Fry, reformer of English prisons, died in 1845. (*Link – Assembly 11*)

This is Christopher Columbus day in South America. In the USA it is celebrated on the second Monday in October.

13th Margaret Thatcher, former Prime Minister, was born in 1925.

The Roman festival of Fontinalia – water worshipping – took place annually on this date.

14th King Harold was killed at the Battle of Hastings in 1066.

The *Literary Digest* of 14th October 1899, carried some comment on the 'horseless carriage' saying that . . . 'it will never, of course, come into as common use as the bicycle.'

Martin Luther King was awarded the Nobel Peace Prize in 1964.

15th P G Wodehouse, author and creator of Jeeves and Wooster, was born in 1881.

Florence Nightingale was appointed to organise the military hospital at Scutari in the Crimea in 1854.

16th This was the date of John Brown's stand against slavery in the Battle of Harper's Ferry in 1859. Seizing the army base there, he thought that nearby slaves would rush to help. They didn't and he was executed. Slavery was only abolished in the USA after the Civil War.

'John Brown's body lies a-mouldering in the grave,
But his soul goes marching on.'

17th This is St Audrey's Day. The daughter of an East Anglian king, Audrey was famous for her good works in the seventh century. (*Link – Assembly 8*)

18th St Luke's Day. As one of the most talented of Jesus' followers, Luke was a practising doctor and artist as well as the writer of a gospel. He was crucified in the year 63 in Syria.

19th Jonathan Swift, author of *Gulliver's Travels*, died in 1745.

20th Grace Darling, lifeboat heroine, died in 1842. In 1838, along with her father, she saved the lives of nine people from the disintegrating ship 'Forfarshire' off the coast of Northumberland. She was awarded several medals but was only twenty-seven when she died of consumption.

Christopher Wren, architect, was born in 1622. (*Link – Assembly 13*)

In 1822 the first of *The Sunday Times* appeared. (*Link – Assembly 6*)

21st Nelson was killed at the Battle of Trafalgar on this date in 1805. The battle lasted four hours and the admiral was killed by a musket bullet.

Thomas Edison invented the light bulb in 1879. (*Link – Assembly 3*)

22nd The first successful parachute jump was made from a balloon on this date in 1797. The event took place in Paris and the parachutist was Andres Jacques.

23rd This is the birthday of Pele (1940), the only footballer ever to score a thousand goals in first class matches.

24th Cranberries were brought to England by voyagers returning from America in 1667. King Charles II was said to have liked them very much.

United Nations Day since 1946.

25th The Battle of Agincourt took place in 1415. Henry V's army of thirty thousand defeated one hundred thousand Frenchmen. In Shakespeare's *Henry V* the reference to this victory on St Crispin's Day is significant.
    St Crispin was martyred by the Emperor Maximilian in 287. He preached his beliefs during the day and earned his living by making shoes at night. Thus, apart from the literary references, he is also the patron saint of cobblers, and perhaps long-distance walkers because . . .

> Dear Saint, the saint of those who make good shoes,
> Thee for my patron saint I also choose;
> Where'er I walk in highway, trail or street,
> Bring thou unblistered home my grateful feet.

In 1854 the Charge of the Light Brigade took place in the Crimean War.

26th Igor Sikorsky, inventor of the helicopter, died in 1972.

The Football Association was founded in 1863.

27th Captain James Cook, the explorer, was born in 1728.

28th Alfred the Great died in 901.

The Statue of Liberty was unveiled in New York in 1886.

29th Sir Walter Raleigh, explorer and seaman, died in 1618.

30th A minor planet, Hermes, just missed a collision with the earth, which would have destroyed both, in 1937.

Jean Henri Dunant, founder of the Red Cross, died in 1910.

31st The heathen festival of Hallowe'en was taken over by Christians for a threefold commemoration of Christian dead on All Hallows' Eve (31st) followed by All Hallows' Day and All Souls' Day.

Religious notes

The Jewish Festival of Rosh Hashanah takes place in the Jewish month of Tishri, which occurs in autumn.

This festival celebrates God's creation of the world; Abraham's sacrifice of a ram instead of his son; God as judge as well as creator; the need for atonement before God. Jewish years are calculated from Rosh Hashanah – thus it is also a new year celebration.

The Torah says: 'In the seventh month, on the first day of the month, shall be a solemn rest unto you, a memorial gathered with a blast of horns . . .'

The festival is started by the blowing of the sofar (ram's horn), which is a reminder of Abraham's sacrifice. Apples and bread are dipped in honey and eaten in the hope that this will bring a 'sweet' new year. New Year cards are sent to friends and relatives. These contain good wishes – L'Shanah Torah Tikatevu.

Despite the seriousness of the festival, it is not a time of gloom because it emphasises God's forgiveness and love. The festival builds up to Yom Kippur (The Day of Atonement), which is the holiest day of the Jewish year, and continuous prayers are said in the synagogue during this day.

Dashara is a Hindu festival which in some parts of India commemorates Rama's victory over Ravanna, whilst in others it is mainly concerned with the worship of the goddess Durga. The main day of the latter festival is Durga Puja. During the celebrations, clay statues of the goddess are made and treated with great respect and honour. After Durga Puja, the last day of the festival, they are symbolically thrown into the river – recognising the fact that the goddess will now have left these temporary homes.

November

1st   All Saints' Day. Saints are people of all ages and backgrounds who have achieved sainthood by being exceptional Christians. Two requirements were laid down for sainthood by Pope Innocent III in 1199: first, that the person concerned should have lived a life of inspiring virtue and second, performed miracles after his or her death. (*Link – Assembly 18*)

An interesting aside to All Saints' Day is that it was customary amongst better-off families in the sixteenth century to present an apostle's spoon to a child at his baptism. This spoon had the figure of the child's patron saint carved on its handle.

2nd   This is the day when the Christian church remembers all its members who have died. A possible link is with Chinese Buddhists who also set aside a day for remembering – and helping – the dead. Of particular concern are homeless spirits without descendants, for whom large paper boats are burned to help them across the 'seas of hunger and thirst'.

This was the date in 1936 when the BBC's first television service began.

3rd   This being the month associated with saints, this date is the one on which St Winefride is remembered. Killed for her beliefs in the fifth century, a well of pure water is supposed to have sprung up on the spot where she died.

4th   Felix Mendelssohn died in 1847. (*Link – Assembly 2*)

5th   'Now boys with squibs and crackers play,
And bonfires' blaze turns night to day.'
(*Poor Robin's Almanack*)

The plot to kill King James I in 1605 was hatched because of his supposedly unfair treatment of Catholics. Robert Catesby was the mastermind and Guy Fawkes the plotter designated to light the fuse to the gunpowder which would have blown up the Houses of Parliament.

A traitor betrayed the plot and the conspirators were all executed by 1606.

An interesting piece of trivia is that at St Peter's School in York, bonfires are lit there but never is a 'guy' burned. Guy Fawkes was an old boy of the school.

6th   In 1893 Peter Tchaikovsky, composer, died. (*Link – Assembly 17*)

7th   Marie Curie was born in 1867.

The River Thames flood barrier was completed in 1982. It took eight years to complete at a cost of four hundred and fifty million pounds.

8th   In 1922 Dr Barnard, the heart transplant surgeon, was born.

9th   The first motor bike was ridden in 1885.

10th   Thirteen-year-old Fritz Kreisler (born in Vienna) made his American debut as a concert violinist on this date in 1888. (*Link – Assembly 11*)

11th   St Martin's Day. Martin, Bishop of Tours, died in 397. Perhaps best known for the story of the torn cloak (*Link – Assembly 18*), the fragment of the cloak given to the beggar was preserved as one of France's most holy relics.

This was also the date on which the Armistice was signed to end the First World War in 1918. Millions of men lost their lives in this conflict and as a permanent memorial to them the Menin Gate in Ypres, Belgium, was engraved with the names of fifty thousand men who have no known graves.

Traffic through this gate is halted every evening whilst the 'Last Post' is played on a bugle. (*Link – Assembly 19*)

12th   King Canute died in 1035. The story of the limit of his powers (being unable to control the incoming tide) is still an effective one with children.

13th   Robert Louis Stevenson was born in 1850. (*Link – Assembly 17*)

14th Prince Charles was born in 1948.

Medzhid Agayer died in the USSR. He was one hundred and forty-three.

15th St Albert's Day. He died in Germany in 1280 and was considered one of the greatest scholars who had ever lived. (*Link – Assembly 17*).

16th The Suez Canal, one hundred miles long, was opened in 1869, after ten years of work.

Jack Sheppard, the infamous highwayman, was hanged in 1724.

17th One of Britain's most famous generals, Monty, or Field Marshall Viscount Montgomery of Alamein, was born in 1887.

18th This was the date, in 1963, on which the Dartford Road Tunnel was opened. This allows traffic to drive under the River Thames between Essex and Kent.

The UK premier of the record breaking film *Titanic* on this date in 1997. It grossed over one billion dollars world-wide.

19th In 1703 a prisoner died in the Bastille prison in France. He had been imprisoned for over twenty years, wore a velvet mask at all times and was mostly in solitary confinement. Later the subject of a famous book (*The Man in the Iron Mask* by Alexandre Dumas), the identity of the prisoner was shrouded in mystery. One supposition was that he was a criminal who looked so much like the king of France that he had to be masked.

20th Princess Elizabeth (now Queen Elizabeth II) was married in 1947.

21st The balloon designed by the Montgolfier brothers first flew in 1783. It attained a height of three thousand feet.

'Schinderhannes' died in 1803. He was the German Robin Hood.

22nd St Cecilia's Day. The patron saint of music, Cecilia was martyred in 230. (*Link – Assembly 24*)

The SOS call sign was adopted internationally: 'Mayday' comes from *m'aidez* (French for 'Help me').

23rd St Clement's Day. Clement was an early Pope who was put to death by being thrown into the sea tied to an anchor. Because anchors were made by blacksmiths, he became their patron saint.

24th In 1815 Grace Darling, heroine of the famous sea rescue, was born.

25th St Catherine's Day. Catherine was a fourth-century martyr.

In 1823 the first pier was opened – Brighton.

8am, 25/11/1872 was the last entry in the log book of the 'Marie Celeste', a ship found sailing in the Atlantic with no one on board.

26th The first Thanksgiving Day was held in the USA on this date in 1789. The original cause for Thanksgiving was the harvesting of the first crops by the Pilgrim Fathers in 1621.

27th The first policewomen (Misses Allen and Harburn) started their duties in Grantham in 1914.

28th Enid Blyton died in 1968. Her books for children have sold over fifty million copies and have been translated into one hundred and sixty-five languages.

Margaret Thatcher resigned as Prime Minister on this date in 1990. After eleven years at No. 10 Downing Street she was the longest serving Prime Minister since the 1820s.

29th Concorde first flew in 1969. The agreement for its English–French joint development was signed on this date in 1962.

30th St Andrew's Day. The brother of Peter, Andrew was a missionary in the Middle East until his crucifixion on this date in 70 AD.

There is an interesting 'weather saying' associated with this date: 'As November, so is the following March.'

Religious notes

One of the movable feasts which occurs in this month is Guru Nanak's birthday.

Chanukah, the Jewish Festival of Light, and a celebration often linked with Diwali and Christmas in primary school RE themes, also occurs at this time of the year.

From a Christian viewpoint, the significance of All Saints' Day has already been mentioned and, at the end of the month, thoughts of Christmas are stirred by the arrival of Advent. This begins on the nearest Sunday to 30th November.

Advent Sunday is the beginning of the Christian church's year, except in the Greek church where it begins on 11th November, St Martin's Day.

December

1st   St Eligius, a French Bishop, died in 659. He is memorable because he is the patron saint of so many groups of people ... goldsmiths, blacksmiths, miners, locksmiths, clock makers, carriage makers, tool makers, cab drivers, farmers and jockeys!

2nd   The rebuilt St Paul's Cathedral was dedicated in 1697. (*Link – Assembly 13*)

3rd   1962 was one of the worst winters ever recorded in England. On this date fog paralysed London for four days and one hundred and six people died as a consequence. (*Link – Assembly 26*)

4th   In 1957 severe fog also contributed to a railway accident at Lewisham, in south London, in which ninety people were killed.

5th   Mozart died on this date in 1791 at the age of thirty-six. Ironically his last composition was a Requiem Mass. (*Link – Assembly 24*)

6th   This is the Feast Day of St Nicholas, Bishop of Myra, patron saint of Russia and sailors, who died in 342. Renowned for his wisdom and generosity, Nicholas has become a figure closely associated with Santa Claus and Father Christmas.

        The reason for his connection with sailors is that in 1807 some Italian seamen from Bari brought his remains back from Myra and lodged them in a church in Bari. (*Link – Assembly 27*)

7th   On the Sunday morning of this date in 1941, Japanese aircraft from six aircraft carriers attacked the United States naval fleet at Pearl Harbour. Nineteen ships were sunk or badly damaged and over two thousand men were killed. (*Link – Assembly 23*)

8th   Horace, the Roman poet, was born on this day in 65 BC. Greatly admired during his lifetime, many of his sayings are ideal assembly starters.

> 'No lot is in all respects happy.'
> 'Once a word has been allowed to escape it cannot
>   be recalled.'
> 'When your neighbour's wall is on fire it becomes
>   your business.'
> 'Seize today, and put as little trust as you can in
>   tomorrow.'
>
> (*Link – Assembly 6*)

9th   The first Christmas card was created on this date in England in 1842.

Arthur Pearson died in 1921. He founded St Dunstan's Home for the Blind. (*Link – Assemblies 7, 16*)

10th   In 1959 the Crowther Report recommended the raising of the school leaving age to 16 in England.

Alfred Nobel, the Swedish engineer who founded the Nobel prizes, died in 1896.
    The Nobel prizes are awarded annually for achievements in physics, chemistry, medicine, literature, and service to the cause of peace. (*Link – Assembly 19*)

This date is Human Rights Day.

11th   Hector Berlioz, the French composer, was born in 1803.

12th   This was the date of Marconi's first transatlantic radio message in 1901.

Robert Browning, author of 'The Pied Piper', a valuable assembly resource, died in 1889.

13th   St Lucy's Day. A native of Syracuse, St Lucy was martyred in 304. She is particularly remembered in Sweden every year in a Festival of Lights, symbolic of her aid to early Christians.

14th   In 1918 women voted for the first time in a British general election.

15th   Alexandre Eiffel, designer of the Eiffel Tower, was born in 1832. The tower in Paris is three hundred metres high.

16th   Ludwig van Beethoven was born in 1770.

Wilhelm Grimm (one of the Grimm brothers) died in 1859.

Camille Saint-Saëns, French composer of 'Carnival of the Animals', died in 1921.

17th In 1903 Orville Wright made the first aeroplane flight, near Kittyhawk in North Carolina, USA. He was aloft for twelve seconds and covered a distance of about forty metres.

18th In 1865 slavery in the USA was abolished.

19th This was the date in 1981 when the tragedy of the lifeboat from Mousehole in Cornwall occurred. Trying to rescue survivors from the freighter 'Union Star', the lifeboat was fighting conditions of eight-knot winds and twenty-metre-high waves when it sank.

20th A fish caught off Madagascar in 1952 was recognised as being of a prehistoric species, a coelacanth.

21st St Thomas's Day. Thomas spread the gospel in the Middle East and India before dying in the first century. He is the patron saint of builders.

22nd Beatrix Potter (creator of *Peter Rabbit*) died in 1943.

George Eliot died in 1880. The plot of her novel *Silas Marner* contains some parts very well suited for assembly material. 'George Eliot' was in fact Mary Ann Evans.

This was also the date when 70mph speed limits were introduced on British roads in 1965.

23rd Christmas Island was discovered by Captain Cook in 1777.

24th In 1933 the British Museum acquired the *Codex Sinaiticus*, an ancient manuscript of the Bible, written in the fourth century.

There is an ancient legend that on Christmas Eve the cock crows all night, thus keeping all evil at bay. (*Link – Assembly 22*)

25th The Queen's Christmas Broadcast was televised for the first time in 1957.

A useful quotation for Christmas Day comes from *Sketches by Boz* by Charles Dickens: 'There seems a magic in the very name of Christmas. Petty jealousies and discords are forgotten ... would that Christmas lasted the whole year through.'

26th Boxing Day derives its name from the time when church poor boxes were opened on this date so that their contents could be distributed to the needy.

This is also St Stephen's Day, Stephen was the Christian church's first martyr, being stoned to death in 33 AD.

27th St John's Day. John was the last of the original disciples to die – in Ephesus in about 100 AD.

28th This was the night of the Tay bridge disaster in 1879. The bridge collapsed in a storm as a train was passing over it. Seventy-five people died.

29th The man who invented the raincoat was born on this date in 1776. His name was William Macintosh.

30th In the severe winter of 1962 this was the day on which the worst snowstorm since 1881 hit England. (*Link – Assembly 26*)

Rudyard Kipling was born in 1865. He won the Nobel Prize for Literature in 1907. (*Link – Assembly 17*)

31st The chimes of Big Ben bringing in the New Year were first broadcast in 1923.

Apart from being Hogmanay in Scotland, it is also a Hindu festival and the Shinto festival of Joya No Kane. Bells are rung at this time to give thanks for the good things of the past year and to prepare for the coming year.

Religious notes

Bodhi Day (Mahayana) is a movable feast in December when Buddhists celebrate the Buddha's enlightenment, as he reflected sitting under a Bodhi tree. 'Buddha' means 'the enlightened one' and the experience took place over two thousand five hundred years ago. (*Link – Assembly 22*)

Chanukah, the Jewish Festival of Lights, is also a November–December movable feast.

Christmas Day on the 25th of the month was not established until the time when Julius I was Bishop of Rome (337–352). Julius fixed this as the date, after various Christian communities had celebrated the birth on dates as diverse as 6th January and 29th March, with others in between.

January

'Then came old January, wrapped well
In many weeds to keep the cold away.'
(*Edmund Spenser, 1552–99*)

The ancient Jewish year, which began on 25th March, held its legal position in Christian countries up until the eighteenth century. It was not until 1752 that 1st January became the legal, as well as the 'popular' start to the English new year.

1st   This is the time for 'New Year Resolutions'. Charles Lamb said: 'The man who does not propose to himself to be better this year than he was last, must be either very good or very bad indeed.' (*Link – Assembly 28*)

Many countries around the world held huge celebrations to welcome 1st January 2000 as the dawn of the third millennium. Due to time zone differences the Pacific islands of Kiribati were the first to see the dawn of the new millennium and Western Samoa the last.

The BBC began broadcasting its first programmes in 1927.

Traffic policemen were introduced in Great Britain in 1931.

In 1954 flashing indicator lights became legal requirements on all motor vehicles in Great Britain. (*Possible assembly starter for a 'signs' theme*)

2nd   The Roman poet Ovid died on this day in the year 18. He is remembered for many thought-provoking 'sayings': 'To be loved, be lovable' and 'While fortune smiles you will have a host of friends, but they'll desert you when the storm descends.'

General 'Tom Thumb' (real name Charles Stratton), probably the most famous dwarf, died in 1883. He was 31 inches (84 cm) tall.

In 1914, at Hendon, a woman pilot looped the loop for the first time. Her name was Trehawke Davies.

In 1984 a report said that acid rain was contaminating Britain's lakes and rivers.

3rd   In 1847 the Californian town of Yerba Buena had its name changed – to San Francisco.

On this date in 1661 Samuel Pepys noted in his diary that he had been to the theatre and that it was 'the first time that I saw women come upon the stage'. Prior to this, boys and young men had taken women's parts.

4th   During the Middle Ages monks compiled a catalogue of flowers for each day of the year, linking each flower with a saint. Today's flower is the common hazel and it is linked to St Titus.

Jacob Grimm (of the Grimm brothers' fairy tales) was born in 1785.

Louis Braille was born in 1809. He was three years old when an accident caused him to lose his sight. According to *The Young Louis Braille* by C H Abrahall, it was feeling the indentations on dominoes which was one inspiration for his devising the system known as Braille. (*Link – Assembly 41*)

This was the date in 1944, during the Second World War, when Hitler ordered the mobilisation of all children over ten.

5th   St Simeon Stylites died in 459. He lived for 36 years on a pillar 60 feet from the ground, wearing an iron collar and animal skins. Twice a day he preached to people who came to hear him. He was greatly admired for his patience, humility and wisdom. He was 69 when he died.

In 1927 in New York the first demonstration of Movietone took place. This was a synchronisation of moving pictures and sound.

6th   This is the feast of Epiphany, which marks the time when three Wise Men first saw Jesus. 'Epiphany' comes from the Greek world which means 'appearance'. The Twelve Days of Christmas end with the Feast of Epiphany. In mediaeval England all twelve days were celebrated, with great festivities on the last night before serious work on the land began the next day. It is traditionally unlucky to have decorations up after Twelfth Night.

In 1928 the Thames burst its banks. Fourteen people were drowned, there was serious flooding and valuable paintings were damaged in the Tate Gallery.

In 1931, during excavations in Iraq, a royal palace dating from 550 BC was discovered.

In 1941 the world-famous pilot Amy Johnson was missing, believed drowned, after her plane disappeared while flying over the Thames Estuary. (Her body was never found.)

7th In some parts of Japan this is a festival date on which rice cooked with herbs is eaten to prevent both bad luck and bad health.

8th St Nathalan's Day. His generosity to others gained him sainthood but he is probably best remembered for losing his temper, then chaining his ankles in repentance. Throwing the key to his chains into the sea, he later bought a fish in Rome and, on cutting it open to cook, found the key inside.

Galileo, the astronomer, died in 1642.

Elvis Presley was born in 1935.

9th Davy's safety lamp was first used down a coal mine in 1816.

In 1920 the Government announced plans to build 100,000 new houses during the year.

In 1948 four hundred Jamaicans arrived in London on the ship *Empire Windrush* to look for work in the rebuilding of post-war Britain.

10th The Penny Post was introduced by Sir Rowland Hill in 1840.

'Buffalo Bill' (William F Cody) died in 1917.

'Tintin', the famous cartoon character, first appeared in Belgium in 1929.

After a twelve-day ordeal in which he tried to save his ship (the *Flying Enterprise*), Captain Henrick Carlsen had to abandon it forty minutes before it sank. This was in 1952 and was an early 'disaster' covered by TV.

11th Tradition has it that if today is mild moles start their tunnelling operations and throw up the first mole hills.

In 1905 the price of liner tickets to cross the Atlantic went up. To get from London to New York now cost £6.

12th Charles Perrault was born in 1628. He wrote: 'Cinderella' and 'Sleeping Beauty'.

In 1807 a ship full of gunpowder exploded at its moorings in the Dutch city of Leyden. One hundred and fifty-one people were killed and 2,000 injured, and 200 buildings were levelled. The blast was heard 50 miles away and the anchor of the ship was later found in a field outside the town.

Britain's first supermarket was opened in Manor Park in 1948.

13th St Veronica died in 1497. She was a poor peasant girl who lived such an exemplary life that she became prioress of a nunnery. How the name Veronica came into being is significant. When Christ was carrying his cross a girl wiped his face with a cloth. After she had done so the cloth miraculously bore an imprint of his features – a *Vera Iconica* ('true portrait'). The cloth still remains in St Peter's in Rome.

During the 'flu epidemic of 1922, 804 people died during the week ending on this day.

14th This is the feast day of St Kentigern, a Scottish saint whose Day is celebrated in Glasgow and elsewhere in Scotland.

On this date in 1205 one of the coldest ever spells hit Europe. A hard frost gripped England until 22nd March. From then on, 14th January was thought of as the coldest day of the year – something borne out in 1734 when Siberia registered temperatures of – 120°F and birds fell frozen from the sky.

Albert Schweitzer was born in 1875.

Lewis Carroll (author of *Alice in Wonderland*) died in 1898.

15th This is the day on which St Paul, the first hermit, died in 342.

This is Martin Luther King Day in the USA. The civil rights leader was born in Atlanta, Georgia, in 1929. He was assassinated in Memphis, Tennessee, in April 1968.

16th Promises! An advertiser said that on this day in 1749, at London's Haymarket Theatre, he would play sounds from every musical instrument on a walking stick, and would then squeeze himself into a quart bottle. A huge crowd bought tickets and turned up – but the 'magician' didn't. There was a riot and the theatre was wrecked.

17th This is the feast day of St Anthony, the patron saint of domestic animals, who died in 356.

On this date in 1939 the Nazi Government in Germany banned Jews from being dentists or vets and they were not allowed to drive cars, or go to cinemas and theatres.

18th   Every year on this date the festival of St Peter's Chair is held in Rome. This is held in St Peter's Church, where the chair on which the saint is said to have meditated is enshrined. The ceremony commemorates the founding of the papacy.

This is the date on which the annual week of prayer for Christian Unity begins.

Rudyard Kipling died in 1936.

In 1923, because of inflation, there were 112,000 Deutschmarks to £1.

19th   James Watt, the inventor (steam engine), was born in 1736.

In 1903 a new bicycle race was announced in Paris – the Tour de France.

20th   This is St Sebastian's Day. Born in Narbonne, he was an early Christian who was killed by the Romans and buried under the Appian Way. During his life he managed to persuade one Roman governor to release many Christian prisoners. He lived during the third century.

John Howard, the prison reformer, died in 1790.

In 1961 John F Kennedy became the USA's youngest president. In his inaugural speech he said: '. . . ask not what your country can do for you; ask what you can do for your country.'

21st   This is the feast day of St Agnes (died 304). She is the patroness of purity.

In 1930 the BBC made the first world broadcast.

In 1935 Snowdonia, the first British National Park, was established.

22nd   Sir Francis Bacon, the great philosopher, was born in 1561. Despite his great mental powers, he was guilty of taking bribes when he was a judge. Hence the poet Alexander Pope described him as: 'The wisest, greatest, meanest of mankind'.

In 1901 Queen Victoria died at Osborne House on the Isle of Wight. She had reigned for 63 years.

In 1959 on this date it was announced that TV was growing rapidly in popularity and that two thirds of the British population now had a set. (*Link – Assembly 50*)

23rd   St Eusebius died in 400. He ate only once every four days.

'Bodyline' bowling by the English cricket team in Australia caused great controversy in 1933.

The first jumbo jet landed at London's Heathrow Airport in 1970.

24th   This is the feast day of St Timothy, bishop and martyr who was killed in 97 AD while trying to quell rioters in his temple.

The Boy Scouts were founded by Baden Powell in 1908.

Winston Church died in 1965. He was ninety.

25th   This is the feast of St Paul and celebrates his conversion to Christianity. (Bible reference: Acts 9, 1–31) Tradition maintains that weather for the year can be foretold by how it is on St Paul's Day:

> 'If St Paul's Day be fair and clear,
> It does betide a happy year.'

Robert Burns, the Scottish poet, was born in 1759. At Burns Night celebrations the haggis is eaten. The recipe for a haggis is minced heart and liver of sheep, suet, oatmeal, and seasoning – sewn into the sheep's stomach and boiled for three hours. (*Link – Assembly 35*)

On this date in 1915 Alexander Graham Bell established a new long-distance record for a telephone call – 4,750 miles from New York to San Francisco. (*Link – Assembly 41*)

26th   Australia Day – commemorating the landing of Captain Arthur Phillips in 1788. On the same day in 1865 the sending of convicts from England to Australia ceased. (*Link – Assembly 43*)

27th   St John Chrysostum's Day. Born in 347 AD in Antioch, John was a brilliant orator ('Chrysostum' means 'golden mouth') whose Christian message made him enemies who succeeded in getting him banished. He died, ill and exhausted, while travelling in 407. Thus he was not a martyr but his sainthood came from his devotion and sincerity.

Mozart was born in 1756.

Lewis Carroll (*Alice in Wonderland*) was born in 1832.

In 1906 the River Thames caught fire as oil on the surface ignited.

In 1926 the first TV pictures were demonstrated in London by John Logie Baird.

28th Henry VII died in 1547.

Francis Drake died in 1596 on his ship off the coast of Panama.

In 1807 London's Pall Mall became the first street in the world to be lit by gaslight.

In 1986 the American space shuttle *Challenger* exploded on lift-off, killing its crew of seven.

29th St Francis's Day. He is the patron saint of writers and journalists. He died in 1662 and is known fully as St Francis de Sales.

The Victoria Cross was first awarded on this day in 1856. The medals were made from guns captured in the Crimea.

In 1947 one of the coldest ever spells of winter weather in Britain saw temperatures at – 16°F. (*Link – Assembly 33*)

30th King Charles I was beheaded in 1649.

Edward Lear, poet, died in 1888.

Mahatma Gandhi was assassinated in New Delhi, India, in 1948. 'Mahatma' means 'Great Soul'.

In 1958 a bill was passed in the House of Lords marking lifetime peerages for men and women. For the first time in over six centuries women were admitted to the House of Lords.

31st Guy Fawkes was executed in 1606.

While on the subject of 'bonfires', on this night in 1804, with the country apprehensive about a French invasion, a warning bonfire was accidentally set alight near Berwick. This triggered off the lighting of many others and by morning all the southern Scottish counties were armed and ready to fight.

In one year, up to this date in 1922, the cost of living in Germany had risen by 73.7%.

Car front-seatbelts became compulsory in the UK in 1983.

Epiphany is the Christian feast which occurs twelve days after Christmas. It was originally associated with the baptism of Christ. An interesting link with the traditional story of the three wise men and their gifts is that these same gifts are presented at the altar in St James Palace, Chapel Royal, by members of the British royal family at this time of year.

January 25th has already been mentioned in the foregoing notes as St Paul's Day. It has another significance in that the week of prayer for Christian Unity is timed to end on this day.

The Hindu festival of Vasanta Panchami takes place in the month of Magha (January/February) and is a celebration of Sarasvati who is the goddess of learning and wisdom.

February

February (along with January) was one of the two months by which Numa Pompilius extended the Roman year from ten to twelve periods. The name came from the word 'februare', meaning 'to purify'.

1st   This is St Bride's Day. She is the patroness of Ireland.

In 1811 the beacon on Bell Rock lighthouse was first lit. In earlier times the Abbot of Aberbrothock had put a bell on this rock, off the Firth of Tay, to warn mariners of its presence. A pirate called Ralph the Rover cut this bell adrift and sent it into the sea. Later his ship was wrecked on the same rock and he was drowned. (Junior children find this a very telling story!)

In 1915 passport photographs were first introduced in Great Britain.

In the same year, Sir Stanley Matthews, possibly England's most famous ever footballer, was born. He played until he was fifty.

2nd   Candlemas. On this date many churches have candlelit processions to celebrate the presentation of Jesus in the temple. In former times candles were thought of as 'representations' of the all-important sun, and were considered a talisman against such dreads as famine and plague. One other reason for the Church's emphasis on candles was to counteract these pagan celebrations. Candles and light symbolise good, truth, knowledge, hope and an early reference to Jesus the child said that he was 'a light to lighten the Gentiles' (Luke 2, 32). Candlemas Day is another of those which has traditional weather lore attached to it:

> 'If Candlemas Day be fair and bright,
> Winter will have another flight;
> But if it be dark with clouds and rain,
> Winter is gone and will not come again.'

Tradition also names the snowdrop as the flower for 2nd February. It is said to have been created from a snowflake by an angel to give Adam and Eve hope when they had been expelled from the Garden of Eden.

3rd   In Japan this is seen as the last day of winter and, to celebrate, people throw beans at each other.

Felix Mendelssohn was born in 1809.

This is the feast day of St Blaise, a saint with the power to cure throat problems.

On this day in 1953 hurricanes and high tides brought disaster to Britain's east coast. Two hundred and fifty people were drowned and thousands were made homeless.

4th   Charles Lindbergh, the first man to fly solo over the Atlantic, was born in 1902.

In 1929 the first Green Belt area round London was approved. This was a five-mile tract near Hendon.

On this date in 1953 sweet rationing ended in Great Britain.

5th   St Agatha's Day. Agatha was being tortured for being a Christian when an earthquake erupted. It stopped when her torture stopped. She died peacefully in 251 AD.

Robert Peel, founder of the British police force, was born in 1788.

The *Reader's Digest* was first published in 1922.

In 1983 an unknown Mozart symphony was found among a pile of old papers in Odense, Denmark. It was calculated that the composer had written it when he was nine years old.

6th   On this day in 1918 the Representation of the People Act came into force, allowing women to vote in General Elections. They had to be over thirty, and householders. (Equal voting rights for all adults were won in 1928.)

In 1927 a ten-year-old boy in short trousers made a sensational debut playing the violin at a concert in Paris. His name was Yehudi Menuhin.

In 1958 the Manchester United football team's aeroplane crashed in Munich following a European cup tie. Seven of the players died immediately.

In 1964 Britain and France agreed to build a Channel Tunnel.

7th   Charles Dickens was born in 1812.

This was the day, in 1845, when William Lloyd went into the British Museum and deliberately broke the priceless 300-year-old Portland Vase, which had been discovered in Rome. He was fined for the vandalism. The vase, shattered into 2,000 pieces, was laboriously repaired by a man called Doubleday. (*Link – Assembly 45*)

On this date in 1960 Israeli archaeologists discovered some parchment scrolls containing Biblical texts. The scrolls were estimated as having been written 1,700 years ago.

8th   Jules Verne, the author of *Around the World in Eighty Days*, was born in 1823.

9th   St Apollonia's Day. During her torture for being a Christian, in Alexandria, Apollonia's teeth were removed to make her renounce her faith, which she would not do. She died in 249 AD and is the patron saint of dentists.

This was the date in 1855 when, after a fall of snow in south-west England, mysterious footprints appeared next morning. These ran for nearly one hundred miles – over roofs and haystacks. They were cloven hooves – the mystery was never solved.

After eighteen days of continuous rain, London suburbs started to flood on this date in 1926.

In 1939 the British Government announced that London families on an income of less than £250 a year would be given free air-raid shelters.

10th St Scholastica's Day. Scholastica died in 543. She was the sister of the better-known St Benedict who founded the Benedictine monastery at Monte Cassino in Italy.

Samuel Plimsoll was born in 1824. (*Link – Assembly 38*)

This was the date, in 1913, when rescuers found the dead bodies of Captain Scott and his two companions in their snow-covered tent near the South Pole. Scott's diary was found with them.

On this date in 1942 the first Golden Disc for a successful recording was presented. It was to Glenn Miller and his band for their hit, 'Chattanooga Choo Choo'.

11th This is a day of celebration in Japan – to commemorate the founding of the country in 660 BC.

12th Alexander Selkirk (the model for Defoe's Robinson Crusoe) was rescued from the uninhabited island of Juan Fernandez on this day in 1709. He had been there alone for five years.

Abraham Lincoln, sixteenth president of the United States, was born in 1809. He was responsible for the emancipation of negro slaves after the Civil War. He made the famous Gettysburg Address: 'This nation, under God, shall have a new birth of freedom; and that government of the people, by the people, and for the people, shall not perish from the earth.'

13th On this date in 1978 Anna Ford became ITV's first female newscaster.

14th St Valentine's Day. In the third century the Roman Emperor Claudius II passed a law against marriage because it was denuding his army of troops. A Christian priest, Valentine, continued to marry couples. He was discovered and sentenced to death. His compassion for all – including his jailer and that man's daughter – earned him sainthood. The sending of Valentine cards was probably at its peak in Britain in the nineteenth century. Postmen in London at this time felt that their task was so onerous on this day that they asked for a special meal allowance. (*Link – Assembly 39*)

15th Galileo Galilei, the astronomer, was born in 1564.

Decimal currency was introduced in Britain in 1971.

16th Desperate unemployment in Britain in 1921 included 368,000 ex-servicemen.

Tutenkhamen's tomb and contents were discovered in Egypt in 1923.

The new synthetic fibre, nylon, was patented in New York on this date in 1937. Its name came from the two cities where work on its development had taken place: NY (New York) and LON (London).

17th   Michaelangelo Buonarotti, the Italian artist who decorated the ceiling of the Sistine Chapel, died in 1563.

In 1920 Britain's police force started to replace its horses with cars.

18th   St Simon, Bishop of Jerusalem, nephew of Joseph and Mary and Christ's cousin, was crucified in 116. He was 120 years old.

Martin Luther died in 1546.

A new planet was sighted and named in 1930 – Pluto.

In 1942, to save fuel and soap during the Second World War, people in Britain were urged to take fewer baths, and to paint a 'plimsoll line' in bathtubs to regulate the amount of water put into them.

In 1949 the millionth ton of airlifted supplies reached the western sector of the beleaguered Berlin.

19th   Nicholas Copernicus, the astronomer, was born in 1473.

20th   Traditionally, old almanacs recommended this date as the date to sow beans. In folklore the bean is associated with ghosts and witches. In days when witches were feared it was recommended that lonely travellers carried a bean in their mouths to spit at a witch if one appeared.

Jimmy Greaves, the international footballer, was born in 1940.

21st   Cardinal Newman, who wrote the hymn 'Lead, kindly light', was born in London in 1801.

In 1842 John Greenough received a patent for the sewing machine.

In 1956 the Duke of Edinburgh announced an award scheme for enterprising young people.

22nd The first Woolworth's store opened in New York in 1879.

In 1910 X-ray machines were first used in medical treatment.

The announcement of the birth of Dolly the sheep was made on this date in 1997. Dolly was the first animal to be born using the technique of cloning.

23rd Samuel Pepys, the diarist, was born in 1632.

George Frederick Handel was born in 1685.

Dame Nellie Melba, the singer who had the 'peach melba' named after her, died in 1931. (*Link – Assembly 46*)

In 1975, Laurence Stephen Lowry, the artist, died. He was born in 1887.

24th This is the feast day of St Matthias. Matthias was the apostle who took the place of Judas Iscariot after the latter committed suicide. (Bible ref: Acts 1, 23–26)

Wilhelm Karl Grimm (of the Grimm brothers' fairy tales) was born in 1786.

25th Sir Christopher Wren, the architect, died in 1723.

So important to Naples and Italy was the great opera singer, Enrico Caruso, born this day in 1873, that the world's largest candle was dedicated to his memory. It was eighteen feet high when new and is lit every year on his birthday. It is expected to last for 1,800 years. (*Link – Assembly 46*)

26th Victor Hugo (author of *Les Misérables*, which contains the story of the Bishop's candlesticks, such a good assembly tale) was born in 1846.

27th This day celebrates St Thalilaeus who died in the fifth century. He is remembered for his constant weeping as penance for his sins.

In 1964 engineers in Italy pronounced the leaning tower of Pisa dangerous. They said it needed straightening by eleven feet to stop it falling over.

28th In 1912 the first parachute jump from a plane was made by Albert Berry in Missouri, USA.

In 1975 the driver and thirty-five passengers died in a London Underground train disaster at Moorgate. (*Link – Assembly 47*)

29th The Leap Year tradition of women asking men to marry them was once taken so seriously in Scotland that a law as passed saying that any man who turned down such a proposal would be heavily fined.

Religious notes

Candlemas, on 2nd February, celebrates Jesus's presentation at the temple. At the time Jesus was born it was customary for every Jewish mother to go to the temple forty days after the birth of her first male child so that he could be 'presented to the Lord'. The mother was also 'blessed' on this occasion. Candles have come to celebrate this day in connection with Jesus being 'the light of the world'.

Lent is the period from Ash Wednesday to Holy Saturday – forty weekdays. During this time Christians remember the temptations of Jesus in the wilderness. It is a time for spiritual preparation for Easter.

March

The word 'March' comes from the Roman 'Martius'. It was originally the first month of the Roman calendar, named after the God of War.

1st St David's Day. The emblem of the leek originated from soldiers wearing them in their hats to distinguish them from the Saxon enemy in battle. A great victory was won on this day and is commemorated by the same emblem.

In Switzerland cow bells 'ring out winter' on this date.

In 1976 a Road Traffic Bill was approved in the British Parliament. Its aim was to make the wearing of car seatbelts compulsory.

2nd John Wesley, the founder of Methodism, died in 1791.

In 1949 on this date the US airforce B-50 Superfortress *Lucky Lady II* completed the first non-stop flight round the world – 23,452 miles.

3rd Alexander Graham Bell, inventor of the telephone, was born in 1847.

In 1937 on this date it was announced that Britain had 824 millionaires.

In 1955 notice was given that London would be a 'smokeless zone' from October onwards.

In 1958 the first parking tickets were issued to British motorists.

4th   In 1824 the Royal National Lifeboat Institution was founded. (*Link – Assembly 38*)

In 1927, 25,000 diggers rushed to stake their claims in the new South African diamond fields.

In 1982 London's Barbican Centre was opened by the Queen.

5th   The Spitfire made its maiden flight in 1936. It was flown from Eastleigh Airport, Southampton, by Captain J Summers.

In 1942, in an effort to save pencils during wartime economies, all civil servants had their pencil sharpeners withdrawn.

6th   Davy Crockett and 86 others died when Mexican forces captured Fort Alamo in 1836.

This is the birthday of Sri Ramakrishna, the Hindu teacher, in 1833.

In 1946, when Great Britain was still suffering from food short-ages, the British food ministry issued a recipe for squirrel pie.

On this date in 1947 Britain continued to suffer one of its worst ever winters when three hundred roads were blocked and fifteen towns cut off. (*Link – Assembly 33*)

In 1987 the *Herald of Free Enterprise*, a Townsend Thoresen car ferry, capsized off the Belgian port of Zeebrugge at 7pm when it was setting out for Dover. It happened so quickly that there was no time to send an SOS and 193 people lost their lives. (*Link – Assembly 38*)

7th   The British and Foreign Bible Society was founded in 1804. It has been responsible for translations into over 1,500 different languages.

St Perpetua's Day. She was martyred in 203 AD when she died before a crowd of thousands in the Rome amphitheatre.

The Albert Medal, for gallantry in saving life, was instituted in 1866.

In 1965 traffic jams blocked roads round Regent's Park, London, where crowds gathered to watch Goldie, a golden eagle who had escaped from London Zoo. He was recaptured on the 10th.

In 1969 the Queen opened the new London Underground line from Victoria to Walthamstow. (*Link – Assembly 47*)

8th   International Women's Day.

In 1834 a Newfoundland dog called Hero saved two boys from drowning in the River Thames. As a result ten Newfoundlands were brought and trained for similar life-saving duties along the Seine in Paris. (*Link – Assembly 43*)

The first British pilot's licence was issued in 1910.

On this date in 1906 the British Empire occupied one fifth of the land surface of the globe and had a population of four hundred million.

In 1925 the 'crossword craze' brought forth conflicting comments. The British Optical Association feared they would cause eye strain and headaches: the Chicago Department of Health announced that their mental stimulation was good for health and happiness. (*Link – Assembly 41*)

9th   C M Howard invented false teeth in 1827.

The French Foreign Legion was founded in 1831.

10th   The first Cruft's Dog Show was held in London in 1886. (*Link – Assemblies 36 and 43*)

Harriet Tubman died in 1913. She was famous for her work in helping slaves to escape during the American Civil War.

The first 'movie' was made in Hollywood in 1910. It was called *In Old California*.

11th   Johnny Appleseed, the famous American apple tree planter, died in 1847.

Sir Alexander Fleming, discoverer of penicillin, died in 1955.

12th   This is the feast day of St Gregory the Great, who sent St Augustine on his mission to England in 597.

In 1908 Benjamin Waugh, founder of the NSPCC, died.

Coins replaced English £1 notes in 1983.

13th   From this day onwards in 1886 British soldiers were allowed to wear beards.

The discovery of the planet Pluto was announced in 1930.

In 1918 the British school-leaving age was raised to fourteen.

14th   Albert Einstein, the physicist, was born in 1879.

In 1934 it was announced that eggs in Britain had dropped to their lowest price since 1914 – 6d (2½p) per dozen.

15th   Julius Caesar, Roman Emperor, was murdered in 44 BC.

The first cricket Test match was played between Australia and England at Melbourne, Australia in 1877. The Australians won by 45 runs.

In 1909 Selfridges opened in London's Oxford Street.

In 1949 clothes rationing (which had been introduced in Britain in 1941) ended.

16th   The first English FA Cup Final took place in 1872. (Wanderers beat the Royal Engineers.)

In 1917 the Czar abdicated in the face of the Russian Revolution.

In 1919 the invention of the wireless telephone enabled air pilots to talk in flight.

In 1912, Lawrence Oates, thinking his death would aid the survival of his four colleagues, left the tent of Captain Scott's South Pole expedition, and walked in the snow to his death.

17th   St Patrick's Day. Patrick died in 464. He was sent to Ireland by Pope Celestine to convert the heathens there. One of the ways in which he did this was to show them a shamrock – where three leaves combine to make a single plant. This he linked to the Trinity and the shamrock became a national emblem.

Feast day of St Joseph of Arimathea – who placed the body of Jesus in the tomb.

18th   John Luther Jones ('Casey Jones') stayed at the controls of his runaway train on the Chicago–New Orleans Line and died saving as many lives as he could when the train crashed. This was in 1900. The famous ballad recalls his story. (*Link – Assembly 47*)

In 1945 all schools and universities were closed in Tokyo. Everyone over six years old was ordered to do war work.

19th   This is the feast day of St Joseph, Mary's husband.

Sydney Harbour Bridge was opened in 1932.

In 1962, the discovery of a 300-year-old skull was made beneath 10 Downing Street.

In 1964, the St Bernard Tunnel between Switzerland and Italy, via the Alps, was opened.

In 1967 an oil tanker, the *Torrey Canyon*, ran aground at Land's End and its cargo of oil began spilling into the sea. RAF planes later bombed it to disperse the oil which was said to be the 'greatest peacetime threat to Britain'.

20th   Sir Isaac Newton died in 1727.

In 1967 Sir Francis Chichester began the last leg of his solo voyage round the world.

The landing of the first successful round the world hot air balloon flight by Bertrand Picard and Brian Jones in the Breitling Orbiter 3 on this date in 1999. The balloon covered a distance of 26,000 miles (42,197 km).

21st   Feast of St Benedict. As Abbot of the monastery at Monte Cassino, he founded the order of Benedictine monks.

Johann Sebastian Bach was born in 1685.

22nd Johann Wolfgang von Goethe, the German philosopher, died in 1832. He was so clever that he could speak French, Italian, Latin and Greek by the time he was eight years old.

The English Football League was founded with twelve clubs in 1888.

23rd   Roger Bannister, the first man to run a mile in under four minutes, was born in 1929.

24th   Queen Elizabeth I died in 1603 after reigning for 44 years.

25th   Lady Day, Feast of the Annunciation of the Virgin Mary. (Luke 1, 26–38)

Opening of London Airport, Heathrow, in 1948.

Some old English tombstones show interesting inscriptions which concern this date. In the graveyard of the parish church of St Mary, North Mymms, Hertfordshire, the tombstone of Thomas Huxley puts his death in 1695/6. This signifies the fact that until 1752 the legal New Year in Britain began on 25th March; the 'popular' New Year was 1st January. Consequently it was not unusual for gravestones recording deaths between 1st January and 24th March to show both years.

26th Ludwig van Beethoven died in 1827.

The first BBC weather forecast was broadcast on this date in 1923.

27th The first international wireless message was sent by Marconi in 1899.

Yuri Gagarin, the Soviet cosmonaut, died in 1968.

28th The first European use of gunpowder was at a battle between Venetians and Genoese in 1380.

The Crimean War began in 1854.

29th The actress Sarah Bernhardt died, aged 78, on this day in 1923. (Traffic came to a halt in Paris for her funeral.)

In 1981 Dick Beardsley of the USA won the first London Marathon.

30th Anna Sewell, the author of *Black Beauty*, was born in 1820.

Vincent van Gogh, the artist, was born on this date in 1853. His painting 'Sunflowers' was sold at Christie's in London for £24,750,000 in 1987.

31st The Eiffel Tower was opened in Paris in 1889. It is 300 metres high but was not universally popular – over a hundred leading French writers, artists and composers claimed it was an affront to French taste and architecture.

In 1911 it was announced in Britain that the Government was seeking to make sixty hours the maximum working time for shop workers.

Religious notes

Purim is the Jewish festival which celebrates how the Jews of Persia were saved from the persecution of Haman. Because he hated the wise Mordecai, Haman and his followers planned a wholesale slaughter of the Jews throughout the kingdom. His plans were foiled when Esther, Mordecai's niece, was chosen by King Ahasuerus as his new queen. She revealed Haman's plot to the king. Modern celebrations at this festival are light-hearted and jolly. Much fancy dress is worn and hisses and noises greet Haman's name whenever it is mentioned.

The same aura of colour, spectacle and jollity pervades the Hindu spring festival of Holi. On the first day of the festival a bonfire is lit, and on the second day people throw coloured water and powder over each other and exchange presents. These activities celebrate the revels of Lord Krishna.

April

Few months make such an initial impact with their first day as does April! It is also a time for obvious, and sage, advice: 'April showers bring May flowers' and "Til April's dead, change not a thread.'

1st   An attempt to trace the origins of April Fools' Day is confused by its popularity in France, where an April Fools' trick is an 'April Fish' ('*un poisson d'avril*'), and by the similar goings-on at the Hindu Holi celebrations. One suggestion is that when New Year's Day used to be 25th March, 1st April presented itself as a day of levity to end the celebrations.

The Royal Air Force was founded in 1918.

2nd   Hans Andersen was born in 1805. Two of his tales which are useful for assemblies are 'The Ugly Duckling' and 'The Emperor's New Clothes'. Appropriately enough, this is also International Children's Book Day. (*Link – Assembly 51*)

3rd   The Pony Express was founded on this date in 1860 when two riders set out in the USA. One was going east from San Francisco, the other west from St Joseph, Missouri. During its short life, 80 riders and 500 horses worked on the 1,900 miles of the organisation's route.

4th   St Ambrose died on this date in 397. A great orator, he is credited with the famous phrase: 'When you are in Rome, do as they do in Rome.'

Martin Luther King, the American civil rights leader, was assassinated in Memphis in 1968. A few days later (on 9th April) over 150,000 people attended his burial in Atlanta.

5th   Robert Raikes died in 1811. He founded Sunday Schools for children throughout Britain. His first school was opened in 1780 in Gloucester, and was for poor children.

On this date in 1955 Sir Winston Churchill resigned as Prime Minister at the age of eighty.

6th   Albrecht Dürer, the artist ('Praying Hands') died in 1528.

Houdini, the great escape artist, was born in 1874.

Robert Edwin Peary became the first man to reach the North Pole in 1909. He and his party had set out from New York by ship in July 1908.

7th   The highwayman Dick Turpin was hanged in York in 1739.

In 1832, at Carlisle, Joseph Thomson sold his wife to Henry Mears for twenty shillings and a dog.

This is World Health Day, when prayers are asked for sick and suffering people all over the world.

8th   This is the date of a Mahayana Buddhist celebration of Buddha Sakyamuni's birthday.

9th   Isambard Kingdom Brunel, the engineer, was born in 1806.

The American Civil War ended in 1865.

A letter appeared in *The Times* of London asking for a new word to describe 'progress by electric power'. Eventually the world 'motor' was chosen.

10th   William Booth, co-founder, with his wife Catherine, of the Salvation Army, was born in 1829. (Salvation Army, 101 Newington Causeway, London SE1 6BN)

The *Titanic*, the world's largest ship, set off on its ill-fated maiden voyage from Southampton to New York on this date in 1912.

11th   St Guthlac, who died in 714, renounced his earlier career as a robber, took to living in a swamp in the English Fens and existed on only bread and water for the rest of his life.

Napoleon was exiled to Elba in 1814.

12th   The American Civil War broke out in 1861.

The Russian cosmonaut, Yuri Alekseyevich Gagarin, made the first manned space flight round the earth in 1961. His space craft was called *Vostok* and the orbit took 89 minutes.

13th   This is the date of Baisakhi, the festival which commemorates the founding of the Sikh Kalsa (brotherhood) by Guru Gobind Singh in 1699. The five symbols of the religion worn by the Kalsa are: the *kesh* (uncut hair), the *kanga* (a comb to hold hair under the turban); the *kara* (a bracelet), the *kirpan* (a sword), and the *kaccha* (shorts).

14th   Traditionally this is the date on which the cuckoo is first heard in Britain.

Abraham Lincoln, US President, was shot by John Wilkes Booth in 1865. Booth was later killed resisting arrest.

15th   Leonardo da Vinci was born in 1452.

This is traditionally Swallow Day in Britain – when swallows return for the spring and summer.

Father Damien, who gave his life treating lepers, was born in 1889.

The *Titanic* sank after hitting an iceberg in 1912 and 1,513 people were drowned.

In 1989 ninety-four people died at the Hillsborough football stadium disaster in Sheffield.

16th   Wilbur Wright, the aeroplane inventor and flier, was born in 1867.

Marie Tussaud, wax modeller and founder of Madame Tussaud's Waxworks in London, died in 1850. (*See also 26th April.*)

17th   Benjamin Franklin, the often-quoted American statesman and scientist, died on this date in 1790. One of his most appropriate 'sayings' was: 'Do you love life? Then don't squander time, for that is the stuff life is made of.'

This was the date, in 1492, when Columbus set sail to 'discover' the New World. He was equipped with a seal from King Ferdinand of Spain giving him the title of 'Admiral and Viceroy' over all the lands he might discover.

18th On this night in 1775, Paul Revere rode through the Massachusetts countryside to warn people that British troops were coming.

This was the date of the San Francisco earthquake in 1906. Devastation and fire caused the death of seven hundred people.

Albert Einstein, the scientist, died in 1955.

19th This is St Alphege's Day. Alphege was the Archbishop of Canterbury when captured by the Danes in the eleventh century. During his captivity he nursed sick Danes who were ill with the plague. He was executed in 1012.

Lord Byron, the poet, died in 1824. Charles Darwin, the naturalist, died in 1882. (*Link – Assemblies 64, 72, 77*)

20th This is the date on which the cuckoo is traditionally first heard in Europe. One old belief associated with this event is that whatever you are doing when your hear its first call – you will be doing most during the rest of the year.

Adolf Hitler was born in 1889.

21st In 753 BC Romulus started to lay the foundations of a city on the banks of the River Tiber. This became Rome. (*Link – Assembly 73*)

Charlotte Brontë, author of *Jane Eyre*, was born in 1816.

Mark Twain (pen name of Samuel Longhorne Clemens) died in 1910. His works included *Tom Sawyer* and *The Adventures of Huckleberry Finn*.

Manfred von Richthofen, the First World War German fighter pilot known as 'the Red Baron', was killed in 1918.

Queen Elizabeth II was born in 1926.

22nd In 1794 Edmund Bon became the first person to qualify as a veterinary surgeon in Great Britain.

Richard Trevithick, an engineer who pioneered locomotive building in the British Isles, died in 1833.

Yehudi Menuhin, world famous violinist, was born in 1916. (*Link – Assembly 66*)

23rd Today is St George's Day. ('Cry God for Harry! England and St George!' – from Shakespeare's *Henry V*). The patron saint of England supposedly saved the Libyan town of Sylene from a man-eating dragon. He did this on condition that the inhabitants of the town would be baptised.

This date is also established as Shakespeare's probable date of birth in 1564. He was baptised on the 26th, and died on 23rd April 1616.

William Wordsworth ('I wandered lonely as a cloud ... saw a crowd, a host, of golden daffodils') died in 1850.

The Pennine Way, the footpath which spans 250 miles (402 km) from Derbyshire to the Borders, was opened in 1968. It was Britain's first long-distance footpath.

24th   Daniel Defoe (author of *Robinson Crusoe*) died in 1731.

Joshua Slocum set out in an eleven-metre-long sloop to sail round the world from Boston, USA in 1895. His single-handed journey took three and a half years.

25th   This is St Mark's Day. He died in AD 68, having served as a secretary to the disciple Peter. His writings appear in the Bible under his own name.

Oliver Cromwell was born in 1599.

Work started on the Suez Canal on this date in 1859.

In 1874 Guglielmo Marconi was born in Bologna, Italy. He invented radio telegraphy and was awarded the Nobel Prize for Physics in 1909.

26th   Alfred Krupp, the German industrialist, was born in 1812.

Madame Tussaud's was opened on its current site in London in 1928.

27th   Ferdinand Magellan, the Portuguese explorer, was killed on an expedition in 1521. He named the Pacific Ocean. His ship, which arrived home in Spain in 1522, had completed the first circumnavigation of the world.

Samuel Morse, inventor of the Morse Code, was born in 1791.

Henry Willis, one of Britain's greatest organ builders, was born in 1821. He was also a church organist.

The *Kon-Tiki* expedition set out on its balsawood raft in 1947.

Betty Boothroyd became the first ever woman speaker in the Houses of Parliament on this date in 1992.

28th   Captain Bligh of the *Bounty*, together with eighteen men, was set adrift on the ocean in a rowing boat by mutineers led by Fletcher Christian in 1789. He survived to become Governor of New South Wales in Australia.

Lord Shaftesbury (Anthony Ashley Cooper) was born in 1801. He was a great reformer who helped poor children especially.

29th   Sir Malcolm Sargent, the orchestral conductor, was born in 1895.

Emperor Hirohito, the 124th of Japan's 'divine' rulers, was born in 1901.

The rose 'Peace' was named on this date in 1945. (*Link – Assembly 69*)

30th   William Lilly was born in 1602. He was one of the first astrologers to become rich and well known for his skills.

Adolf Hitler died in 1945.

Religious notes

While not strictly religious festivals, two important modern Jewish festivals which usually fall in April or May are Yom HaShoah which commemorates the victims of the Holocaust, and Yom HaAtzmaut which celebrates Israel's independence.

The Sikh festival of Baisakhi takes place on 13th April (see the note for this date).

Although it is a movable feast, Easter often occurs in this month. The build-up to Easter is considerable. Lent is preceded by Shrove Tuesday when worshippers went to church to be 'shriven' – confess their sins. Ash Wednesday, as the first day of Lent, is a time when Christians daubed ash on their faces as a further reminder of the need to repent sins. The forty days of Lent then follow, as a spiritual preparation for Easter. It should be remembered that these forty days do not include Sundays – which always remain feast days, not fast days. Holy Week precedes Easter Sunday, which is the joyous celebration of Jesus's resurrection and which activates thoughts through the next forty days to Ascension Day.

The Jewish Pesach (Passover) festival is held to celebrate the escape of the Children of Israel from Egypt. This happened under the leadership of Moses, more than three thousand years ago. Passover occurs in the Jewish month of Nisan and lasts for eight days – the first two and the last two are full festival days.

213

The house is thoroughly cleaned and a meal prepared. No leaven (yeast) must be used. On the first evening of the festival, the family, dressed in their best (or new) clothes, come to the table for the Seder. Each member of the family has a cup of wine and certain food (bitter herbs, a lamb's shank bone, a roasted egg, a mixture of apples and nuts in a paste, watercress and unleavened bread). These foods are symbolic. Exodus 12 tells the story of the Passover.

May

May, named after the Roman goddess Maia, could certainly be said to be one of Northern Europe's most popular months. In Britain it is looked upon as the beginning of summer and the month of flowers.

> A trout peeped out
> From his shady nook,
> A butterfly too
> Flew lazily by,
> And the willow catkins
> Shook from on high
> Their yellow dust
> As I passed by:
> And so I know
> That summer is nigh.'
>
> (Anon.)

1st   This date is celebrated as Labour Day in many countries. Parades and other displays of human achievements are held.

The General Election of 1997 saw the election of the first Labour government for 18 years.

David Livingstone, the Scottish missionary and explorer, died in Africa in 1873.

This was the date in 1928 when footballer Dixie Dean of Everton and England scored a record number of goals in a season: sixty. (Link – Assembly 71)

2nd   This date has an amazing number of connections with flight and flying.

Leonardo da Vinci died in 1519.

Baron von Richthofen ('the Red Baron') was born in 1892.

Robert Hewitt began America's first aeroplane passenger service in 1919.

The airship *Hindenburg* left Europe for America on this date in 1937. It exploded when about to land in America and thirty-three people were killed.

The British Overseas Airways Corporation began the first jet airline service in 1952 (England to South Africa).

The spacecraft *Pioneer X* was launched by the USA in 1972. It sent back information about the planet Jupiter.

3rd   In 326 St Helena found the cross on which Jesus was crucified in Jerusalem. (*Link – Assembly 73*)

The Royal Festival Hall was opened on London's South Bank in 1951.

Margaret Thatcher became Britain's first woman Prime Minister in 1979.

4th   In 1626 Peter Minuit, arriving with four shiploads of settlers and their cattle, reached Manhattan Island, New York. He 'bought' it from the Indians there for some scarlet cloth and brass buttons – valued at $24.

The first Epsom Derby horse race was run in 1780.

5th   Napoleon Bonaparte died in 1821.

The first General Strike in Britain's history began in 1926.

Amy Johnson took off for her single-handed flight to Australia in 1930.

Fossils and tools used by people 250,000 years ago were found near Nairobi in Kenya on this date in 1944.

6th   'Penny Black' stamps were first put on sale on this date in 1840. Some are very valuable, but by no means all are, as millions were printed.

Maria Montessori, the nursery school pioneer, died in 1952.

On the evening of this date in 1954, at Oxford, Roger Bannister became the first man to run a mile in less than four minutes (3 mins 59.4 secs).

7th   Nelson's flag ship. HMS *Victory*, was launched in 1765. It took between two and three thousand oak trees to build it.

Peter Ilich Tchaikovsky, the Russian composer, was born in 1840.

The Second World War in Europe ended when Germany surrendered at 2.41 am on this date in 1945.

In 1959 British Rail announced it was going to close two hundred and thirty BR stations.

8th   Jean Henri Dunant was born in 1828. He founded the International Red Cross and was the first winner of the Nobel Peace Prize (shared with Frédéric Passy), in 1901. Today is World Red Cross Day.

The Thames Barrier was officially opened in 1984.

9th   This was the date, in 1671, when Thomas Blood, disguised as a priest and with three accomplices, attempted to steal the Crown Jewels. He was captured but pardoned by King Charles II.

John Brown, leader of the anti-slavery movement in America, was born in 1800.

> John Brown's body lies a-moulderin' in the grave,
> But his soul goes marching on.

(*Link – Assembly 75*)

Tensing Norgay, the Sherpa climber who reached the summit of Mount Everest with Sir Edmund Hillary in 1953, died in 1986.

10th   An eight-day holiday from England to the French Riviera cost £8 in 1938. (Thomas Cook)

US *Triton*, a nuclear submarine, completed a submerged journey round the world in 1961.

11th   Baron Münchhausen was born in 1720. He became famous as a teller of outlandish stories. (*Link – Assembly 67*)

Irving Berlin, writer of more than three thousand popular songs, was born in 1888. His compositions included 'God Bless America' and 'White Christmas'.

In 1941 London endured its worst air raid of the war. Westminster Abbey, St Paul's Cathedral and the British Museum were all damaged and 1,400 people were killed.

12th Florence Nightingale was born in 1820.

> A lady with a lamp I see
> Pass through the glimmering doom.
> (Longfellow)

In 1937 George VI was crowned king. His elder brother Edward VIII had abdicated in 1936.

This date in 1949 marked the end of the Berlin Blockade. The city had been supplied by air since June 1948.

In 1958 it was decided to establish one hundred and sixty square miles of Surrey countryside as an area of outstanding natural beauty. (*Link – Assemblies 64, 72, 77*)

13th Fridtjof Nansen died in 1930. He was a famous Norwegian Arctic explorer who later won a Nobel Peace Prize for his welfare work after the First World War.

14th In 1796 Edward Jenner established smallpox vaccinations. (*Link – Assembly 62*)

Henry John Heinz, the America food manufacturer who created '57 varieties' of food products, died in 1919.

In 1948 the new state of Israel was proclaimed.

15th The Romans celebrated this date as the birthday of Mercury, the messenger of Zeus.

In 1970 Ann Hays and Elizabeth Holsington became the first female generals in the US army.

16th This is St Brendan's Day. An Irish saint who died in 587, Brendan is believed by some people to have been the first European to have discovered America.

The Woman's Voluntary Service (WVS) was founded in Britain in 1938. In 1966 it became the Women's Royal Voluntary Service.

In 1980 inflation in the United Kingdom reached 21.8%.

17th Paul Dukas, French composer (*The Sorcerer's Apprentice*) died in 1935.

18th This is the birthday of Karol Wojtyla – Pope John Paul II. He was born in 1920.

19th St Dunstan's Day. Dunstan was Archbishop of Canterbury, and a goldsmith, and died in 988. He is credited with devising the coronation service.

Dame Nellie Melba, the famous opera singer, was born in 1861.

In 1980, Mount St Helens in the USA, a long dormant volcano, erupted killing eight people.

20th Albrecht Dürer, the painter, was born in 1471.

Christopher Columbus died in 1506.

Charles Lindbergh flew *The Spirit of St Louis* from New York to Paris – the first solo non-stop flight across the Atlantic. This was in 1929.

This was the date, in 1913, of the first Chelsea Flower Show.

The BBC opened its new headquarters in Portland Place in 1932.

The Nature Conservancy Council announced in 1952 that eight areas of England and Scotland were to become nature reserves. (*Link – Assemblies 64, 72, 77*)

21st There was an earthquake in Britain in 1382. Some churches in Kent were 'thrown down to the earth' according to *Stow's Chronicle*.

Elizabeth Fry, the prison reformer, was born in 1780.

In 1964 a BBC survey revealed that the Beatles were Britain's most popular tourist attraction.

22nd Richard Wagner, the composer, was born in 1813.

Sir Arthur Conan Doyle was born in 1859.

Victor Hugo died in 1885. His novel *Les Misérables* contains the story of the Bishop's candlesticks which is marvellous assembly material. (*Link – Assembly 80*)

In 1959 the US state of Alabama banned a children's book because it showed a black rabbit marrying a white one.

In 1987 one of Mozart's notebooks was sold for £2.3 million at Sotheby's.

23rd John D Rockefeller, the American businessman and philanthropist, died in 1937. (*Link – Assembly 75*)

In 1956 it was announced that self-service shops, which were springing up all over Britain, had resulted in quadruple sales.

24th   Carl Linne, the Swedish naturalist, was born in 1707. He said, 'If a tree dies, plant another in its place.' (*Link – Assembly 72*)

Samuel Morse sent the first message by Morse Code on this date in 1844. It was from Washington to Baltimore, USA and it said, 'What hath God wrought?'

This was the date of a great sea tragedy in 1941. The British battleship HMS *Hood* was hit by a shell from the German ship *Bismarck*. The magazine exploded and only three of the 1,421 men on board survived.

25th   Captain Cook set out on his first voyage of discovery, in the seas around Australia. New Zealand and Indonesia, in 1768.

Igor Sikorsky, designer of the first helicopter in 1939, was born in 1889.

26th   Samuel Pepys died in 1703. The famous diarist kept his journal from 1660 to 1669 and it encompassed three outstanding events – the Great Plague, the Fire of London and the Dutch attack on the Medway.

Petrol rationing in the UK ended on this date in 1950, five years after the end of the Second World War.

27th   This is the Feast Day of the Venerable Bede who died at Jarrow in 735. Known as the Father of the English Church, and a celebrated writer about early Christianity in England, his tomb is in Durham Cathedral. Thought to be the first person to draw up a calendar of the Christian year, he was widely revered in his day. (*Link – Assemblies 62, 68*)

In 1936 the *Queen Mary* (80,773 tons) set sail from Southampton on her maiden voyage.

28th   This was the birth date of Solomon in 970 BC.

Sir Francis Chichester ended his solo round-the-world voyage on his arrival in Plymouth in 1967. He had completed 15,517 miles and was later knighted by Queen Elizabeth II at Greenwich. She used the sword of Sir Francis Drake for this ceremony. (*Link – Assembly 76*)

29th   This is Oak Apple Day – when King Charles II rode into London on his thirtieth birthday in 1660, as newly proclaimed king. He had escaped from Cromwell's army in 1651 by hiding in an oak tree. A traditional old school jingle linked to the day was:

> The twenty-ninth of May
> Is Royal Oak Day;
> If you cannot give us a holiday,
> We'll all run away.

The summit of Mount Everest was reached for the first time on this day in 1953 by Edmund Hillary and Tensing Norgay.

In 1951 eighty-three miners died after an explosion at Easington Colliery in County Durham.

In 1977 Nigel Short (aged eleven) became the youngest ever qualifier in the UK national chess championships.

In 1985, rioting in the European Cup Final football match between Liverpool and Juventus at the Heysel Stadium in Brussels resulted in forty-one people being killed.

30th King Arthur is said to have died in 542.

Many historians believe this was the date that Joan of Arc was burned at the stake in Rouen in 1431.

31st This was the date, in 1678, of Lady Godiva's famous naked ride through Coventry. Her husband agreed to remit heavy taxes on the town's people if she did this.

Religious notes

In the Christian Church Ascension Day is the Thursday which is the fortieth day after Easter. This commemorates the last time the disciples saw Jesus before his ascension. This happened on the Mount of Olives and Jesus blessed his followers with the words: 'Lo, I am with you always, even unto the end of the world.' Biblical references for this event are Mark 16, 19; Luke 24–51; Acts 1, 1–11.

There then follow the ten days between Ascension and Whitsun. The latter festival, also known as Pentecost, is the fiftieth day after Easter and celebrates the giving of the Holy Spirit to the followers of Christ. ('Pentecost' comes from the Greek word meaning 'fiftieth'.) It was from this moment that these followers began to preach about Jesus, and therefore it is considered the birthday of the Christian Church. This is also the time which begins the second half of the Christian Year.

This is also the time of the Jewish festival of Shavuoth, which celebrates the giving of the Torah on Mount Sinai. Synagogues are decorated with flowers and plants.

June

June is a month of many associations, including marriage, roses, midsummer, and well dressing. Northern Europeans hope that the weather in reality matches the promise and they can agree with James Lowell's comment: 'What is so rare as a day in June.'

1st   Captain Robert Falcon Scott's ill-fated expedition to the South Pole set out in 1910.

The *Queen Mary* arrived in New York in 1936 on its maiden voyage.

Helen Keller died in 1968. She was eighty-eight and had become a world-famous lecturer and writer despite being deaf and blind since the age of nineteen months. She was noted for her work with the handicapped.

2nd   Thomas Hardy, the author, was born in 1840.

Queen Elizabeth II was crowned in 1953.

3rd   The game of lacrosse was introduced into Britain in 1876. A group of Canadians gave an exhibition game.

In Japan, this is the day on which a Buddhist ceremony takes place when all broken dolls are taken to priests.

Johann Strauss died in 1899.

4th   In 1913 Emily Wilding Davison, a suffrage campaigner, threw herself in front of the king's horse, Anmer, in the Epsom Derby. She was killed, but her action attracted more attention to the suffrage campaign for the vote for women.

On this date in 1940 the evacuation was completed of British troops from Dunkirk during the Second World War.

5th   In 1783 Joseph and Etienne Montgolfier gave the first public demonstration of a hot air balloon. This was at Annonay, in the Languedoc in France. The balloon was airborne for ten minutes.

6th   In 1930 frozen peas were sold in America for the first time. That this was possible was due to a 'quick-freeze' technique invented by Clarence Birdseye.

In 1944 the Allied troops landed on the Normandy coast in the D-Day operations.

In 1977 beacons were lit all over the country at the start of Queen Elizabeth II's jubilee celebrations – twenty five years on the throne.

7th   Robert the Bruce died in 1329. (*Link – Assembly 60*)

Paul Gauguin, the artist, was born in 1848.

8th   The prophet Muhammad died in 632. He was the founder of Islam. (*Link – Assemblies 57, 67, 80*)

In 1786 commercially-made ice cream was sold for the first time in New York.

In 1978 Naomi James beat Sir Francis Chichester's record for a solo round-the-world voyage by two days.

9th   This is the feast day of St Columba. He died in 597 and is considered the spreader of the gospel over the northern part of the British Isles. (*Link – Assembly 68*)

George Stephenson, inventor of railways, was born in 1781.

Charles Dickens died in 1870. Queen Victoria said of him, 'He is a very great loss. He had a large and loving mind.'

In 1958 Queen Elizabeth opened the new and improved facilities at Gatwick Airport.

10th   Feast day of St Margaret (b. 1050) in England.

The first World Cup Soccer Final was played in Rome in 1934. The score was Italy 2, Czechoslovakia 1.

The 'biro', a ball point pen, was patented by Hungarian Laszlo Biro in 1943.

The 750th anniversary of the signing of the Magna Carta was celebrated in St Paul's Cathedral in 1965.

11th   This is the feast day of St Barnabas. He accompanied St Paul on his gospel-spreading journeys and is believed to have been put to death for his beliefs in Cyprus.

John Constable, the painter, was born in 1776.

Britain's first North Sea oil was pumped ashore in 1975. (*Link – Assembly 75*)

In 1982 forty-two British soldiers were killed in the fighting at Fitzroy in the Falklands War.

12th Auguste and Louis Lumière showed the first newsreel film in Paris in 1895. Many among the audience were frightened by its realism.

Bryan Allen 'pedalled' across the Channel in a pedal powered aircraft in 1979. The flight took three hours.

In 1980 Billy Butlin, the founder of Britain's popular holiday camps, died aged eighty.

13th The Virgin Mary, mother of Jesus, died in AD 40.

St Anthony, patron saint of the illiterate, died in 1231.

The MCC was founded in 1787. (*Link – Assembly 71*)

Jesse Boot, Lord Trent, founder of Boots the Chemist, died in 1931.

In 1956 Real Madrid won soccer's first European Cup, beating Stade de Reims, 4–3.

14th Captain Bligh, set adrift from the *Bounty*, arrived in Timor in 1789. With the barest of supplies, he and his eighteen companions had completed a journey of 3,618 miles in an open boat.

This is Flag Day in the USA – to commemorate the adoption of the 'Stars and Stripes' as the national flag in 1777.

The first non-stop flight of the Atlantic was made by William Alcock and Arthur Whitten-Brown in 1919.

John Logie Baird, who pioneered the invention of the television, died in 1946 aged fifty-eight.

In 1961 push-button controlled pedestrian crossings were introduced into Britain.

15th World Children's Day.

This is St Vitus's Day. This fourth-century saint and martyr is the patron of actors and dancers.

In 1215 King John signed the Magna Carta – the first documentation of human freedom.

Benjamin Franklin proved the existence of electricity in lightning in 1752. This was done by flying a kite in a storm. It was struck by lightning and the electricity ran down it to make a spark near the ground.

In 1952 Anne Frank's diary was published. She had kept it from 1942 to 1944, before her family was discovered and sent to a concentration camp. (*Link – Assembly 69*)

16th Henry Ford founded the Ford Motor Company in Detroit, USA, in 1903.

General William Bramwell Booth, founder of the Salvation Army, died in 1929.

Edmund Hillary and John Hunt received knighthoods for their parts in the successful 1953 Mount Everest expedition.

In 1963 Russia put the first woman in space when Lieutenant Valentina Tereshkova circled the earth in a *Vostok* spacecraft. She was twenty-six.

17th John Wesley, the founder of Methodism, was born in 1703. Wesley preached thousands of sermons all over the country. He travelled mainly on horseback, lived abstemiously and gave away an estimated £30,000 in his lifetime. ('Give all you can'). (*Link – Assembly 61*)

18th The Battle of Waterloo took place in 1815. This finally ended the ambitions of Napoleon, who abdicated on 22nd June and was banished to St Helena. (*Link – Assembly 69*)

19th The French genius Blaise Pascal was born in 1623. A brilliant mathematician (he invented a digital calculator, and a syringe) he was also a very religious man and a philosopher. 'If you want people to think well of you, do not speak well of yourself.'

James Barrie (author of *Peter Pan*) died in 1937.

In 1961 archeological evidence relating to Pontius Pilate was found a few miles from Haifa in Caesarea, Israel. A stone slab was discovered on which were two names: Pontius Pilate and Emperor Tiberius. (*Link – Assembly 72*)

In 1978 Ian Botham achieved England's greatest all-round performance in a cricket test match. This was against

Pakistan at Lords, when he scored a century and had bowling figures of 8–34. He was twenty-two at the time. (*Link – Assembly 71*)

20th This day in 1837 saw Queen Victoria's accession to the British throne. Her coronation was held on 28th June 1838.

The medal, the Victoria Cross, was created in 1856. The first person to be awarded it was Lieutenant Charles Lucas who threw a live bomb off a ship's deck. It exploded immediately.

21st This is the longest day of the year in the northern hemisphere (except on leap years)

22nd In 1923 runaway inflation meant that there were 622,000 German marks to the £1.

On this date in 1941 Germany invaded Russia in the Second World War. (*Link – Assembly 69*)

In 1964 Francis Chichester set a new record for a solo boat crossing of the Atlantic in under thirty days.

In 1970 it was announced by the Methodist Church that women would be recognised as full ministers.

23rd In 1683 William Penn arranged the signing of a treaty between settlers and indigenous people in the State of Pennsylvania. This established peace in the state – something very different from other states in America. (*Link – Assembly 58*)

24th This is John the Baptist's Day. This is unusual in that the Christian Church usually celebrates saints on the day of their death – not so in John's case.

This is Midsummer Day.

25th This was the date of 'Custer's Last Stand' in 1876. At a battle by the Little Big Horn River in Montana Custer's force was wiped out by Sioux Indians.

The Korean War began in 1950.

26th According to legend, in 1284 the Pied Piper lured away one hundred and thirty children from the German town of Hamelin. This was because the town fathers refused to honour his fee of 1,000 guilders for ridding the town of rats. (*Link – Assembly 56*)

225

Delegates from fifty states met in San Francisco to sign the World Security Charter in 1945. This was to establish an international peace-keeping body called the United Nations.

27th Helen Keller was born in 1880.

28th Queen Victoria was crowned at Westminster in 1838.

Archduke Franz Ferdinand, heir to the throne of Austria-Hungary, and his wife were assassinated in Sarajevo. The assassin was a Serb called Gavrilo Princip and the act was to contribute to the outbreak of the First World War.

Prince William was born in 1982.

29th St Peter, the disciple, was crucified in 68.

The Automobile Association was founded in 1905. The annual membership then was two guineas.

In 1925 a law was passed in South Africa banning all black people from holding skilled jobs.

In 1968 Britain's first credit card – the Barclaycard – was introduced.

30th Tower Bridge was opened by the Prince of Wales in 1894.

In 1938 a new comic appeared in the USA – *Superman*.

In 1948 this was the date the Berlin Airlift began. The beleaguered city was supplied entirely by air.

Religious notes

At the time of publication the birthday of the prophet Muhammad (pbuh) falls in June.

The Christian feast of Corpus Christi ('the body of Christ') is celebrated on the Thursday after Whit week. It commemorates the institution of the Eucharist at the Last Supper.

July

'Then came hot July, boiling like to fire'.

So said Edmund Spenser, but as well as its reputation for heat, this month has strong links with wet weather as it contains St Swithin's Day. It was Mark Antony who named the month in honour of Julius

Caesar; the Anglo-Saxon name, 'Hey Monath', simply reflected the time of hay harvesting.

1st   Prince Charles became the Prince of Wales in 1969.

Louis Blériot, the French airman who made the first flight across the English Channel, was born in 1872.

Hong Kong is returned to Chinese control by Britain in 1997 after 156 years as a British colony.

Diana, Princess of Wales was born on this date in 1961. She died in a car crash in Paris on 31st August 1997; her death was mourned by many people around the world.

2nd   Nostradamus, the astrologer and prophet, died in 1566.

In 1964 the Civil Rights Act was signed in the USA. This was intended to prevent racial discrimination of any kind.

3rd   This is the beginning of the period known to the Romans as 'the dog days' (3rd July to 11th August). The name derives from the fact that the Dog Star (Canicular) rose at this time. These days were considered the hottest of the year, when 'dogs grew mad, other animals languid and men prey to fevers, hysterics and frenzies'.

4th   This is Independence Day in the USA. The Declaration of Independence was made in 1776 and contained some memorable phrases, notably: 'We hold these truths to be self evident, that all men are created equal . . .' (*Link – Assembly 55*)

Thomas Barnardo was born in 1845. It was while training to be a medical missionary in London, that the Irishman discovered the orphans that led to his work with Dr Barnardo's homes.

In 1968 Alec Rose, aged fifty-nine, completed his solo round-the-world voyage when he returned to Portsmouth. His boat was *The Lively Lady* and he had sailed her 28,500 miles in 354 days.

5th   Sir Thomas Stamford Raffles, founder of Singapore, died in 1826.

The first Thomas Cook excursion took place in 1841 (from Leicester to Loughborough).

Phineas T. Barnum, the circus proprietor and presenter of 'The Greatest Show on Earth', was born in 1810.

In 1952 this was the last date on which trams ran in London.

6th   Sir Thomas More, Chancellor of England, was executed in 1535 because he refused to sanction the marriage of Henry VIII to Anne Boleyn. He was canonised in 1935, and the 6th is now his feast day.

Louis Armstrong, the jazz trumpeter and singer, died in 1971. His song 'Black and Blue' provides thought-provoking assembly material for top juniors.

7th   Another 'first' in Channel crossings took place on this date in 1981. Stephen Ptacek made the first solar-powered flight.

Sir Arthur Conan Doyle, creator of Sherlock Holmes, died in 1930.

8th   La Fontaine, French writer of stories and 'thoughts for the day', died in 1621. His material is still a richly rewarding source for assemblies. (*Link – Assemblies 58, 61, 65, 78, 80*)

9th   Edward Heath, the former British Prime Minister and advocate of European Union, was born in 1916.

The seven-hundred-year-old York Minister was hit by a bolt of lightning in 1984. The ensuing fire caused over a million pounds worth of damage.

10th The Emperor Hadrian died in 138. Hadrian's Wall covers a distance of seventy-three miles across the north of England.

A survey in 1951 discovered that British housewives worked a seventy-five-hour week.

11th Robert the Bruce, King of Scotland, was born in 1274.

12th Julius Caesar was born in 100 BC.

George Eastman, the photographer, inventor of roll films and cheap cameras, and founder of Kodak, was born in 1854.

13th Bertrand de Guesclin, 'the founder of French chivalry', knight and statesman, died in 1380.

14th Bastille Day. This is a national holiday in France and commemorates the storming of the Bastille Prison in 1789. It marked the beginning of the Revolution and is a symbol of the victory of democracy over aristocratic rule.

Emmeline Pankhurst, the suffrage leader who organised the Women's Social and Political Union, died in 1928.

15th Feast of St Swithin, who died in 862. (*Link – Assembly 80*)

In 1945, after more than two thousand nights of official 'black-out' during the war, lights came on again all over Britain.

Officially the beginning of the Muslim age in 622. (*Link – Assemblies 57, 67, 80*)

16th In 1439, in an effort to stop the spreading of plague germs, kissing was banned in England.

Roald Amundsen, the Norwegian explorer and navigator who was the first man to reach the South Pole, was born in 1872.

17th St Alexius's Day. Alexius, having left home, returned in disguise to live under his father's rule as a servant as badly treated as his peers. He revealed his identity just before he died.

In 1981 Queen Elizabeth II opened the Humber Estuary Bridge – a total length of 1.37 miles.

18th WG Grace, the legendary cricketer who scored 54,896 runs, including 126 centuries, and took 2,876 first-class wickets, was born in 1848. (*Link – Assembly 71*)

In 1955 Disneyland was opened in California, USA.

19th This is the feast day of St Vincent de Paul, carer for galley slaves, whose story makes very good assembly material. (*Link – Assembly 73*)

The first Wimbledon Lawn Tennis Championships were held in 1877.

20th This was the date, in 1969, when men – Neil Armstrong and Edwin Aldrin – landed on the moon for the first time.

21st Ancient Egyptians believed the world was created on this day.

Daniel Lambert, recorded as England's fattest ever man, died in 1809. He weighed 739 pounds (approximately 336 kilos).

22nd The Reverend William Spooner, a nervous speaker, became famous for his 'Spoonerisms'. One example was: 'Sir, you have tasted two whole worms.' (Sir, you have wasted two whole terms.) He was born on this day in 1844 and served both as dean and later warden of New College, Oxford.

The World Health Organisation was founded in 1946.

23rd In 1904 Charles E Menches of St Louis, USA, thought of a new way to serve ice cream – in a cone.

24th Alexandre Dumas, author of *The Three Musketeers*, was born in 1802.

Captain Webb, the first man to swim the English Channel (in 1875), drowned while attempting to swim Niagara Falls in 1883.

25th This is the feast day of St James, disciple of Jesus and elder brother of St John. He was martyred in 44. This is also St Christopher's Day. He is the patron saint of travellers and is symbolised by a palm-tree staff.

The English Channel was crossed for the first time by plane in 1909 (the pilot was Louis Blériot). On the same day in 1959 the first Hovercraft crossing was made.

26th This is the feast day of St Anne, the mother of the Virgin Mary.

John Wilmont, Earl of Rochester, a poet and wit, and leader of the court of King Charles II, said of the king: '. . . never says a foolish thing; nor ever does a wise one.'

27th Tradition has it that this was the day Noah sent the dove out of the ark. (*Link – Assembly 56*)

Jim Laker took the most wickets ever in a cricket test match. This was nineteen – for England against Australia at Old Trafford, Manchester, in 1956.

28th Johann Sebastian Bach, the composer, died in 1750.

Hans Andersen, the Danish author, died in 1875. (*Link – Assembly 56*)

In 1964 Sir Winston Churchill, then eighty-nine, made his last appearance in the House of Commons.

29th The Spanish Armada was defeated in 1588.

William Wilberforce, the social reformer, died in 1833. One month after his death the Slavery Abolition Act was passed by Parliament.

In 1981 Prince Charles married Lady Diana Spencer.

30th Henry Ford, of motorcar fame, was born in 1863.

In 1966 England won the World Soccer Cup for the first time when they defeated Germany 4–2 at Wembley.

31st This is the feast of St Ignatius Loyola. He founded the order of the Jesuits and wrote one of the most famous prayers of all time:

> Teach us, good Lord, to serve thee as thou deservest; to give and not to count the cost; to fight and not to heed the wounds; to toil and not to seek for rest; to labour and not to ask for any reward save that of knowing that we do thy will.

Assemblies linked by theme

This section seeks to aid teachers who wish to present a number of assemblies linked by *themes* which are popular ones in a primary school and RE context. The assemblies are shown by their number and title.

Those who help us

Wisdom

The stories

This section classifies the stories according to source categories – *folk, original or contemporary, religious, true* – for teachers who wish to use them in groupings of this nature. The assemblies are shown by their numbers and titles.

Folk stories, myths, legends

6	For good and evil
8	A tale of two sisters
10	Learning a lesson
11	Honesty
14	The friend
17	Know your strengths
20	A long tongue makes for a short life
21	Giving
23	Tough?
25	What's in a carol?
29	The hero
30	A helping paw
35	The recipe
37	Patience
39	Two's company
44	Tell the truth
54	Learning a lesson
58	I don't like you
60	It's not fair
61	Enough is enough
63	The grave
65	Once too often
67	A wise man
76	The traveller's gift
78	Stick together

Original or contemporary stories

1	She's new
9	Mums
16	John and Errol
55	The tooth
59	The move
66	Down and out?
71	The disappointment
79	Locked in

Religious stories

3	Laurence
5	What do we see?
12	A father's choice
15	Happiness
18	The beggar
22	*Stop!*
32	Here he comes
40	The plot
48	The lost sheep

True stories

Resources

Addresses

SAEs are welcomed when you contact the following addresses, which are useful for specially produced material.

General
Save the Children, 17 Grove Lane, London, SE5 8RD. www.oneworld.org/scf/

The National Society's RE Centre, 36 Causton Street, London SW1P 4AU. The centre distributes the annual journal of the SHAP Working Party on World Religions in Education, which is particularly valuable for precise annual dates of religious festivals. www.namss.org.uk/fests.htm

Independent Publishing Company, 38 Kennington Lane, London SE11 4LS. They publish a large selection of books, posters and cards relating particularly to South East Asian countries.

Christianity
Christian Education Movement, Royal Buildings, Victoria Street, Derby DE1 1GW. By subscribing to the CEM schools receive a termly mailing of material which is always useful for RE, and sometimes specially aimed at assemblies. www.cem.org.uk

Hinduism
Hindu Centre, 7 Cedars Road, London E15 4NE.

ISKCON Educational Services, Bhaktivedanta Manor, Hilfield Lane, Aldenham, Watford, Herts WD2 8EZ. www.iskcon.org.uk

Islam
IQRA Trust, 24 Culross Street, London W1Y 3HE. www.iqratrust.org

Muslim Educational Trust, 130 Stroud Green Road, London
N4 3RZ.

Judaism
Jewish Education Bureau, 8 Westcombe Avenue, Leeds LS8 2BS.

Books and Stories

One of the difficulties of recommending books is that, particularly
in recent years, titles have not only gone out of print but have also
changed publishers at a bewildering rate.

The wise teacher, therefore, will seek to build up a range in two
areas. The first would be the background information type of book.
A Bible dictionary is a useful reference and there are many good
information books on festivals and celebrations from around the
world.

The second collection will consist of folk tales which often
produce marvellous assembly material. New anthologies appear with
great regularity and should always be examined carefully. Old
favourites like *Anansi*, the *Hodja, Brer Rabbit* and Aesop's *Fables* are
suitable for many re-tellings and adaptations.

Other books published by Stanley Thornes in the area of
Assemblies and Religious Education include:

Join With Us Book One by Jeanne L. Jackson (a book of assembly
stories covering the whole school year)

Join With Us Book Two by Jeanne L. Jackson (a book of assembly
stories covering the whole school year)

Red Letter Days by Jeanne L. Jackson (the Christian year in story
for primary assembly)

Stanley Thornes Infant RE by Louis Fidge and Christine Moorcroft
(two teacher resource books covering Years 1 and 2 (P2–P3) and
each accompanied by 12 full colour, A2-sized posters)

Stanley Thornes Junior Steps in RE by Michael Keene and Jan
Keene (teacher resource books covering the four junior years and
supported by a pupil book at each year)

Resources for Music

The BBC's *Come and Praise* anthologies are the source for all the hymns recommended in this book. It would be hard to better this series for primary hymns.

Festivals by Jean Gilbert (Oxford University Press, Music Department, Great Clarendon Street, Oxford OX2 6DP) is a very useful anthology with suggestions for songs and musical activities related to festivals.